Communicator-in-Chief

LEXINGTON STUDIES IN POLITICAL COMMUNICATION

Series Editor: Robert E. Denton, Jr.

Virginia Polytechnic Institute and State University

This series encourages focused work examining the role and function of communication in the realm of politics including campaigns and elections, media, and political institutions.

TITLES IN SERIES:

Communicator-in-Chief

How Barack Obama Used New Media Technology to Win the White House

Edited by John Allen Hendricks and
Robert E. Denton, Jr.

LEXINGTON BOOKS
A division of
ROWMAN & LITTLEFIELD PUBLISHERS, INC.
Lanham • Boulder • New York • Toronto • Plymouth, UK

Published by Lexington Books
A division of Rowman & Littlefield Publishers, Inc.
A wholly owned subsidiary of The Rowman & Littlefield Publishing Group, Inc.
4501 Forbes Boulevard, Suite 200, Lanham, Maryland 20706
http://www.lexingtonbooks.com

Estover Road, Plymouth PL6 7PY, United Kingdom

British Library Cataloguing in Publication Information Available

Library of Congress Cataloging-in-Publication Data

Communicator-in-chief : how Barack Obama used new media technology to win the white house / edited by John Allen Hendricks and Robert E. Denton Jr.
    p. cm. — (Lexington studies in political communication)
Includes bibliographical references and index.
    ISBN 978-0-7391-4105-2 (cloth : alk. paper) — ISBN 978-0-7391-4106-9 (pbk. : alk. paper) — ISBN 978-0-7391-4107-6 (electronic)
    1. Presidents—United States—Election—2008. 2. Political campaigns—United States. 3. Obama, Barack. 4. Communication in politics—United States. 5. Mass media—Political aspects—United States. I. Hendricks, John Allen. II. Denton, Robert E., Jr.
    JK5262008 .C655 2010
    324.973'0931—dc22
                                                2009037695

Printed in the United States of America

To my wife, Stacy, and my children, Abby and Haydyn. I am thankful and fortunate that my wife is accepting and supportive of my career as an academic. I am especially thankful to my young children, who are very patient and understanding when their dad's attention is focused, sometimes too much, on a computer screen or the pages of a book. I hope they have the same opportunities one day to pursue their intellectual pursuits, whatever they may be.

—John Allen Hendricks

To my wife and sons. It is family members who sustain us, encourage us, and provide a sense of belonging, love, and security that frees us to read, write, think, and pursue projects of interests. And, thankfully, they provide the joys of life beyond academe. Thanks to my wonderful wife Rachel and my now-grown sons Bobby (and his precious wife Christen) and Chris—together they, with my most beloved dog Daisy (who snuggles and accompanies me wherever I go), enrich and fulfill every moment of my life.

—Robert E. Denton, Jr.

Contents

Tables

Preface

The 2008 presidential campaign was one of the most remarkable and fascinating in this nation's history due to a confluence of several intriguing precedents that occurred during the battle for the White House. First, the 2008 campaign offered the electorate the most diverse slate of candidates from which to choose in the nation's history including the first African American candidate to obtain the Democratic Party's nomination, the first time a former First Lady sought the role of president, the Republican Party's nominee was the oldest individual to ever vie for the presidency, and finally, the Republican Party chose a female for the vice presidential running mate. Second, the 2008 campaign witnessed a precedent-setting number of voters from diverse demographics participating in the campaign, especially among the technologically savvy Millennial generation of eighteen- to twenty-four-year-olds. Third, the candidates who were vying for the White House during 2008 campaign raised a staggering amount of money to fund their race for the ultimate prize.

Most interestingly, the 2008 campaign was unique in that it became the first national campaign in which traditional media such as television, radio, and newspapers were overshadowed by new media technologies and the Internet. Although the 2008 presidential campaign was not the first time candidates utilized new media technologies to communicate with the electorate, it was the first campaign in which candidates used it extensively and effectively. Effective political communication is important because a candidate's success hinges on his or her ability to convey messages to voters. Unlike in previous presidential campaigns, the Internet was not used in a static manner where candidate policy positions were posted on rarely updated Web sites for voters to read and for fundraising purposes; but instead, the Internet was used strategically and dynamically to motivate, involve, and generate enthusiasm among the electorate during the 2008 campaign more than in any prior presidential campaign in history.

Mass media and politics naturally go hand-in-hand. New communication technologies have always transformed electoral politics. Sometimes the impact was incremental, like with the invention of the telegraph or even the telephone. Other times the impact of technology changed the dynamics and practice of political campaigns forever, such as with radio and television. Since 1992, the role of technology and the Internet have fundamentally changed how campaigns raise money, target audiences, and disseminate messages.

However, the 2008 presidential campaign of Barack Obama has changed forever the use of the Internet and Web 2.0 technologies in not only presidential campaigns, but for campaigns at all levels. The Web site for the Obama campaign organized over one hundred fifty thousand events, created more that thirty-five thousand groups, had over 1.5 million accounts, and raised over $600 million from three million donors. The campaign used YouTube for free advertising, sending the address of ads to supporters, and encouraging them to pass the address along to friends and family. His campaign material was watched for 14.5 million hours—on broadcast television, that would have cost $47 million.[1] Obama's Facebook site had 3,176,886 supporters and he had 987,923 MySpace friends.[2] The campaign used text messaging to stay connected to youth voters and send e-mails to counter attacks. In general, Obama's high tech campaign used the Internet to fact-check information, counter attacks, strengthen connection to supporters, and have an "always on," 24/7 presence. In short, the Obama campaign utilized every type of new media technology to reach voters of all ages and ethnic and social class backgrounds.

This book examines the use of new media technologies in the 2008 campaign and contemplates its future ramifications in the democratic process. This book is one of the first to focus on how the Obama campaign used new communication technologies to win the White House. Each chapter examines the campaign's use of a specific technology and its effectiveness in reaching people, motivating them, and getting votes. Specifically, this book examines the presidential candidates' use of cell phones and PDAs, texting, Twitter, blogging, social networking on sites such as Facebook and MySpace, YouTube, electronic mail, and advertising in video games to reach out to and communicate with a twenty-first-century electorate. Technology is updated and changes rapidly, so it is difficult to predict how its usage will develop and be used in future campaigns at the local, state, and national levels. However, one thing is indisputable and that is the Internet and new media technologies will play a prominent and influential role in all political campaigns of the twenty-first century, as the 2008 presidential campaign and Barack Obama made a certainty. Finally, both editors wish to note that this book is not "pro-Obama." A concerted effort was made to objectively review what occurred during the 2008 presidential campaign regarding the use of new media technologies in the political campaigning process and Barack Obama was the undisputable leader of the pack—thus, the focus of the book.

John Allen Hendricks
Robert E. Denton, Jr.

NOTES

1. Claire Cain Miller, "How Obama's Internet Campaign Changed Politics," *New York Times*, 7 November 2008, bits.blogs.nytimes.com/2008/11/07/how-obamas-internet-campaign-changed-politics/ (10 August 2009).

2. "Facebook Supporters," TechPresident.com, techpresident.com/scrape_plot/facebook (10 August 2009).

Acknowledgments

An edited book is by its very design a huge collaborative project that could not be accomplished without the hard work of many very intelligent and highly respected scholars. Accordingly, I am most grateful to each contributor of this book for their outstanding work and contribution toward better understanding new media technology and its role in the political and democratic process. Moreover, for many years I have read and respected the work of Robert E. Denton, Jr., and it has been my honor that he agreed to serve as coeditor on this project. This project was completed at Stephen F. Austin State University and I thank the institution for its support of scholarly and intellectual pursuits.

I am appreciative of the assistance offered to me in preparation of the book's proposal by Alan Albarran (University of North Texas) and David Schultz (Hamline University). Also, without the assistance and complete support of Lexington Books's acquisition editor, Matthew R. McAdam, this book would not have come to fruition, and I am most grateful for his participation in this project at its outset. My appreciation is also extended to Rebecca Mc-Cary, assistant acquisitions editor for communication at Lexington Books, for guiding the final manuscript through completion in a timely manner. Finally, and most importantly, I am blessed and thankful to have a supportive family. My wife of nearly twenty years, Dr. Stacy Nason Hendricks, has been very understanding and supportive of my career and without her support there would have been far fewer successes in my life. My children, Abby and Haydyn, are patient with me when I am glued to the computer screen and I thank them and love them for their support and understanding.

—J.A.H.

I want to thank my colleagues in the Department of Communication at Virginia Polytechnic Institute and State University (Virginia Tech) for their continued collegiality, encouragement, and rich environment that support differing thoughts, views, and scholarship. It is a genuine pleasure to serve as head of the department. I also thank Sue Ott Rowlands, dean of the College of Liberal Arts and Human Sciences and Richard Sorensen, dean of the Pamplin College of Business, for their continued support of administrative, professional, and scholarly activities. They understand the importance of the "right mix" that makes my job a privilege and pleasure. Finally, countless thanks to my wonderful wife, Rachel, a true blessing, friend, colleague, and partner in my life. For me, life simply could not be any better or filled with more blessings.

—R.E.D., Jr.

Political Campaigns and Communicating with the Electorate in the Twenty-First Century

John Allen Hendricks and Robert E. Denton, Jr.

Human communication has long been an essential element of politics. Over twenty-three hundred years ago Aristotle recognized the natural kinship of politics and communication. In his writings in *Politics*, Aristotle proclaimed that humans "are political beings [who] alone of the animals [are] furnished with the faculty of language." Human speech "serves to indicate what is useful and what is harmful, and so also what is just and what is unjust. For the real difference between man and other animals is that humans alone have perception of good and evil, just and unjust, etc."[1]

More contemporary scholars of political communication view politics, broadly defined, as talk, social conversations, argument, and persuasion.[2] Human communication is the vehicle for political thought, debate, and action. Communication channels the inputs, structures the outputs, and provides feedback from political system to the environment. The vast multitude of interactions literally constructs our political, economic, and social institutions.[3] Robert E. Denton, Jr., and Jim Kuypers argue that one cannot separate the notion of politics apart from how it is communicated. Thus, politics—in all its varied forms—takes place through communication.[4]

Denton and Kuypers also argue that while the types and forms of political messages are virtually limitless, there are commonalities among them. For them, the most general characteristics of political communication include the elements of (1) a short-term orientation, (2) communication based on specific objectives, (3) primarily mediated, and, above all, (4) audience-centered.[5] And because political communication is largely mediated communication, the mass media are basic to the study of politics.

MASS MEDIA AND POLITICS

Mass media and politics have gone hand-in-hand since the founding of this nation. During the Revolution, early Patriots passed out pamphlets, newspapers were highly partisan, and books were written providing statements of political philosophy. Public speaking became the main avenue to public success and popularity. Politicians made frequent and long orations. Political gatherings were complete with banners, bands, slogans, and often concluded with fireworks. Even through the Civil War, newspapers continued to be partisan in tone and content.

Public oratory began to change after the Civil War. There was a trend toward shorter and more simplistic speeches. There was a shift of public attention from politics to business. This shift reflected the virtues of directness, conciseness, and pragmatism.[6] Interestingly, the number of magazine articles and newspaper stories increased while their length decreased. Likewise, political speeches became shorter and more colloquial. The focus was more on utility of message and the sharing of information.

Radio changed the dynamics of governance and campaigns. President Harding during the early 1920s spoke directly to the American public. In 1924 the Democratic convention was broadcast to over five million Americans who had radio receivers.[7] President Coolidge gave the first broadcast State of the Union address on radio. Herbert Hoover made eight nationally broadcast radio speeches during his 1928 presidential campaign, making radio the dominant media for politics until 1952, with the invention of television. As a medium, radio introduced discussion shows, "new reports" (unlike news stories), and time constraints for both speaker and audience. There were political implications as well. Radio messages crossed ethnic and geographic boundaries. It was unwise for a politician or government official to say one thing on the East Coast and something different on the West Coast. Members of the press became filters of, rather than vehicles of, political communication and discourse.

Other media were also used in the 1920s. In 1924, Republicans had William Fox (founder of Twentieth Century Fox) make a silent film about Calvin Coolidge.[8] By 1928, newsreels had sound and candidates as well as political parties began using them to target the distribution of, political messages to the public.

As with radio, television also changed the dynamics of the art and practice of politics. Television became a major player in politics in 1952 with the broadcast of the party conventions and the first purchases of airtime for political ads. The medium transformed the form and content of political discourse. The effective use of television became more important than party organizations. In the age of television, we come to know our leaders through the privacy of our living rooms rather than packed auditoriums. Kathleen Jamieson argues that the illusion of interpersonal, intimate context created through television required a new eloquence, one in which candidates and presidents adopt a personal and revealing style that engages the audience in conversation.[9] This essentially means shorter speeches, a more conversational tone, and self-disclosure in discourse. Television allows higher levels of intimacy and expressiveness. The false "intimacy" allows the audience to feel as if they know the official or politician as a "dear friend." Frequent "conversations" of politicians or candidates with citizens lead to feelings of friendship, trust, and intimacy with the nation.[10]

The introduction of new communication technology results in a corresponding effect on the way officials and politicians communicate with the public. It changes the form and content of the communication. We are now being bombarded with literally waves of new communication technologies. Computers, fiber optics, satellites, and the Internet introduced the era of high-speed and greatly enhanced communication. In addition to impacting the creation, collection, and dissemination of information, the new technologies promise better citizen issue understanding and political engagement. They further transcend the time and space constraints of traditional forms of media.

Bruce Gronbeck argues that we are transitioning from candidate-centered campaigns to citizen-centered campaigns.[11] Citizen-centered campaigns encourage not only more general participating, but multiple types or ways of participation. This transition, according to Gronbeck, "is a paradigm shift in American politicking" where the classic media theories relating to campaigns are no longer informative.[12] In the digital age, we are moving very rapidly from "mediated communication" to "electric communication."[13]

CAMPAIGNS AND NEW COMMUNICATION TECHNOLOGIES

Just a little more than a decade ago, new campaign technologies included computerized interactive telephone calls, continued cable segmentation of audiences, and nearly one hundred channel offerings. Satellites were used for distance media interviews and conferences. Video press releases were created for local media and video mail was targeted to specific constituent groups or geographic areas.

The 1992 Clinton campaign was the first to extensively use the Internet, although it was limited to e-mail and listserv distribution of information. Interestingly, the largest expansion of the Internet resulted from a $2 trillion dollar investment by the Clinton administration on the infrastructure and the establishment of the Office of Electronic Publishing and Public Access Electronic Mail.[14]

While there were numbers of candidate sites on the Web in 1994, political Web presence was dominated by nonprofits and interest groups. Sites such as Project VoteSmart contained candidate profiles, voting records, political philosophies, and histories. The vast majority of the sites were informational rather than partisan. A few candidates attempted to collect e-mail lists and provide issue information but the Web sites were crude compared with the increasing sophistication of e-commerce and online gaming sites.[15]

In 1996, just twenty-five thousand of the more than one hundred thousand candidates who ran for public office posted home pages on the World Wide Web.[16] However, more importantly, all the major news networks and organizations expanded their online coverage of the election. Network sites carried video of campaign events and posted poll results.[17]

In 2000, growth of using the Web was in fundraising and voter mobilization. Early success stories in fundraising were Republicans John McCain and Steve Forbes. The Internet was also most useful in mobilizing third-party and opposition groups. Ralph Nader supporters organized "vote swaps" with Democrats online. Overall, the Internet had little impact swaying voters. At the time, observers argued that the Net functioned as an echo chamber. Partisans and like-minded folks were doing most of the interactions. Thus, the Web served more for candidate and attitude reinforcement than persuasion.[18]

By 2004, sixty-three million used the Internet for political information, forty-three million discussed the election by e-mail, thirteen million even used the Internet to make a political contribution, and 52 percent of online users indicated that information obtained from the Internet influenced their vote.[19] Nearly half of the ads appeared online, campaign e-mails were routine, and blogs gained importance for both campaigns and media outlets as a means of interactivity with constituents.[20]

Also during this timeframe, the political influence of the social networks increased in importance. First there was MySpace in 2003, then Facebook in 2004, and YouTube in 2006. Savvy campaigns utilized these networks from their beginning. Innovation of activity on the Web follows new technological software and hardware.

In 2004, it was the presidential campaign of Howard Dean that set the standard in terms of using social media tools in campaigns. The Dean campaign used social media as a virtual and physical organizing tool, as a fundraising tool, and to help design a campaign.

Weise and Gronbeck argue there were six major developments in "cyber-politics" that emerged during the 2004 presidential election: the introduction of network software and theory to online campaign strategy; the move to expand database functions to enhance e-mail and wireless uses; the incorporation of coproduction features to increase citizen participation for online campaigns; the entrenchment of Web video and Web advertising for online messages; the evolution of candidate Web sites into a standard genre of Web text; and, as already mentioned, the introduction of blogs.[21] Social networking software allowed grassroots events to happen where supporters could find events nearest their location. Extensive databases allowed e-mail targeting where a single voter profile could generate a more personalized message. A rich Web environment with interactive features, video, animation, and so on provided incentives for continual and multiple campaign site visits. The big story was the impact of blogs in 2004. Traffic on many surpassed major television news network coverage. Election night, the most popular sites crashed, unable to handle the volume of hits.

In 2006, for the first time, the Internet ranked among the top sources of information for campaigns. In fact, citizens seeking campaign information more than doubled between 2002 and 2006. Thirty-one percent of Americans went online for information during the 2006 mid-term elections.[22] Historically, Republicans, because of the monetary advantage, were the first to embrace early technology such as polling, the use of computers, and marketing techniques. However, Democrats have mastered the use of new media in campaigns. This was most evident during the 2006 elections. Motley Winograd and Michael Hais observe that the Republican "YouTube-induced losses" of George Allen and Conrad Burns cost the party control of the Senate and demonstrated their lack of understanding of today's communication technology. They also note that during the 2006 election cycle the Democratic National Committee spent $7.4 million on Web-oriented campaigning compared with just $600,000 by the Republican National Committee during the same timeframe.[23]

Without question, the Internet is becoming one of the defining scientific and social innovations of the twenty-first century. Users can share data, communicate messages, transfer programs, discuss topics, and connect to computer systems all over the world. The potential of the Internet as a tool for retrieving information is almost limitless. As a result of the freedom of expression allowed, the possibilities for learning and enrichment are endless. However, there is also growing concern about the material readily available to anyone accessing the Internet, from the most perverse pornography to instructions for building bombs.

The uses of computer-based communication systems have evolved rapidly over the past decade or so.[24] The first computer-based communication systems were developed to gather voter information such as focus groups, public opinion polling, and dial technologies. More recently, voter mapping or profiles are established by looking at voting records, meeting attendance, contribution lists, Web site affiliations, etc. Such information would be used from creating campaign messages, to creating ads, to determining where to place advertising, to name only a few.

Also more recently, computer-based communication systems were developed to reach voters directly. In the digital age that includes such tactics as listserv mailings, use of personal blogs, sending photos and video to PDAs, positing podcasts, and establishing links to networking sites, for example. The effect is to establish increasing ways to not only contact voters, but do so with great frequency.

Finally, the Internet has generated another new group of political activists that provides sources of information and acts as interpreters of political events. The political/news Web site Drudge Report started in the mid-1990s. It gained notoriety in 1998 when it broke the story of Clinton's relationship with intern Monica Lewinsky. The Drudge Report demonstrated the potential power of bloggers. However, the "revolution" started during the 2004 political season. Within the "blogosphere" there are hundreds if not thousands of sites that provide political information and commentary. Few are neutral and most are advocates for a specific candidate, issue, or perspective. Some sites, such as Moveon.org or the HuffingtonPost have become essential players in elections. Staffers even began showing up as panel members on news programs as political analysts.

According to Winograd and Hais, there have been five major political realignments in American history. Each was triggered by a crucial event such as the Civil War or the Great Depression. They argue that we are witnessing another political realignment with the advances in communication technologies: "Technology serves to enable these changes by creating powerful ways to reach new voters with messages that relate directly to their concerns."[25] In terms of politics, Winograd and Hais also observe a generational transition. They predict that the "political world is about to be shaken to its core by the arrival of these new capabilities for reaching voters, especially the generation that uses them every moment of every day."[26] An interesting characteristic of Millennials is that they are in a constant and steady state of connection and interaction with friends. And their friends play an important role in decision-making about all types of things. Thus, Net interactions influence political decisions, especially in terms of voting. In addition, today's eighteen- to twenty-one-year-olds rely on the Net even more frequently as their primary source of news and information. For Winograd and Hais, both the generational and technological changes will cause a new civic realignment favoring the Democratic Party. The 2008 presidential election signaled the political realignment. They suggest that the impact of 9/11 upon this generation encourages even a larger electoral turnout of the Millennial generation, who by their nature favor the Democratic Party.

TRADITIONAL MEDIA VS. NEW MEDIA AND THE YOUTH VOTE

During presidential campaigns, the social responsibility of the media is to serve in a manner that informs the electorate with sufficient information to make decisions as voters and citizens. This goal has always existed, but the way in which the goal has been achieved has changed as advancements in technology have emerged.[27] Moreover, candidates hire media savvy campaign teams to play an influential role in what is reported by the media during presidential campaigns.[28] As advancements in technology emerge, there also emerges a new manner in which candidates communicate with the electorate. Although Governor Howard Dean's 2004 presidential bid was the first to use the Internet successfully to campaign, it was the Obama campaign that actually won the White House using the relatively new mass medium.[29] In the 2008 campaign it was the Internet that became a substantial component in the mix of mass media offerings for the electorate: "Today, the World Wide Web is the single best medium for allowing candidates to communicate directly, without any filter, to a multitude of constituencies simultaneously while maintaining a great deal of control over their own message."[30]

As his predecessors had done with partisan newspapers, news reels in movie theaters, radio, and later television, Senator Barack Obama successfully communicated with the electorate by using the popular and rapidly emerging mass medium of the time—the Internet. The Internet had been utilized by presidential candidates prior to the 2008 campaign, but not to the extent, nor level of success, as Obama during the campaign. Paul Harris and David Smith noted, "Obama's embrace of new ways of communicating—comparable to John F. Kennedy's mastery of the relatively new medium of television—means he can bypass the traditional political media in a way no other President can have dreamt of. It will put the Washington media establishment in the unusual position of being outsiders on a relationship between a President and his public."[31] The Obama campaign's goal was to utilize the Internet to motivate both young and new voters and it achieved great success. Sixty-six percent of voters under the age of thirty supported Obama and an impressive 69 percent of new voters supported Obama.[32]

The campaign created an entire department, called Triple O, whose sole responsibility was to create and post Obama campaign propaganda on the Internet. Chris Hughes (a cofounder of Facebook), Kate Albright-Hanna (a former CNN.com producer), and Scott Goldstein (owner of a Washington,

D.C.-based public relations firm) were the first three members of Triple O.[33] In total, the Obama campaign had a staff of ninety people working on the Internet campaign and spent approximately $8 million on Internet advertising.[34] Utilizing the Internet, the Obama campaign raised a staggering $711,741,924 compared to McCain's $296,124,438.[35] McCain's campaign team did not embrace the Internet and its capabilities to the extent of the Obama campaign.

NEW MEDIA AND THE 2008 PRESIDENTIAL CAMPAIGN

Stephen Coleman and Jay G. Blumler assert, "The 2008 presidential campaign was the first to occur with the existence of an online media platform that offered the would-be presidents the reach of a mass medium, but with a markedly different architecture and aesthetics than radio and television."[36] A senior producer for CNN.com, Manuel Perez, observed that Obama's "'grassroots' efforts on Twitter, Facebook, and other social media sites has gone a long way to engage young voters."[37] But the grassroots effort with the traditional social media was just the start. Obama had a presence on Asian Avenue.com, MiGente.com, and BlackPlanet.com, which targeted Asian, Latino, and black communities.[38] On Election Day in 2008, young voters turned out in large numbers.[39] An estimated twenty-three million voters under the age of thirty voted in the 2008 election; this was 3.4 million more than had voted in the previous presidential election.[40] Obama garnered 66 percent of the under age thirty vote. Michael Cornfield asserts, "The sheer size of this subpopulation, along with the traditional role of young people as enthusiastic campaign volunteers, made social networking sites valuable territory to stake out this cycle."[41]

Obama's media team realized the potential of utilizing the social networking sites on the Internet such as Facebook, MySpace, and other peer-to-peer Internet hubs. Brandon Waite suggests that politically minded individuals are sought after in online social settings just as they would be in the real world if their friends who were not politically minded, needed political information. Waite states, "Those people naturally emerge as the discussion leaders in politics, and they emerge online." This has become more prevalent with social networking sites, leading Waite to cleverly assert, "It's not word of mouth. It's word of mouse."[42] When Web users exchange information and ideas on the Internet using social networking technologies it is referred to as Web 2.0. With Web 2.0 technologies, political candidates can "aggregate supporters based on interest and demographics, raise money, publish information and urge action through e-mail. And they can communicate instantly with supporters."[43]

In addition to the social networking sites like MySpace and Facebook, the Obama campaign team utilized the Internet to establish a portal that allowed for videos to be posted by the campaign which bypassed traditional media outlets. One way to communicate with the electorate online was via video portals such as YouTube—the most popular Web video portal on the Internet. Other portals exist such as Dailymotion.com, Metacafe, MySpaceTv, and peer-to-peer platforms such as BitTorrent.[44] The Obama campaign team created BarackTv.com and used it, along with YouTube, to post videos. Those video portals enabled viewers to leave comments, forward the videos to friends, and donate money to the Obama campaign. As of August 2008, the videos posted on the Obama YouTube Channel had been watched almost fifty-two million times.[45] The widespread popularity of YouTube is impressive given the fact that it was established in 2005 and later sold to Google, Inc. for $1.65 billion. It was *Time* magazine's "Invention of the Year" for 2006.

Perhaps more importantly than the medium in which they were being delivered, the videos were being produced by individuals who were not connected to a political party or a candidate and their videos were being watched millions of times. Robert Greenwald, a Hollywood film producer, created several videos that showed John McCain contradicting himself.[46] In total, his videos were viewed more than five million times on YouTube. This new media technology has allowed many people who previously were unable to participate in the system to be a part of it now. One observer notes, "Four years ago, the Internet was a Wild West that caused the occasional headache for the campaigns but for the most part remained segregated from them. This year, the development of cheap new editing programs and fast video distribution through sites like YouTube has broken down the barriers, empowering a new generation of largely unregulated political warriors who can affect the campaign dialogue faster and with more impact than the traditional opposition research shops."[47]

Blogs, the twenty-first-century version of a diary, are simply Web pages where an individual can post thoughts on any subject. The thoughts posted on the blog are available for anyone with Internet access to read, and most blogs permit readers to post their thoughts in response to the original posting. Thus, an online community is created where individuals who share common interests meet on the Internet and conduct online conversations. Blogs began growing in popularity beginning in 1999 and have become a common feature of Internet activity.

Because of the growing popularity of blogs, politicians and political enthusiasts began using them to communicate with the electorate. Blogs have become very attractive to political enthusiasts, especially beginning with the Howard Dean run for the presidency in 2004.

David D. Perlmutter notes, "it seemed like everyone running, from alderman to commander in chief, was blogging or trying to use blogs to raise money, rally supporters, and achieve every politician's dream of bypassing mainstream press and communicating directly to the voters (for a lot less money than a televised ad)."[48] In order to remain competitive, the twenty-first-century politician must "live in MySpace, see in YouTube, and write in blog."[49] The 2008 campaign was the year that blogs appeared to have made a significant difference in political campaigning. Perlmutter asserts, "the year blogs arrived was 2004, and in the 2006 election, blogs became full-time players in the game; 2008 will be the year political professionals thoroughly explore what blogs can do in all political races, including the run for the White House."[50]

Triple O established a unit within the Obama campaign Chicago headquarters that was responsible for sending text messages to the electorate to communicate Obama's message. This was a strategy designed to appeal to younger voters, with custom-made wallpapers, ring tones, and a personalized text message number of 62262, which spelled "OBAMA" on cell phones.[51] The Obama campaign even created an iPhone and iTouch application that could be downloaded for free that organized an individual's personal contacts based on whether they lived in a state considered a battleground state.[52] Winograd and Hais report that Millennials are community and group oriented and share their thoughts and activities with each other. They communicate with twenty-first-century technologies such as e-mail, text messaging, and instant messaging. Winograd and Hais found "half of Millennials report that they have in the past twenty-four hours sent or received an e-mail (50 percent) and/or cell phone text message (51 percent), and almost a third (30 percent) an instant message."[53] It was that sense of community and staying connected with friends that the Obama campaign successfully tapped into during the 2008 campaign.

To reach the Democratic Party's base of African Americans, Hispanics, and the youth votes, the Obama campaign team devised an elaborate text messaging strategy that included more than three million people registering their phone numbers with the campaign. Christopher Stern notes, "Studies show that texting is among the most effective and cheapest ways of getting supporters, particularly blacks, Hispanics and younger voters, to the voting booth."[54] There was a lot of anticipation leading up to Obama's announcement of his running mate for the vice presidential position because the announcement was going to be made via a text message sent to cell phones that had been registered with the campaign.

Observers suggest this campaign tactic was a failure because news leaked early of Obama's pick as a running mate before registered cell phones were sent a text. Approximately 40–50 percent of the registered users did not receive the text message announcing that Senator Joe Biden was the running mate.[55] Moreover, the Obama campaign sent the text message at 3:00 a.m., preventing major newspapers throughout the United States from having the story on the front pages the next day.[56] The Obama campaign team believed strongly in utilizing new media technologies to communicate with the electorate. Scott Goodstein, responsible for the Obama text messaging campaign, stated, "New Media and the Internet and text-messaging all have millions of people communicating in unique ways, and I don't think it's going to be going anywhere for a very long time."[57]

Similar to text messaging on a mobile phone, but usable with or without a phone, is an Internet-based mass medium known as Twitter. It is a social messaging application and micro-blogging application that allows users to send messages to people by using 140 characters or less. Each message is referred to as a "tweet" and users must have a Twitter account to send tweets and read tweets sent by other users. In order to read tweets sent by others using the service, you must subscribe to their account and become a "follower." Twitter was founded in 2006 and is utilized by media savvy politicians. Arnold Schwarzenegger, governor of California, utilizes Twitter to communicate with his constituents and he has more than sixty-five thousand followers.[58] In total, more than six million people have Twitter accounts and this was attractive to the Obama campaign team during the 2008 presidential election.[59] During the campaign, Obama had more than one hundred thousand followers subscribed to receive his tweets, which contained campaign messages that reminded people when and where to vote and requested donations. As with most new media, the Millennials are attracted to this technology. One in five people with Internet access between the ages of eighteen and thirty-four have accessed Twitter to update their profiles at least once.[60]

Viral videos, or videos that are forwarded from Internet user to Internet user, emerged in the 2008 campaign. The videos were a very effective marketing tool for the presidential candidates, especially for Barack Obama. During the 2008 election, candidates had their own YouTube channel and posted videos there promoting their positions on issues and other significant announcements relating to their campaigns. In total, Obama posted 1,820 videos that were viewed more than ninety million times compared to his most ardent opponent, Hillary Clinton, who posted only seventy-six videos.[61] During the 2008 presidential campaign, candidates posted videos and advertisements on YouTube without having to pay expensive rates for television advertising: "At times, both campaigns called press conferences to announce a new ad, hoping that reporters would provide free coverage of the ad's message, even though the ad was rarely shown in paid media slots."[62]

In the final days of the 2008 presidential campaign, Barack Obama even resorted to placing advertising in online video games such as the Xbox 360 game *Burnout Paradise* that spanned ten battleground states including Ohio, Florida, Iowa, Colorado, Indiana, Montana, North Carolina, New Mexico, Nevada, and Wisconsin.[63] The Obama campaign spent nearly $45,000 placing advertising in eighteen different games leading up to Election Day. Obama's Republican challenger, John McCain, was approached by the same company and his campaign declined to advertise in the video games.[64] The advertisement in the Xbox game was in the form of a roadside billboard that encouraged early voting and directed gamers to the voteforchange.com Web site.[65] Advertising in video gaming systems is used to reach the eighteen- to thirty-four-year-old demographic.[66] Barack Obama was the first presidential candidate to ever buy advertising space in an online video game.[67]

NEW MEDIA AND FUTURE CAMPAIGNS

The Internet, and Web 2.0 politicking, is sure to continue playing a major role in American politics in the twenty-first century. Girish J. Gulati asserts, "As today's younger generation become the leading trendsetters of tomorrow and more households gain access to high-speed Internet service, it is not inconceivable that the Internet will be the number one source for campaign news in 2012."[68] Technological advancements are developing rapidly and the 2012 presidential campaign could rely even more on the Internet to communicate with the electorate. The politicians must follow the voters and it is clear that the voters are relying heavily on Internet based technologies to deliver the latest information, ranging from things as simple as news, weather, and driving directions to basic human needs such as interpersonal communication via social networking sites. Astutely, Perlmutter notes "successful mass political communication is that which best approximates successful personal communication."[69]

Lois Kelly suggests the use of social media during the 2008 presidential campaign changed the landscape of political campaigning in three ways. First, the manner in which candidates raise funds has given average citizens with middle class incomes a larger role in the democratic process. In the 2008 campaign, Obama raised $40 million from 1.5 million donors giving small amounts of money ranging from $5 to $100 donations. Second, the role of traditional media has been diminished due to new media which allows citizens to go directly to candidate Web sites and get information unfiltered. The voters who are thirty years of age and under prefer the Internet to traditional mass media to obtain information. Thus, as this demographic grows, the agenda setting function of traditional media will continue to diminish. Third, the power of traditional advertising is diminishing as younger voters are seeking information about candidates via Internet videos through YouTube and other video portals as opposed to traditional media.[70]

As the popularity of the Internet continues to grow and technological advancements continue emerging, the role it will play in future political campaigns is significant. Richard Davis states, "Since communication is so vital to a campaign, and candidates and voters are turning to the Internet to transmit and receive information, the Internet must be studied as a communication tool."[71] Moreover, Kartik Hosanagar, a Wharton School professor, posits: "The web will create a participatory culture and unprecedented levels of civic engagement. The web itself is becoming more decentralized with user-generated content and open platforms. I think that the same sort of culture will spill over into how this segment wants to engage politically. Citizens [these days] want to create and distribute political messages themselves, endorse candidates and spread those messages they find most appealing. I think these trends will have a lasting impact on politics."[72]

Although the Internet and its use during the 2008 campaign was a very successful endeavor, there are concerns that arise from the emergence of and rapid adoption rate by consumers of an unregulated mass medium such as the Internet. For political purposes, its role will continue to be to communicate with the electorate, raise funds for campaigning, and identify new supporters. The Internet will also create a need for tech savvy staffers on political campaign teams to stay abreast of technological advancements and devise ways to target demographics on the Internet with very specific messages that appeal to the interests and concerns of specific and unique demographics. Marjorie Randon Hershey states: "With new applications appearing regularly, political use of the Internet should continue to expand in 2010 and 2012. Because the Internet has become the main source of information for people younger than thirty about the presidential election, any successful national campaign will need to bring Internet strategies into the core of its efforts. That, in turn, should increase the opportunities for younger and more Web-savvy people in running campaigns."[73]

Political communication has evolved dramatically in the twenty-first century and the 2008 presidential campaign is evidence of that evolution. In politics, effective communication is imperative because, as Judith S. Trent and Robert V. Friedenberg astutely note, "communication is the heart of the modern political campaign."[74] As a result of John F. Kennedy's effective use of the then new mass medium of television, political communication in the twentieth century was changed. After Kennedy, no serious presidential contender could succeed without effectively utilizing the medium of television.

Likewise, Barack Obama used the Internet to change political communication making him a truly twenty-first-century communicator. The *New York Times* observed, "One of the many ways that the election of Barack Obama as president has echoed that of John F. Kennedy is his use of a new medium that will forever change politics. For Mr. Kennedy, it was television. For Mr. Obama, it is the Internet."[75] Without question, Obama established a precedent for how future contenders for the White House must communicate with the electorate, especially a technologically savvy electorate.

Barack Obama's campaign utilized every type of new media technology that existed during the 2008 presidential campaign to reach voters of all ages, ethnicities, socioeconomic backgrounds, and sexual orientations to inspire and motivate Americans to participate in the country's democratic process of electing its leaders. Obama, the first Web 2.0 president, used social networking technologies such as Twitter, Facebook, My Space, YouTube, e-mail, blogs, video games, and text messaging to communicate with voters. Girish J. Gulati asserts, "For better or worse, the new forms of media that came of age in the 2008 elections are here to stay. The youngest generation of voters is the most attached to the Internet and soft news sources for learning about campaigns and are unlikely to abandon them in favor of the media of yesterday."[76] It was Barack Obama, and the Triple O campaign team, who "signed, sealed, and delivered" the guide that will be followed by future presidential contenders when using the Internet to communicate with the electorate.[77]

NOTES

1. Aristotle, *The Politics of Aristotle*, trans. Ernest Barker (New York: Oxford University Press, 1970), 5.

2. See, for example, Lloyd F. Bitzer, "Political Rhetoric," in *Handbook of Political Communication*, ed. Dan Nimmo and Keith Sanders (Beverly Hills, CA: Sage, 1981), 228; Dan Nimmo and David Swanson, "The Field of Political Communication: Beyond the Voter Persuasion Paradigm," in *New Directions in Political Communication: A Resource Book*, ed. David Swanson and Dan Nimmo (Newbury Park, CA: Sage, 1990), 33; G. R. Boynton, "Our Conversations about Governing," in *Political Communication Research*, ed. David Paletz (Norwood, NJ: Ablex, 1996), 102; or Robert E. Denton, Jr., and Jim Kuypers, *Politics and Communication in America* (Long Grove, IL: Waveland Press, 2008), 21–39.

3. As quoted in Dan Nimmo and David Swanson, "The Field of Political Communication: Beyond the Voter Persuasion Paradigm," in *New Directions in Political Communication: A Resource Book*, ed. David Swanson and Dan Nimmo (Newbury Park, CA: Sage, 1990), 33.

4. Robert E. Denton, Jr., and Jim Kuypers, *Politics and Communication in America* (Long Grove, IL: Waveland Press, 2008), 4.

5. Denton and Kuypers, 5–9.

6. See, for instance, Walter Dill Scott, *Influencing Men in Business* (New York: The Ronald Press Company, 1911).

7. Samuel Becker and Edward Lower, "Broadcasting in Presidential Campaigns," in *The Great Debates: Carter vs. Ford, 1976*, ed. Sidney Kraus (Bloomington: Indiana University Press, 1979), 22.

8. Joanne Morreale, "American Self-Images and the Presidential Campaign Film, 1964–1992," in *Presidential Campaigns and American Self-Images*, ed. Arthur H. Miller and Bruce E. Gronbeck (Boulder, CO: Westview Press, 1998), 19–39.

9. Kathleen Hall Jamieson, *Eloquence in an Electronic Age* (New York: Oxford University Press, 1988), 166.

10. Robert E. Denton, Jr., *The Primetime Presidency of Ronald Reagan* (New York: Praeger, 1988), 84.

11. Bruce E. Gronbeck, "The Web, Campaign 07-08, and Engaged Citizens," in *The 2008 Presidential Campaign*, ed. Robert E. Denton, Jr. (Lanham, MD: Rowman & Littlefield, 2009), 229.

12. Gronbeck, *The 2008 Presidential Campaign*, 229.

13. Gronbeck, *The 2008 Presidential Campaign*, 229.

14. Gronbeck, *The 2008 Presidential Campaign*, 230–31.

15. Danielle Wiese and Bruce E. Gronbeck, "Campaign 2004 Developments in Cyberpolitics," in *The 2004 Presidential Campaign: A Communication Perspective* (Lanham, MD: Rowman & Littlefield, 2005), 218.

16. Robert Friedenberg, *Communication Consultants in Political Campaigns* (Westport, CT: Praeger, 1997), 204.

17. Friedenberg, *Communication Consultants in Political Campaigns*, 218.

18. Wiese and Gronbeck, 220.

19. Andrew Williams and John Tedesco, "Introduction," in *The Internet Election* (Lanham, MD: Rowman & Littlefield, 2006), 1.

20. Clifford A. Jones, "Regulating Web Messages in the 2004 Election and Beyond," in *The Internet Election*, ed. Andrew Williams and John Tedesco (Lanham, MD: Rowman & Littlefield, 2006), 14; see also Kaye Trammell, "The Blogging of the President" (133–46), in the same source.

21. Wiese and Gronbeck, 220.

22. Morley Winograd and Michael Hais, *Millennial Makeover: My Space, YouTube, and the Future of American Politics* (New Brunswick, NJ: Rutgers University Press, 2008), 166.

23. Winograd and Hais, 175.

24. Gronbeck, 231–33.

25. Winograd and Hais, 1.

26. Winograd and Hais, 155.

27. John Allen Hendricks and Shannon K. McCraw, "Coverage of Political Campaigns," in *American Journalism: History, Principles Practices*, ed. W. David Sloan and Lisa Mullikin Parcell (Jefferson, NC: McFarland & Company, Inc., 2002), 181–88.

28. Jose Antonio Vargas, "Obama's Wide Web: From YouTube to Text Messaging, Candidate's Team Connects to Voters," *Washington Post*, 20 August 2008, C01.

29. Michael Wolff, "Candidate.com," *New York Magazine*, 8 September 2003, nymag.com/nymetro/news/media/columns/medialife/n_9188/index1.html (14 May 2009).

30. Girish J. Gulati, "No Laughing Matter: The Role of New Media in the 2008 Election," in *The Year of Obama: How Barack Obama Won the White House*, ed. Larry J. Sabato (New York: Longman, 2010), 193.

31. Paul Harris and David Smith, "Obama's Wi-Fi White House Speaks to the YouTube Age," *The Observer*, 16 November 2008, 38.

32. Chuck Todd and Sheldon Gawiser, *How Barack Obama Won: A State-by-State Guide to the Historic 2008 Presidential Election* (New York: Vintage Books, 2009), 30–31.

33. Vargas, *Washington Post*, C01.

34. Adam Nagourney, "In Election's Wake, Campaigns Offer a Peek at What Really Happened," *The New York Times*, 9 December 2008. www.nytimes.com/2008/12/09/us/politics/09webnagourney.html (27 February 2009).

35. Marian Currinder, "Campaign Finance: Fundraising and Spending in the 2008 Elections," in *The Elections of 2008*, ed. Michael Nelson (Washington, DC: CQ Press, 2010), 177.

36. Michael Cornfield, "Game-Changers: New Technology and the 2008 Presidential Election," in *The Year of Obama: How Barack Obama Won the White House*, ed. Larry J. Sabato (New York: Longman, 2010), 207.

37. Stefanie Olsen, "Insiders Debate Social Media's Influence on Election '08," *CNET News*, 29 April 2008. news.cnet.com/8301-10784_3-9931171-7.html (27 February 2009).

38. Vargas, *Washington Post*, C01.

39. Laura Olson, "Obama Team Capitalizes on Link to Youth: Online Outreach Lays Groundwork for New Way to Govern," *ChicagoTribune.com*, 26 November 2008, www.chicagotribune.com/news/nationworld/chi-youth-obama nov26,0,5441030.story (27 February 2009).

40. "Young Voters in the 2008 Presidential Election," The Center for Information and Research on Civic Learning and Engagement, Tufts University, 19 December 2008, www.civicyouth.org (27 February 2009).

41. Cornfield, *The Year of Obama: How Barack Obama Won the White House*, 220.

42. Gerald Witt, "This Election, It's 'Word of Mouse' for Voters," *News-Record.com*, 7 September 2008. www.newsrecord.com/content/2008/09/06/article/this_election_its_word_of_mouse_for_voters (17 February 2009).

43. "Marketing Presidential Candidates on the Web Goes Mainstream: But Does It Get Votes?" *Knowledge@Wharton*, 9 January 2008. knowledge.wharton.upenn.edu/printer_friendly.cfm?articleid=1874 (27 February 2009).

44. Fred Aun, "Over Long Campaign, Obama Videos Drew Nearly a Billion Views," *Clickz*, 7 November 2008, www.clickz.com/3631604 (27 February 2009).

45. Vargas, *Washington Post*, C01.

46. Jim Rutenberg, "Political Freelancers Use Web to Join the Attack," *New York Times*, 29 June 2008, www.nytimes.com/2008/06/29/us/politics/29opposition.hrml?pagewanted=print (27 February 2009).

47. Jim Rutenberg, *New York Times*, 29 June 2008.

48. David D. Perlmutter, *Blog Wars* (New York: Oxford University Press, 2008), xiv.

49. Perlmutter, *Blog Wars*, xv.

50. Perlmutter, *Blog Wars*, 105.

51. Vargas, *Washington Post*, C01.

52. Ari Melber, "Obama's Web-Savvy Voter Plan," *The Nation*, 8 October 2008, www.thenation.com/doc/20081027/melber (19 May 2009).

53. Winograd and Hais, 83.

54. Christopher Stern, "Obama Counts on Text Messages to Drive Turnout of Youth, Blacks," *Bloomberg.com*, 4 November 2008.

55. Stephanie Condon, "Whoops! Obama's VP Text-Messaging Idea Didn't Work Out So Well," *CNET.com*, 28 August 2008, wwwnews.cnet.com/8301-13578_3-10028614-38.html (20 May 2009).

56. Anne E. Kornblut and Ed O'Keefe, "Tale of the Obama Text Message," *Washington Post*, 23 August 2008, voices.washingtonpost.com/44/2008/08/23/tale_of_the_obama_text_message.html (20 May 2009).

57. Kate Linthicum, "Barack Obama's Text Message Guru Talks to the Ticket," *Los Angeles Times*, 7 January 2009, latimesblogs.latimes.com/washington/2009/01/obama-chief-tec.html (20 May 2009).

58. Scott Bauer, "Politicos Get Taste for Twitter's Tiny Sound Bites," *Herald Democrat*, 3 May 2009, B4.

59. Michael Liedtke, "Can All That Twitters Turn to Gold Amid the Gloom?" *Herald Democrat*, 15 February 2009, B1.

60. Liedtke, *Herald Democrat*, B1.

61. Stern, *Bloomberg.com*, 4 November 2008, www.bloomberg.com/apps/news?pid=20670001&sid=av91P3tyvybU (20 May 2009).

62. Marjorie Randon Hershey, "The Media: Coloring the News," in *The Elections of 2008*, ed. Michael Nelson (Washington, DC: CQ Press, 2010), 138.

63. Brendan Sinclair, "Obama Campaigns in Burnout, 17 Other Games," *Gamespot*, 14 October 2008, www.gamespot.com/news/6199379.html?print=1 (27 February 2009).

64. Brendan Sinclair, "Obama's In-Game Ad Bill: $44.5K," *Gamespot*, 29 October 2008, www.gamespot.com/news/6200232.html?sid=6200232&print=1 (27 February 2009).

65. Craig Daitch, "Obama Says 'Yes We Can!' to In-Game Advertising: Billboard in 'Burnout Paradise' Promotes Early Voting," *Advertising Age*, 13 October 2008, adage.com/digitalnext/article?article_id=131675 (27 February 2009).

66. Daitch, *Advertising Age*, 13 October 2008.

67. Devlin Barrett, "Obama Ads: 'It's in the Game,'" *MSNBC.com*, 14 October 2008, www.msnbc.msn.com/id/27184857/ (27 February 2009).

68. Gulati, *The Year of Obama: How Barack Obama Won the White House*, 188.

69. Perlmutter, *Blog Wars*, 153.

70. Lois Kelly, "Social Media and the 2008 Presidential Campaign," blog posted 17 May 2008, blog.foghound.com/265/ (27 February 2009).

71. Richard Davis, *The Web of Politics: The Internet's Impact on the American Political System* (New York: Oxford University Press, 1999), 96.

72. "Marketing Presidential Candidates on the Web Goes Mainstream: But Does It Get Votes?" *Knowledge@Wharton*, 9 January 2008, knowledge.wharton.upenn .edu/printer_friendly.cfm?articleid=1874 (27 February 2009).

73. Hershey, *The Elections of 2008*, 140–41.

74. Judith S. Trent and Robert V. Friedenberg, *Political Campaign Communication: Principles & Practices*, sixth ed. (Lanham, MD: Rowman & Littlefield, 2008), 415.

75. Claire Cain Miller, "How Obama's Internet Campaign Changed Politics," *New York Times*, 7 November 2008, bits.blogs.nytimes.com/2008/11/07/how-obamas -internet-campaign-changed-politics/ (7 June 2009).

76. Gulati, *The Year of Obama: How Barack Obama Won the White House*, 201.

77. Stevie Wonder's 1970 hit song, *Signed, Sealed, Delivered I'm Yours*, was one of the Barack Obama campaign theme songs.

2

Gadgets, Gismos, and the Web 2.0 Election

Jenn Burleson Mackay

Cell phones, BlackBerrys, and iPhones allowed Americans to connect to the presidential candidates as though they were old college pals. Wielding a tiny gadget in the palm of their hand, they sifted through text message announcements from candidates, and checked for updates on Facebook and My Space. They could watch YouTube campaign clips while they rode the train to work or as they sat in traffic jams. Voters were intimately connected to the campaigns through the single object that goes with them everywhere they go—their wireless phones.

Barack Obama was not the only winner in the 2008 presidential election. The technologically savvy cell phones that became a powerhouse of political proportions joined him. As described by Merrie Spaeth, "It's not just a phone. It's an e-mail vehicle, a written or text device, and a small screen TV in a way that computer-based instant messaging never reached."[1] Those multipurpose devices gave candidates a direct connection to potential volunteers and campaign contributors across the country. The popularity of Web 2.0, the growing sophistication of handheld devices, and the merger between social networking and the mobile Internet changed the dynamic of this campaign and campaigns of the future.

This chapter will explore how cell phones and other handheld gadgets played a role in the presidential election. It will discuss how candidates used phones to mobilize volunteers and to develop massive lists of potential voters and contributors. This chapter also will delve into the constant access to information that Web 2.0 technology and the mobile Internet provided the owners of smart phones and other devices.

19

THE GROWTH OF THE CELL PHONE

While cell phones are so commonplace now that many of us cannot imagine life without them, it took three decades for them to become a staple in American culture. Motorola employee Martin Cooper made the first cell phone call in 1973. Motorola invested some $100 million in the cell phone industry from the 1960s to the 1980s. Those earliest phones were not practical for the average consumer. They weighed nearly two pounds each. A single phone cost nearly $4,000 as of 1983. With time, those phones became more practical. Both the price and the size changed and from 1985 to 2002 the number of cell phone subscribers increased from 350,000 to almost 150 million.[2]

The first smartphone came onto the scene in 1993. IBM's "Simon" phone had some basic applications such as a calendar and an address book. Whereas original cell phones were designed specifically for wireless calling, smartphones added additional features that gave them capabilities similar to a Palm Pilot PDA. Smartphones have evolved to become even more advanced. Today, they are similar to miniature computers.[3]

There are several different types of smartphone operating systems. The Research in Motion Blackberry was introduced in 1999. The first BlackBerry looked a bit like a pager and featured services that were useful to the business world such as an organizer, paging, a calendar, and e-mail. It also included a "qwerty" keyboard, but lacked phone capabilities.[4] In 2002 the first phone-equipped BlackBerry hit the streets.[5] At the time this chapter was written, the BlackBerry corporate Web site boasted that more than twenty-one million people were using BlackBerry smartphones around the world.[6]

The BlackBerry has its smartphone rivals. The Apple iPhone was introduced in 2007, just in time for the presidential campaign. Consumers waited outside stores overnight hoping to be one of the first to grab the shiny new gadgets.[7] The phones were described as being an iPod-style music player, as well as a cell phone and an Internet device. The Obama campaign wasted little time in taking advantage of the device by launching an iPhone application. The free software allowed iPhone owners to organize their personal contacts according to the battleground states in the election. It also showed users caller statistics to demonstrate how their personal calling statistics stacked up against other iPhone owners across the country. Individuals could receive automatic updates and access to videos and photos from the campaign, among other features.[8]

TEXTING THE ELECTION

Vodafone and Airwide Solutions employee Neil Papworth typed the words "Merry Christmas" into a computer and sent them to a cell phone in 1992. It was the first text message and the beginning of a phenomenon. The Vodafone employees originally saw their text messaging experiments as a potential enhancement for pagers, but the technology eventually became a major facet of cell phone technology. It is not clear how many text messages now are sent on a daily basis, but some suggest that it is more than one trillion.[9]

Text messaging became a major tactic during the 2008 campaign. One writer even suggested that that "this year's campaign speeches may be asking for your text messages as often as they ask for your vote."[10] But this was not the first election that tested the power of the text message. During Howard Dean's run for the presidency in 2004, supporters could join Dean Wireless—a text messaging service that sent subscribers regular campaign updates. Research also has suggested the importance of text messaging on a campaign. A study of the 2006 elections found that 26 percent of the participants surveyed suggested that text messages increased the likelihood that they would vote. In addition, the experimental study found that those who received text messages cast ballots at a 3.2 percent higher rate than the participants in a control group who did not receive the messages.[11]

The 2008 presidential candidates found several ways to utilize text messaging. On one hand, companies offered rally attendees the opportunity to send text messages that were shown on a screen to everyone else attending the event. A single individual could screen each message before it displayed on the screen. This text-to-screen technology previously has been used in concerts, sporting events, and other venues, but it was a relatively new addition to the political arena.[12]

Messages sent to the screen were limited to 160 characters. One advantage to candidates who used the method was that they could use the messages to create a contact list of people who attended the event. Then they could keep in touch with them long after the event ended, by sending thank-you messages or other campaign-related comments.[13] Campaign organizers found some creative ways to take advantage of the technology. When Republican vice presidential candidate Sarah Palin went to a rally at the Home Depot Center in Carson, California, an electronic billboard greeted her. The California Democratic Party placed the board in a parking lot across from the stadium where she was speaking. Throughout the day of the rally, the board showed questions that were sent in via text message or e-mail. Questions such as "Why do you make victims pay for rape kits?" appeared on the board.[14] Also, the Obama Minute, a grassroots campaign aimed at electing the president, organized a text messaging campaign, which encouraged supporters to text a message that would appear on an enormous screen in New York's Times Square.[15]

As a whole, the Obama campaign placed more emphasis on the use of text messaging than the other candidates. Nonetheless, reports suggest that some of Obama's supporters were skeptical when Scott Goodstein unveiled his text message program for the campaign. The plan incorporated Obama phone wallpaper as well as ring tones into the campaign. While those features have been popular in the commercial market, they had not previously found a place in politics. Democrat candidates Hillary Clinton and John Edwards, as well as Republican candidate Mitt Romney, had text message programs as well, but they did not go so far as to create custom-made wallpapers. Republican John McCain's troop did not rely on text messaging.[16]

The Obama campaign used the text messages to build an enormous database of supporters and to keep individuals engaged throughout the campaign. Those who signed up for text messages were reminded of upcoming debates and events. The texting program also enabled voters to contact the Obama camp whenever they had general questions such as where they could cast their ballots.[17] Of course, this meant that the Obama campaign needed to have workers ready to answer questions quickly and efficiently.

Those who signed up with the Obama campaign received a variety of messages. One text read "Please REPLY to this message with your five-digit zip code to receive local Obama campaign news and periodic updates."[18] The system allowed the campaign to collect a list of cell phone numbers that could be sorted by area code, zip code, and demographics.[19] Eventually, text messages asked supporters to volunteer in precincts, and to vote on January 26 in South Carolina—a state that Obama won by twenty-eight points. Goodstein told a journalist that the success of the South Carolina vote helped the campaign to develop their overall strategy for the entire campaign.[20] Obama supporters in Democrat stronghold California were asked via text message to man phone banks and field offices in Colorado and Nevada.[21] Perhaps taking a cue from the commercial industry, the Obama campaign even found a way to promote campaign memorabilia via text messages. One message read "A holiday gift from the Obama store: get a 20% discount on all Store.BarackObama.com items through Dec. 31. Use coupon code: TEXT at checkout."[22]

Arguably, the most significant text message sent during the campaign was Obama's announcement that Joe Biden would be his running mate. Before the announcement was made, newspapers regularly reminded readers of the text messaging plan, giving the candidate even more publicity. Reports suggested that the message reached 2.9 million people. While those who signed up to receive the text were promised that they would receive the news of the vice presidential announcement before anyone else, there were perhaps some flaws in the messaging system. Initially, some fake text messages were sent out to text subscribers.[23] The political blog Wonkette posted instructions on how the fake messages could be delivered.[24] To further complicate matters, CNN and other major news organizations broke the news that Obama had selected Biden on a Friday night. To keep up with their promise that texters would receive the message first, Obama campaigners sent out their text messages at roughly 3 a.m. Eastern time—when many voters were in bed.[25]

In addition to the campaigners, other organizations relied on text messaging to motivate young potential voters. The nonpartisan organization Rock the Vote worked with AT&T to initiate a program that allowed potential voters to get election news through text messages.[26]

Text messaging gave the candidates an efficient and inexpensive way to reach out to voters. One text message can be sent to droves of voters at a fraction of the cost of a television advertisement or a bulk mailing. E-mail also is an inexpensive way to reach voters, but is easy to ignore and runs the risk of ending up in a junk mail folder. Also, text messaging gave the candidates a way to reach voters no matter where they were. Candidates did not have to wait for supporters to be in front of their computer in order to receive the message. If the campaign needed a last-minute volunteer to man a post, he or she could be reached immediately. Text messaging also gave the candidates a way to develop a massive cell phone list of voters. With no comprehensive cell phone list currently in existence, this new method gave Obama an edge over candidates who were less aggressive with text messaging. The campaigners had an intimate way to reach voters throughout the campaign and developed a list that may still be very useful during the next presidential campaign.

INTRODUCING WEB 2.0

In previous elections, candidates uploaded static Web pages to the Internet to share some basic facts and their political platforms. The pages may have provided an e-mail address for a candidate, but they did not give voters the chance to enter into a real dialogue with the representatives. The pages were created using programming languages such as hypertext markup language. They were not designed for frequent updates but rather gave the candidate a constant, rarely changing presence online. The development of Web 2.0 opened up a host of new opportunities for candidates.

Web 2.0 is characterized as the second stage of the Web. The new Web style replaces those static, difficult to update Web pages with blogs and other social networking sites that allow users to share and frequently update their personal opinions, photos, and videos without any computer programming expertise. It allows users to enter into discussions with the world by posting comments directly to a Web page—rather than sending an e-mail that can only go to a handful of people.[27]

There is some debate as to who coined the phrase Web 2.0. Some people suggest that the concept of Web 2.0 was initiated during a conference between O'Reilly Media and MediaLive International.[28] Darcy DiNucci also discussed the term in a 1999 article: "The first glimmerings of Web 2.0 are beginning to appear, and we are just starting to see how that embryo might develop."[29]

A classic example of Web 2.0 is blog—a Web site that allows individuals to create their own Web page within moments. Individuals simply choose how they want their page to appear, and what features they want to include by clicking on a Web page. Users are able to post updates to the page regularly, without knowing anything about the computer lingo that created the Web page. Other examples of Web 2.0 are sites such as YouTube and Vimeo, which allow individuals to upload videos to the Web to share with millions of people with only the click of a few buttons. Users essentially develop their own personal video Web pages. Social networking sites such as Facebook and MySpace represent another form of Web 2.0, as users without any use for computer programming create Web pages, post regular updates, upload photos, link to news clips, and enter into online conversations with friends. Once a user sets up a page on these social networking sites, others are invited to follow them. For example, individuals can ask to be "friends" with someone who has a personal page on Facebook. If the other individual acknowledges the friend request, both individuals are able to follow each other's comments online.

This new technology created a new online political environment. Politicians were able to connect to citizens on a different level, by creating their own Facebook pages that were frequently updated with new information. Rather than buying commercial time on television, they were able to upload free videos to YouTube. Even potential voters were able to create and post their own campaign videos in support or opposition to various candidates. In some cases, they were even encouraged to create their own videos by contests. Add to that the presence of the mobile Internet on cell phones and other wireless gadgets, and candidates had a whole new playing field for a political match of epic proportions.

CAMPAIGNING WITH SOCIAL SAVVY

Voters had a host of ways that they could use their cell phones to keep up with the election in addition to text messages. The sophistication of cell phones allowed users to also link to the Internet to search for information, read blogs, download YouTube videos, etc. The Obama campaign took advantage of these capabilities and hired the California-based company iLoop Mobile to create a mobile site, my.barackobama.com, that would allow cell phone users to easily access campaign information.[30]

Social networking created a new dimension for the political campaign. Web sites such as Facebook and MySpace gave candidates easy-to-use options for creating social networking sites. They provided candidates with a way to connect with younger voters who stay connected to social networking sites all day via computers and cell phones. Social networking sites also provided candidates with a way to potentially mobilize campaign volunteers. Research suggested that by the February before the 2008 election, some fifty million people were already using their cell phones for social networking.[31]

Candidates also experimented with creating their own social networking sites. Obama's my.barackobama.com was operational the day that Obama announced his candidacy.[32] Obama hired the small privately owned firm Blue State Digital to help with his campaign. The market research and new media company was formed in 2004 by four members who worked on Howard Dean's presidential campaign. The company helped develop Obama's Web site. The Web site encouraged communication between individuals, allowing them to share ideas and organize events. Obama campaign staffers monitored the discussion and used the Web site to help workers respond to supporters in a personal fashion.[33] The site allowed users to customize their pages, as they can with other programs such as iTunes and Mobile Me. They could upload photos, and use other interactive features on the site.[34] The ability to have an individual page on a candidate's Web site allowed users to feel connected to the campaign in a personal way. It also gave voters a way to show the world which candidate they were supporting in a fierce campaign. The customizable features made those pages even more individualized.

WeTheCitizens developed software that allowed campaigns with less cash than the Obama campaign to develop similar social networking sites. The software is similar to Facebook, in that it allows users to create personal profiles that become part of a larger site. Other features make it more effective for political campaigns, however, such as the program's ability to keep track of who is doing what for the campaign. Sonny Perdue used the software for his gubernatorial race in Georgia. Rudy Giuliani also used it. His social network, my.joinrudy2009.com, was online in November 2007. The network had between fifteen and twenty thousand members by January 2008. Similar to Obama, Giuliani had his own Facebook and MySpace pages, but Giuliani's deputy e-campaign director Katie Harbath said it was difficult to use those sites to connect groups of people together.[35]

Every presidential candidate had links from their homepage to various social networking sites such as Facebook, MySpace, and Digg. Those sites allowed users another way to stay connected to the campaign.[36] They also gave users a way to connect to other individuals who had similar interests. Some suggest that the use of those free social networking sites allowed Republican candidate Ron Paul to stay in the campaign longer than he would have otherwise. The candidate reportedly raised about $500,000 to develop a Web site. That was roughly half of what it would have needed to develop a savvy social networking site. Instead of trying that path, the candidate set up several free social networking sites. The approach prevented Paul from having an easy-to-track, centralized system, but it gave him a way to stay connected with potential voters. The campaign posted their needs on those various sites and relied on its supporters to fulfill those needs. The candidate managed to save enough money that he was able to lease a blimp during the campaign.[37]

The candidates received much attention from their presence on Facebook. The Web site Techpresident.com tracked the candidates as they pursued social networks. The site indicated that Obama had more than two million Facebook supporters, while McCain had more than six hundred thousand, Ralph Nader and Bob Barr each had a little less than eleven thousand, and Cynthia McKinny had about five thousand.[38] Some candidates also relied on MySpace, but they had significantly fewer friends. Obama had more than eight hundred thousand, McCain had about two hundred thousand, Nader had a little less than eight thousand, and Barr had about six thousand.[39] Even corporations joined social networking political extravaganza. Burger King and Qdoba Mexican Grill set up pages on Facebook and MySpace to allow visitors to discuss their political opinions.[40] As individuals visited those sites, they left information, such as demographic details, about themselves behind. That process left candidates with some valuable information. As explained by Bruce Gronbeck, "Knowing who comes and goes, when, and for how long can help guide campaign strategy."[41] It can not only help candidates to target volunteers, but it also can help them to target specific messages to particular audiences.

Campaigns found some off-the-beaten-path methods for taking advantage of social networking, too. The Republican National Committee launched a Facebook parody site called BarackBook that "linked" Obama to friends that might reflect poorly upon his candidacy. The Obama camp followed the incident by posting a series of policy documents on the social networking site Scribd. Similar to other social networking sites, Scribd allows users to interact by commenting on content.[42]

YouTube may have been the major social networking player in this campaign, although the number of subscribers to each candidate's YouTube page may distort its value. Obama had a little more than thirty-one thousand subscribers while McCain had a little less than three thousand subscribers.[43] Those numbers may have some value, in that they show which candidate was considered more popular in some sense, but unlike some online applications, users of YouTube are not required to subscribe to a particular feed in order to receive information so thousands of additional people could have visited each of the candidate's YouTube pages in a single day.

During this election, the candidates were able to use YouTube as an inexpensive alternative to pricey television advertisements. The Obama campaign clearly valued their video presence as they hired an Emmy winner and former CNN journalist to lead their video team. There were at least nine staff members who contributed to the video productions. Some of those staff members traveled with Obama while others worked in the field developing other aspects of the campaign. Some of the videos were less than five minutes long while others ran up to twenty-five minutes. In addition to posting the clips to YouTube, Obama's team also made them available on the candidate's homepage.[44] There were videos of campaign speeches and clips of campaigners talking with voters. Obama's Iowa victory speech received three million hits and his "Yes We Can" speech in New Hampshire garnered 2.5 million hits. Residents no longer needed to make sure that they were at home in front of the TV in order to catch the debates. YouTube gave them a new flexibility.[45]

The candidates also used YouTube to throw a little dirt into the election. McCain's campaign released a video in July 2008 that compared Obama's stardom to Paris Hilton and Britney Spears. Less than a month later the video had been viewed two million times. Obama's team responded by releasing a video that ridiculed McCain's straight talk reputation. In addition to the campaign-sponsored videos, the election saw a surge of videos developed by other people. A group of women calling themselves the McCain Girls released a video called "Raining McCain" on YouTube. During the first four months it was available, it received 1.9 million views.[46] The video "Yes We Can," which was created by will.i.am of the Black Eyed Peas, was viewed millions of times. It initially was posted on YouTube. Later it was available through Obama's homepage.[47] Obama supporters uploaded more than 1,800 videos to the my.barackobama.com channel, while supporters uploaded 330 videos to JohnMcCain.com.[48] YouTube also entered the debate realm through a partnership with CNN. Citizens were invited to videotape themselves asking the candidates questions. The video questions, which were selected by CNN, were played back to the candidates during live debates. During the Democrat debate, the candidates faced questions about lesbian rights, why Democrats had not ended the war in Iraq, and even a global warming question posed by a snowman.[49] The Republicans faced questions about their belief in the Bible as well as their views on homosexuals in the military. The YouTube-driven debates marked a major change in American politics. Some suggest that the transition forced candidates to reveal aspects of themselves that might not traditionally appear during routine debates.[50]

BLOGGING FOR THE PRESIDENCY

The blogosphere had a twofold influence on this campaign. First, there were scores of bloggers who devoted hours to writing about the candidates on their own Web sites. Secondly, there were candidates who were micro-blogging, or Twittering, on the campaign trail. As a result, there was a great deal of room for the blogging phenomenon to leave a footprint on this election.

Research has suggested that blogs can be important information sources to those who are interested in politics. Internet users who are interested in politics tend to find blogs moderately credible information sources. In fact, research suggests that politically interested blog users tend to find blogs more credible than the traditional media. Some researchers have suggested that individuals like blogs because they offer a variety of perspectives and the opportunity to engage in political discussions.[51]

Blogs, or online diaries, have been making their mark on American politics for a few years now. In 2006, former presidential candidate John Edwards spent weeks videotaping his responses to videotaped questions. All of the questions and answers were posted to his own blog. Mark Warner, former Democratic governor of Virginia and a former vice presidential hopeful, hired a well-established blogger when Warner began his campaign for the 2008 election.[52]

In this election, the candidates invited supporters to create blogs on their own Web sites. Obama had a regular podcast that supporters could download, while Edwards and fellow Democratic candidate Tom Vilsack frequently posted video updates on their pages.[53] Meanwhile, political bloggers across the country were posting their own comments about the candidates. The Technorati Web site tracked how often bloggers mentioned each of the candidates during 2008. The site found that Obama was mentioned nearly twelve thousand times, McCain was mentioned more than two thousand times, Palin was mentioned nearly four thousand times, and Biden was mentioned a little more than one thousand times.[54] Some Web sites invited individuals to post about the candidates on their own sites. The snack company LesserEvil's Web site invited site visitors to blog about their "salty-sweet" opinions about the election.[55] In the words of freelance writer Michael Baumann, "Not only have blogs changed the way citizens participate in political discourse, but they have forced candidates, even Barack Obama and John McCain, to watch their backs."[56]

For the individual candidates, there was a major emphasis on Twittering during the campaign. Tweets are essentially one-line blogs that can be viewed through the computer or via cell phones. Individuals can set up their own Twitter accounts and publish 140-character messages. Others follow those accounts and receive each micro-blog that the writer publishes. Obama, McCain, and the vice-presidential candidates had Twitter accounts. In October 2008, one news organization reported that Obama had more than ninety thousand followers. McCain had fifteen hundred followers.[57]

In the case of the political candidates, Twitter allows individual supporters to feel as though they have a direct line of communication with the candidate. One subscriber to Obama's Twitter page typed "Luv Obama, luv luv luv y'all." Another poster wrote, "Why does every McCain advert look like a horror-film trailer?"[58] The posts allow the political candidate the opportunity to promote events. One of Obama's own posts read, "At a New Energy for America town hall meeting in Elkhart, IN. Watch the event live at my.barackobama.com/."[59]

THE FUTURE OF POLITICS AND GADGETRY

The 2008 presidential election showed that handheld technology can be utilized as a potent presidential campaign tool. The cell phone, or whatever the next major phone/computer/music handheld gadget is, will likely continue to be a major hub of political activity. Those devices offer candidates a way to directly and instantly contact people around the clock. As the technology continues to evolve, smart politicians will find new and creative ways to build campaign strategies that embrace that technology. For example, the Apple iPhone went on sale in June 2007.[60] By September of the next year, Obama's campaign released an application that could be used with the popular new device. As mentioned earlier, that application encouraged volunteers to call their friends to tell them about the candidate.[61] If candidates hope to keep the attention of an increasingly technologically savvy population, that sort of quick reaction needs to become a permanent facet of American politics. In the coming years, candidates will likely search for ways that they can release similar phone applications that will be available to people regardless of what type of cell phone they carry.

Many new gadgets will likely be unleashed before the next presidential campaign is in full swing. In addition to the iPhone, the newly released Palm Pre provides a tiny taste of what may be available in the coming years. Released in 2009, the phone incorporated the ability to synchronize the Pre's calendar and contacts with the phone owner's Facebook contacts and

Google's Web-based services.[62] Google has a variety of online programs such as a personalizable online calendar. Obama's iPhone application may evolve into an application that takes advantage of those features. Perhaps a political Palm Pre application will allow users to keep up with campaign events that are happening in their own regions by inserting them automatically into their own Google calendar. Perhaps a new application also will evolve to allow phone users a way to track how many of their Facebook contacts have discussed the election with them. That could be a valuable application since some people have far more Facebook contacts than they have contacts stored in their phone address books. A phone application that connects with Facebook also might give politicians a better way to organize people who are members of their Facebook group. It might allow group members a better way to contact one another to discuss campaign needs without having to rely on an expensively developed Web site like my.barrackobama.com.

Online videos, that can be downloaded or streamed on cell phones and other devices, will likely continue to be a major part of upcoming campaigns. Technology may evolve to allow users to subscribe to certain types of candidate's videos to be sent to their phones. For example, phone owners might be able to request that they receive all videos relating to health care reform or candidate debates.

In essence, these new cell phone programs may make campaign texting obsolete. That certainly won't happen until the vast majority of the population has become addicted to cell phone applications. Phones that are capable of downloading applications also must become more affordable for the average cell phone consumer before that can happen. Right now, texting is the most potent cell phone option that politicians have in their bags of campaign tricks because it is widely available on even moderately priced phones.

There are ways that politicians could likely improve their texting programs. For instance, politicians may soon develop short codes that they use on all of their political paraphernalia. Short codes are essentially five or six letters or numbers that individuals can dial when they want to quickly send a text to an organization. Because they are short, they can be easier for an individual to remember. The corporate world already is using them. By placing them in television advertisements and on all other paraphernalia, the candidate makes it easier for people to know how to quickly contact campaign headquarters.[63] Essentially, it makes sense for a short code to become a major part of the marketing process just as Web addresses and e-mail addresses already are.

The world of avatars may soon become a major facet of the campaign process, too. During the 2008 campaign, private individuals developed avatars—virtual people—that discussed politics in the 3-D interactive Internet world of Second Life. The avatars represented computer users. There were no official campaign sites in the virtual world, but computer users found their own ways to dive into political debates in places such as the Straight Talk Café.[64] San Francisco Bay Representative George Miller had his own Second Life avatar discussing politics in 2007.[65] To make the avatars even more enticing, the Vollee company is expected to create an application that will make Second Life available to cell phone users.[66] As the application becomes more easily accessible from cell phones, campaign teams may choose to develop their own virtual campaign sites. They can periodically set up group discussions with the candidate. They might even run virtual campaign events that allow avid computer users the opportunity to attend virtual campaign events without leaving their homes—or at least without leaving their cell phones. The concept might sound a bit strange to those who are not avid gamers, or who have not tested the waters of virtual worlds, but there is much untapped potential in avatars.

At the local level, there is plenty of room for individuals running for offices to also embrace new technology. The text messaging program that Obama used easily could be implemented. It also may be a more cost effective way for local candidates to run a campaign, rather than relying on paper flyers. The catch, of course, is that local candidates will only be able to use these methods if they are running campaigns in areas where the majority of the population already is embracing this new technology.

Local candidates may not be able to afford to develop sophisticated social networking Web sites. They will likely begin placing more emphasis on the free software that already is available online such as Facebook and YouTube. They may discover old-fashioned static Web sites are no longer useful for their campaigns. An easily updatable blog might be a cheaper and better option for candidates during future elections. If they adequately use free social networking sites, candidates can simply link all of those sites back to their own personal blog site. Technology has made that process quick and easy. For example, candidates might post campaign platform documents on Scribd, as Obama did, and then link their blog to those documents. They can load videos to YouTube and then embed them in Facebook and on their personal blogs. They can subscribe to free photo hosting sites such as Flickr or Photobucket to showcase a host of campaign photos. The list goes on and on.

FINAL THOUGHTS

We have entered a new age in American politics that is inspired by technological innovation. Television first brought candidates face-to-face with voters. Now, new technology is allowing campaigners to have direct, individual contact with potential voters. Text messaging has made it easier for candidates to develop massive lists of volunteers and supporters. The merger between social networking and mobile phones adds to that connection. Social networking has made it easier for candidates to set up quick and easy Web sites with little to no expense. YouTube also allows extensive distribution of videos that individuals can view at their convenience rather than catching them at specific times on television. Candidates with less money may find it easier to run campaigns through the Internet. In essence, candidates constantly can tap into the lives of supporters in a million new ways now, courtesy of modern technology.

It is difficult to say specifically what will happen in future campaigns. To some extent, that will depend on what happens with new technology. With new types of cell phones available on a regular basis as well as other handheld gadgets such as the Apple iPod, the Amazon Kindle e-reader, and the Archos wireless multimedia device, there is a host of new opportunities for candidates to reach audiences in the multimedia world. The question no longer is, how or should we use the new technology? Rather, the question is, where will the technology take us next?

NOTES

1. Merrie Spaeth, "Presidential Politics and Public Relations in 2008: Marshall McLuhan 2.0," *Journalism Studies* 10, no. 3 (June 2009): 442.

2. Paul Levinson, *Cellphone: The Story of the World's Most Mobile Medium and How It Has Transformed Everything!* (New York: Palgrave MacMillian, 2004): 31–32.

3. Jamie Lendino, "Smartphone 101: A Look at the Past, Present & Future," *PC Today*, 2006. www.pctoday.com/editorial/article.asp?article=articles%2F2006%2Ft0 402%2F12t02%2F12t02.asp (13 July 2009).

4. Michael Smith, "All Thumbs: Research in Motion's Thumb-Operated Black-Berry—A Sort of Uber-Pager Beloved of Go-Go Executives has Made the Little Waterloo Company into a Superstock," *The Globe and Mail*, 31 March 2000, 46.

5. Ian Austen, "News Watch: Mobile Technology 'Call Me When You Get This': A Pager Turns Into a Cellphone," *New York Times*, 7 March 2002, 3(G).

6. "Get the Facts," *Blackberry.com*, n.d., na.blackberry.com/eng/ataglance/get_ the_facts/ (16 July 2009).

7. Kim Hart and Sabrina Valle, "Hype Meets Reality At iPhone's Debut," *Washington Post*, 30 June 2007, 1(D).

8. "Obama '08 The Official iPhone Application," *my.barackobama.com*, n.d., my.barackobama.com/page/content/iphone (16 July 2009).

9. Victoria Shannon, "15 years of Text Messages, a 'Cultural Phenomenon,'" *New York Times*, 5 December 2007. www.nytimes.com/2007/12/05/technology/05iht-sms .4.8603150.html (13 July 2009).

10. "Texting, One, Two, Three . . ." *Politics (Campaigns & Elections)* 29, no. 1 (January 2008): 62.

11.   Allison Dale and Aaron Strauss, "Text Messaging as a Youth Mobilization Tool: An Experiment with a Post-Treatment Survey" (paper presented at the annual meeting of the Midwestern Political Science Association, Chicago, Illinois, 2007), 1–34.

12. "Texting, One, Two, Three . . ." *Politics*, 62.

13. "Texting, One, Two, Three . . ." *Politics*, 62.

14. Gene Maddaus, "Palin Goes on the Offensive," *Press-Telegram*, 4 October 2008, www2.presstelegram.com/ci_10641675 (17 July 2009).

15. Michael Whitney, "Reprise of $1 Million 'Obama Minute,' but now with Internative Times Square Billboard," *Techpresident.com*, 5 October 2009, techpresident.com/node/6408 (17 July 2009).

16. Jose Antonio Vargas, "Obama's Wide Web: From YouTube to Text Messaging, Candidate's Team Connects to Voters," *Washington Post*, 20 August 2008, 1(C).

17. Vargas, "Obama's Wide Web," 1(C).

18. Vargas, "Obama's Wide Web," 1(C).

19. Brian Stelter, "Enticing Text Messengers in a Get-Out-the-Vote Push," *New York Times*, 18 August 2008, 12(A).

20. Vargas, "Obama's Wide Web," 1(C).

21. Larry Rohter, "Obama Backers Get the Message," *New York Times*, 31 October 2008, 22(A).

22. Jose Antonio Vargas, "Getting Out the Vote with Text Messages," *The Trail: A Daily Diary of Campaign 2008*, 19 December 2007, voices.washingtonpost.com/44/2007/12/19/getting_out_the_vote_with_text_1.html (21 July 2009).

23. Jim Puzzanghera, "Obama's VP Text Message Reached 2.9 Million People, Nielsen Reports; No Data on How Many Were Awake When it Arrived," *Los Angeles Times*, 26 August 2008, latimesblogs.latimes.com/technology/2008/08/obamas-vp-text.html (21 July 2009).

24. "Freak Out Your Friends With Fake Obama VP TXT," *Wonkette*, n.d., wonkette.com/402054/freak-out-your-friends-with-fake-obama-vp-txt (21 July 2009).

25. Puzzanghera, "Obama's VP Text Message."

26. Vargas, "Getting Out the Vote."

27. See Tim O'Reilly, "What is Web 2.0: Design Patterns and Business Models for the Next Generation of Software," *O'Reilly.com*, 30 September 2005, oreilly.com/web2/archive/what-is-web-20.html (14 July 2009); and Gwen Soloman and Lynne Schrum, *Web 2.0: New Tools, New Schools* (Washington, DC: International Scoiety for Technology in Education, 2007).

28. Tim O'Reilly, "What is Web 2.0."

29. Darcy DiNucci, "Fragmented Future," *Print* 53, no. 4 (July/August 1999): 32–33.

30. Gary E. Salazar, "The 2008 Presidential Race: A Baseline for the Future of Wireless Campaigns," *RCR Wireless News*, 3 November 2008. Retrieved from Lexis Nexis Academic database.

31. Victoria Shannon, "Social Networking Moves to Cellphone," *New York Times*, 6 March 2008, 7(C).

32. Michael Learmonth, "Social Media Paves Way to White House," *Advertising Age* 80, no. 11 (March 2009): 16.

33. Tom Lowry, "Obama's Secret Digital Weapon," *Business Week*, 7 July 2008, www.businessweek.com/magazine/content/08_27/b4091000977488.htm (22 July 2009).

34. Peter Feld, "What Obama Can Teach You About Millennial Marketing," *Advertising Age* 79, no. 31 (August 2008): 1–23.

35. Joel Berg, "Trickle-Down Webonomics," *Politics (Campaigns & Elections)* 29, no. 11 (November 2008): 59.

36. Bruce E. Gronbeck, "The Web, Campaign 07-08, and Engaged Citizens: Political, Social, and Moral Consequences," in *The 2008 Presidential Campaign: A Communication Perspective*, ed. Robert E. Denton, Jr. (Lanham, Md: Rowman & Littlefield Publishers, Inc., 2009), 228–43.

37. Ira Teinowitz, "Note to Politicians: It's not the Spending, Stupid," *Advertising Age* 79, no. 11 (March 2008): 17.

38. "Facebook Supporters 2008," *TechPresident.com*, n.d., techpresident.com/scrape_plot/facebook/2008 (10 July 2009).

39. "MySpace Friends 2008," *TechPresident.com*, n.d., techpresident.com/scrape_plot/myspace/2008 (10 July 2009).

40. Mike Beirne, "Marketers Find Facebook, MySpace Ripe for Politics," *Brandweek* 40, no. 34 (September 2008): 10.

41. Gronbeck, "The Web, Campaign 07-08," 236.

42. Heather Havenstein, "'Politics 2.0' Heating Up Summer Doldrums in D.C." *Computerworld* 42, no. 32 (August 2008): 10.

43. "YouTube Subscribers 2008," *TechPresident* 2008, techpresident.com/scrape_plot/youtube/2008 (10 July 2009).

44. Vargas, "Obama's Wide Web."

45. Gronbeck, "The Web, Campaign 07-08," 228–43.

46. "Flickring Here, Twittering There," *Economist* 388, no. 8593 (16 August 2008): 30–31.

47. Noam Cohen, "The Wiki-Way to Nomination," *New York Times*, 8 June 2008, 4(WK).

48. Matthew Fraser and Soumitra Dutta, "Opinion: Obama and the Facebook Effect," *MediaWeek*, 2008, www.mediaweek.com/mw/content_display/esearch/e3id4ae6ffc50a7784963bd4aba0287b4f9?imw=Y (10 July 2009).

49. Susan Page, "Via YouTube, Public Presses Democratic Hopefuls," *USA Today*, 24 July 2007, 5(A).

50. Linda Feldmann, "GOP YouTube Debates: Good Marks for New Views of Candidates," *Christian Science Monitor*, 30 November 2007, 1.

51. Thomas J. Johnson, Barbara K. Kaye, Shannon L. Bichard, and W. Joann Wong, "Every Blog Has Its Day: Politically-Interested Internet Users' Perceptions of Blog Credibility," *Journal of Computer-Mediated Communication* 31, no. 1, 2007, jcmc.indiana.edu/vol13/issue1/johnson.html (10 July 2009).

52. Adam Nagourney, "Internet Injects Sweeping Change into U.S. Politics," *New York Times*, 2 April 2006, 1(A).

53. Helen Kennedy, "Blogs Show Strength For E-lection '08," *Daily News*, 21 January 2007, 7.

54. "Blog Mentions Via Technorati 2008," *TechPresident.com*, n.d., techpresident .com/scrape_plot/technorati/2008, (10 July 2009).

55. Mike Beirne, "Marketers Find Facebook," 10.

56. Michael Baumann, "Campaign '08: The Power of the Post," *Information Today* 25, no. 9, 25.

57. Rob Waugh, "When Obama Tweets, 90,000 Listen," *Mail on Sunday*, 12 October 2008, 18.

58. Rob Waugh, "When Obama Tweets," 18.

59. Howard Kurtz, "Political Coverage That's All A-Twitter," *Washington Post*, 26 August 2008, 19(1).

60. Fred Vogelstein, "The Untold Story: How the iPhone Blew Up the Wireless Industry," *Wired Magazine*, 9 January 2008, www.wired.com/gadgets/wireless/mag azine/16-02/ff_iphone (13 July 2009).

61. Ari Melber, "Obama's iSuccess," *Nation* 287, no. 13 (October 2008): 8.

62. Rob Pegoraro, "A New Hope For Smartphones," *The Washington Post*, 14 June 2009, 1(G).

63. Dane Strother, "Get Text-Savvy—Or You're Toast," *Politics (Campaigns & Elections)* 29, no. 11 (November 2008): 62–63.

64. Carolyn Davis, "Candidates Wage Virtual Campaigns in a Real Election," *Philadelphia Inquirer*, 28 October 2008, 1(A).

65. Paul Bedard, "YouTube Not Just for White House Hopefuls," *U.S. News & World Report* 143, no. 5 (August 2007): 15.

66. Daniel Terdiman, "'Second Life' Coming to Mobile Devices?" *CNET News*, 19 February 2008, news.cnet.com/8301-13772_3-9874366-52.html (27 July 2009).

3

"RT @BarackObama We just made history": Twitter and the 2008 Presidential Election

Frederic I. Solop

Democratic political systems are built upon a foundation of ongoing interactions between citizens and policy-makers. These interactions are locked into an essential relationship with prevailing technology. Technology shapes mechanisms of political participation and helps define how political campaigns are conducted. As the first president to be born in the Vietnam era, Barack Obama was comfortable introducing new technology into his campaign for the presidency. As reported by Brian Stelter, the BlackBerry-wielding candidate had this to say about the topic: "One of my fundamental beliefs from my days as a community organizer is that real change comes from the bottom up, and there's no more powerful tool for grass-roots organizing than the Internet."[1] Technology played a critical role in helping Obama distribute his message to a wide audience, organize volunteers throughout the nation, and raise unprecedented amounts of money. Today, Obama is building upon lessons learned in the presidential campaign and integrating technology into a strategy of governance.

BARACK OBAMA'S SOCIAL MEDIA STRATEGY

There is no question that Barack Obama feels comfortable using technology in his life. He is familiar with social media and he understands the power of technology in shaping world events. Candidate Obama turned to one of the most successful social media figures in the world for help on his campaign. That figure was Chris Hughes, one of the founders of Facebook. Facebook is arguably the most successful social media tool in existence today, with more than two hundred million active users, one hundred million of whom log in every day.[2] A population of this size locates Facebook in the position of being the fifth largest nation in the world, behind the United States and ahead of Brazil.[3]

Hughes began working with the Obama campaign in February 2007.[4] The centerpiece of Hughes's work was to create an online social networking community, much like what had emerged on Facebook. He did this by taking charge of a Web site titled "my.barackobama.com," or "myBO" for short.[5] MyBO allowed visitors to create personal profiles, create blogs, share information with their neighbors, organize and advertise local events, and solicit donations. By July 2008, the site recorded more than nine hundred thousand subscribers. Stelter writes that the site was particularly useful during the primary election season, allowing Obama to raise more than two million donations of $200 or less.[6] By the time the campaign was over more than two million profiles were created on myBO. In addition, volunteers "planned 200,000 offline events, formed 35,000 groups, posted 400,000 blogs, and raised $30 million on 70,000 personal fund-raising pages."[7]

MyBO was an unqualified success in soliciting donations, organizing volunteers, and promoting the candidacy of Barack Obama. Understanding the power of different social media tools, Obama and Hughes were not content to stop there. They created a huge presence on other social media sites and employed other Internet tools to distribute the Obama message. Like myBO, these sites helped distribute the Obama message unfiltered by the mainstream media and created an image of Obama as a young, tech-savvy candidate. Twitter was one of these sites.

TWITTER

Barack Obama introduced Twitter, a social media tool, into his campaign. Also known as "micro-blogging," Twitter users communicate using short text messages of up to 140 characters in length. The Twitter model differs from other social media sites like Facebook. Whereas Facebook users invite others to be their "friend" and people can allow or not allow others to access information on their Facebook sites, Twitter users simply choose to "follow" information posted by other Twitter users. No permission is needed to follow another's Twitter posts. Users do not authorize others to see their posts. Information is available to all who subscribe to the Twitter postings produced by others.

Despite being a relative newcomer in the world of social media, many agree that Twitter is the fastest growing social media service available today. People working at Odeo Corporation developed the service in 2006.[8] Compared to Facebook with two hundred million active accounts as of May 2009 and MySpace with fifty-six million active accounts,[9] almost twenty million people now have Twitter accounts.[10] Many of these users established Twitter accounts after the 2008 presidential election.

One unique feature of Twitter is that the service lacks central direction. Unlike other top social media sites, Twitter users are the engine of ingenuity and the spark of creative energy in developing uses for the service. Twitter users, in fact, have developed a language of their own. Some aspects of this language include the following:[11]

- @Replies: Twitter users can publicly reply to other users using @ followed by the user ID.
- D or Direct Message: Refers to Twitter users sending private messages to other users.
- RT or Retweet. Refers to Twitter users reposting messages sent by other users.
- Follower: Someone who subscribes to another's Twitter feed.
- Following: The process that occurs once someone subscribes to a Twitter feed.
- Tweets: Short messages of up to 140 characters sent by Twitter users.
- Twitter Feed: The string of messages posted by a Twitter user.
- # (Hashtag): Twitter users can categorize their tweets with a # followed by Labelname to help others find similar information. Twitter users search Twitter postings by hashtags for specific keywords.

Twitter usage has grown substantially as applications allowing access to Twitter have become available for the iPhone, Blackberries, and other mobile devices. People can now monitor Twitter postings and author tweets while traveling throughout a typical day. This creates an environment where information is being posted instantaneously on a 24/7 schedule. In fact, on several occasions recently, Twitter users were first on the scene reporting disasters before the mainstream media were available. This was true when an airplane landed in the Hudson River (January 15, 2009)[12] and when a plane missed the Schiphol airport runway outside Amsterdam (February 24, 2009).[13] Mobile Twitter users actively shared information and coordinated strategy in the recent Moldovia revolution[14] and Iran uprising.[15]

Perhaps the greatest impetus to the growth of Twitter use in the United States comes from celebrity use of Twitter. Twitter use spiked after Oprah Winfrey, a popular talk show host in the United States, signed up for an account and wrote her first tweet while on air. As of this writing, Winfrey has more than 1.65 million followers. Other celebrities with large Twitter followings include singer Britney Spears (2.1 million followers), comedian Ellen DeGeneres (2.2 million followers), and actor Ashton Kutcher (2.5 million followers).

Today, Twitter is being used for a variety of purposes, including individuals posting personal impressions, news outlets generating current event feeds, companies advertising products, entrepreneurs promoting services, politicians and public figures sharing insights and impressions, and activists and organizations disseminating information and mobilizing followers.

CNN encourages viewers to communicate directly with the cable channel using Twitter, as well as Facebook and MySpace. CNN regularly posts subscriber tweets on air, giving Twitter users a chance to publicly comment on the news and directly post questions to reporters. Conferences held by professional organizations such as the American Association for Public Opinion Research (AAPOR) conference (May 2009) are encouraging attendees to Twitter about their conference experiences. Twitter users simply include a hashtag (#) with a predesignated code allowing other conference attendees to easily search and find conference-related posts on Twitter.

New uses for Twitter are constantly emerging. Senator John McCain broke new ground in March 2009 when he participated in a Twitter interview with news commentator George Stephanopoulos.[16] Recently, more than fifteen thousand Twitter users signed a petition circulated through the service encouraging AT&T to offer current iPhone 3G users discounted rates for purchasing a 3GS phone. AT&T heard the call and changed their pricing policy.[17] Many search programs are available allowing Twitter users instant access to information at any time of the day or night.[18] Because information is constantly being posted to Twitter, information about current event topics appear on Twitter more quickly than on other standard search engines. Or take Portland, Oregon's new Twisitor Center where Twitter users can ask questions of the visitor center using Twitter.[19] There is no doubt that Twitter is a dynamic service that many people find exciting to access. As new uses for Twitter emerge, the service is poised to continue growing as a major social media service.

BARACK OBAMA USES TWITTER
IN HIS PRESIDENTIAL CAMPAIGN

Twitter was one of many social media tools in Barack Obama's campaign toolbox, though not a major focus of Obama's social media strategy. At the time of the November election, only about 3.5 million Twitter accounts were in existence[20] and Barack Obama had about 118,000 followers. As one tool among several, Obama used Twitter in tandem with other social media tools to fine-tune his message to a technology-savvy population.

Barack Obama's first tweet was posted on April 29, 2007. In this short tweet Obama encouraged followers to sign a petition against the war in Iraq. He also referenced his campaign Web site in the tweet. The message read as follows:

> Thinking we're only one signature away from ending the war in Iraq. Learn more at www.barackobama.com.

The Obama campaign went on to post a total of 262 tweets over a seventeen-month period, from April 29, 2007, through the day after Election Day, November 5, 2008.

Looking at the corpus of tweets, one finds that Obama's Twitter strategy changed over time. Obama's first few posts, rolled out over a period of two weeks, focused attention on the candidate's opposition to the war in Iraq, his concern about U.S. dependence on foreign oil, and criticisms of the George W. Bush presidency. These policy-related tweets helped distinguish Obama's candidacy within a crowded field of early presidential contenders. Although he started using Twitter to announce his opposition to the war in Iraq and to stake out positions on other policies, he soon dropped this approach and moved on to using Twitter for other purposes.

Obama's use of Twitter was guided by two factors. The first factor was the preset schedule of presidential election milestones, from pre-primary campaigning to the primary elections, and then the general election. Obama employed social media tools to achieve different goals in each of these phases of the election. A second factor affecting Obama's Twitter strategy was an evolution that occurred as the campaign matured in its understanding of the strengths and potentiality of Twitter and the uses of social media.

This researcher employed a content coding strategy for the purpose of discerning Obama's campaign strategy using Twitter. All 262 Obama tweets were coded. Thirteen codes were utilized in this process with multiple codes being assigned to tweets as appropriate. Codes were then aggregated and analyzed to represent changes in posting strategy over time.

The coding analysis demonstrates that Twitter served two primary functions for the Obama campaign. The first function served was to announce where the candidate was at any one moment. Seventy-nine percent of all tweets included a reference to location. The second major function was to direct followers to the campaign Web site. Almost two-thirds of Obama's election tweets (63 percent) included a reference to the campaign site.

Obama began using Twitter to announce where campaign appearances were taking place. He was at the Detroit Economic Club (May 7, 2007), heading to Des Moines (May 10), and in Trenton, New Jersey, at an AFL-CIO Town Hall meeting on May 14. He was in New Hampshire (May 19), Washington, DC (May 24), and at the University of Iowa (May 29).

Table 3.1.   Content of Barack Obama Campaign Tweets

Tweet Content	Number of Tweets	Percent of Tweets
Location Information	206	79%
Campaign Web site Reference	166	63%
Notice of Live Event Streaming	101	39%
Campaign Announcement	59	23%
Reference to TV/Cable Show	35	13%
Policy Statement	25	10%
Get-Out-the-Vote Message	21	8%
Other Event Announcement (e.g., debates)	17	6%
Famous People Named	17	6%
Text Messaging Service Reference	10	4%
Other Web site Reference	6	2%
YouTube Reference	4	2%
Personal Comment	3	1%

In Cedar Rapids, IA at Coe College (October 29, 2007)

Meeting folks in South Carolina today (January 23, 2008)

Had a great three days in Florida (May 23, 2008)

Location matters, both as a way of communicating the breadth of territory Obama was covering in the campaign season and as a way of tracking Obama's presence in primary election states: from Iowa (December 4, 13, 16, 17, 26, 29, 2007), to New Hampshire (December 19, 2007, January 5, 2008), to South Carolina (January 10, 21, 22, 23, 24, 2008), Nevada (January 13, 15, 19, 2008), and onward. Using Twitter, followers maintained a regular relationship with the campaign, knowing where the candidate was at any one time, which group the candidate was speaking to, and where he was going next.

Obama typically included the address to his campaign Web site in his tweets. Followers were constantly encouraged to go to the campaign Web site and read recent speeches, see videos of campaign appearances, watch live-streaming of events, and learn the location of polling sites. While Obama never posted a tweet asking for donations, he did direct traffic to his Web site where followers were asked to donate money. The campaign Web site proved to be a successful tool for motivating many first-time contributors to make relatively small donations to the campaign. Thus, by constantly referring people to the campaign Web site, Twitter played a passive fundraising role.

Obama also used Twitter to refer people to other media sites. Two percent of posts referred followers to non-campaign-related Web sites and 2 percent of posts included references to YouTube videos. Followers were encouraged to look at MySpace to see live streaming of the MTV Presidential Dialogue (October 29, 2007). Thirteen percent of posts referenced a TV show, some serious (e.g., encouraging followers to watch the presidential debates or to watch an interview on CNN) and some more lighthearted:

> Campaigning in South Bend, IN and will then be on Letterman tonight at 11pm ET/PT on CBS (May 1, 2008)

> Going to be on The Daily Show with Jon Stewart tonight. 11:00 pm ET on Comedy Central (April 21, 2008)

On June 19, 2007, Obama announced that he established a text messaging service for the campaign. By texting the word "GO" to the phone number OBAMA, followers would receive a free bumper sticker. Nine days later he used Twitter to encourage followers to text comments about the recent presidential debate to this phone number. Followers were encouraged to text the site with their post-debate comments or to be on guard for a text message announcing Obama's vice presidential choice:

> Announcing the VP candidate sometime between now & the Convention by txt msg & email. Text VP to 62262 or visit (candidate Web site) (August 16, 2008)

In all, 4 percent of Obama tweets helped direct traffic to his text messaging service.

Major campaign announcements were made using Twitter. Almost one-quarter of Twitter posts (23 percent) included an announcement of some type. Announcements included information about when the candidate would be delivering critical speeches, when the presidential debates were being held, and which primaries were taking place next. Critical endorsements and won primaries were also announced on Twitter.

> In Iowa this week. Just announced plan today to "Reclaim the American Dream" (November 7, 2007)

> Meeting folks in South Carolina today. Excited to have received Columbia's The State, Rock Hill Herald & Greenville News endorsements (January 23, 2008)

> Energized by the news of winning Mississippi. We've won the most states, the most votes and the most delegates (March 11, 2008)

Candidates often try to enhance their stature among constituencies by making campaign appearances with famous personalities. Obama tried using Twitter to shape his public image by referencing famous people supporting his candidacy; names of people appearing with Obama at campaign rallies were included in his tweets, as well as references to those endorsing his candidacy. Six percent of posts included the name of a famous person. Names of national-level political leaders were included in Obama tweets (e.g., Bill Clinton, Hillary Clinton, Bill Richardson), as well as the names of famous entertainers (e.g., Macy Gray, Usher, Oprah Winfrey).

By January 2008, and coinciding with the start of the primary season, Barack Obama posted tweets to his site more regularly. This was a departure from previous months, when posting first occurred every week or so and then, by fall 2007, moved to every few days. In February 2008, Obama began making direct appeals to his followers to get more involved in the election. He asked followers to appeal to their friends to participate in Super Tuesday states (February 5), encouraged followers to vote in the District of Columbia, Maryland, and Virginia elections (February 12), and to vote in the Wisconsin (February 19) and Wyoming (March 17) primaries.

> In McKeespo & Pittsburgh, PA today finishing the "On Track for Change" Tour and reminding everyone in PA to vote tomorrow! (April 21, 2008)

> Holding get out the vote events in both IN and NC. To find your polling locations for tomorrow's elections visit barackobama.com (May 5, 2008)

Eight percent of Obama's Twitter posts fit into Obama's get-out-the-vote strategy, including the last three posts to appear on Obama's Twitterfeed just before the end of Election Day.

> Asking you to help Get Out the Vote in these last few critical hours of our campaign for change. Visit www.barackobama.com (November 4, 2008)

> Asking for your vote today. For polling location info visit www.barackobama .com or call 877-874-6226. Make sure everyone votes! (November 4, 2008)

> Asking you to vote Nov. 4th. Visit www.barackobama.com, call 877-874-6226 or text VOTE to 62262 to find your polling locations. (November 3, 2008)

As one tracks Obama's Twitter posts across time, one sees a reflection of Obama's increasing sophistication with the uses of technology. By August 1, 2008, after Obama had enough support to win his party's nomination but before the Democratic National Convention, Obama began to regularly include live-streaming campaign events on this Web site. He began to regularly announce on Twitter when the live-streaming would be available on his Web site. In the posting of a video schedule, we can see the benefits of a social media service that is so immediate in nature. Followers could know instantaneously when a live video stream would be available for viewing.

At the same time, Obama's Twitter posts began to be structured differently. At an earlier time, the campaign tweets had a freer flowing feel about them. By the beginning of August, more posts reflected a preset format:

Holding a town hall on economic security in St. Petersburg, FL. Watch it live at my.barackobama.com/live (August 1, 2008)

At a New Energy for America town hall meeting in Berea, OH. Watch it live at my.barackobama.com/live (August 5, 2008)

Overall, 37 percent of Obama's Twitter posts during the election season fit this format. Most tweets posted after September 1 and continuing through the end of the general election reflected this pattern (fifty-six of seventy-nine general election posts).

In Tampa, FL at an "Early Vote for Change" rally. Watch it live at my .barackobama.com/live (October 20, 2008)

In Miami, FL. At a "Change We Need" rally. Watch it live at my.barackobama .com/live (October 21, 2008)

In Fort Collins, CO. At an "Early Vote for Change" rally. Watch it live at my.barackobama.com/live (October 26, 2008)

Barack Obama posted his final tweet of the election on the morning of November 5, 2008. The final tweet said "We just made history. All of this happened because you gave your time, talent and passion. All of this happened because of you. Thanks." This message was retweeted often by many of Obama's followers, thus the source of the title of this chapter.

Technologies such as Twitter played a central role in Barack Obama's presidential campaign. These technologies allowed candidate Obama the freedom to deliver a crafted, unfiltered, message to voters and nonvoters alike. They allowed Obama the ability to shape an image of being a young, modern leader in touch with the future of the nation. Importantly, Twitter served many purposes for Obama. He used Twitter to announce events, direct traffic to his campaign Web site, refer followers to other media, and engage and mobilize his constituency. Ultimately, Twitter and other social media services allowed Obama to connect with a huge donor base. Barack Obama's reliance upon the power of technology did not end on Election Day. He continues to employ these same technologies as he struggles to govern the nation.

BARACK OBAMA'S CONTINUED USE OF TWITTER

The transition from candidate to elected leader is never easy. In two short months, the newly elected president must select cabinet heads, construct a team of advisors and make scores of political appointments, and grasp the major issues confronting the United States. Obama wants to continue engaging the public as he goes about governing the nation. He continues to rely upon technology to help him achieve this goal.

Obama's campaign Web site, my.barackobama.com, is still online, only now it is known as "Organizing for America" and it is funded and maintained by the Democratic National Committee.[21] The Obama White House is actively using social media today. The official White House Web site can be found at www.whitehouse.gov. This site delivers current information about legislation, position papers, personal information about key administration figures, blog information about what the president is doing at all times, information about government agencies, and contact information. The site also links to the White House presence on Facebook, Twitter, Flickr, MySpace, YouTube, Vimeo, and iTunes. *USA Today* commented that the White House thinks of this presence as "WhiteHouse 2.0."[22]

Obama has continued to post tweets since Election Day, though some time passed between the November 4, 2008, election and when Obama began regularly posting new tweets. As of Election Day, Obama had 118,107 followers on Twitter.[23] In comparison, John McCain only had 4,942 followers by Election Day. Today, Barack Obama's Twitter site shows 1.8 million followers, making his site one of the most popular sites on Twitter today.

As of July 30, 2009, there were fifty post-election tweets on Obama's Twitter site. The first post-election season tweet was put up on January 15, 2009, almost a month and half after the general election and immediately prior to Obama's inauguration as the forty-fourth president of the United States. It was not until the middle of May, however, that Obama began regularly posting messages to his Twitter site. Recent messages ask followers to support his policy agenda in areas such as health care and clean energy. He is using the site to inform the public about meetings he is attending, House and Senate activities, new initiatives he is taking, and progress with Judge Sotomayor's nomination to sit on the Supreme Court.

On July 27, 2009, Obama introduced a new feature on this Facebook page: "Tweet Your Senator." Once Facebook followers click on the "Tweet Your Senator" icon, they are taken to a page that allows them to send a precomposed tweet (assuming they have an active Twitter account) supporting Obama's healthcare agenda to a random senator in their state. If the senator is an active Twitter user, the message is preceded by the @ sign and the message is sent directly to the senator's Twitter account.

Here's an example of a tweet that came from this site:

To Sen. Jon Kyl: Every American family deserves quality health insurance now bit.ly/lr1qC #hc09 #AZ #86004

Facebook followers can remain on the site and watch a map of the United States display locations from where tweets are being sent and what the tweets are saying. This demonstrates how Obama continues to use social media to communicate directly with the American people. His social media strategy is coordinated across sites, with one site referring traffic to other sites. He is also experimenting with using social media to actively engage the public in his presidency at all times, not just for the purpose of winning an election. Social media may prove to be helpful in broadening Obama's base of support in the nation to pursue a broad policy agenda. This sends a unique message to the public, as it seems recently that political leaders are only interested in engaging with the public during election season.

CONCLUSION

In the book *Downsizing Democracy*, Matthew Crenson and Benjamin Ginsberg lament the loss of a democratic system that required public officials to actively mobilize constituents on an ongoing basis.[24] Power was linked to individual success in mobilizing people. Democracy in the United States today, they note, moves according to its own momentum. The public has become superfluous to the system as democracy moves forward along its own momentum. From this perspective, Barack Obama's approach to governance recalls a time when public officials took constituent organizing seriously. Obama remains the consummate organizer today and the Internet is a key building block in this program.

Involvement in Web 2.0 media has exploded in recent years. The technology engages people and encourages them to participate in networks of like-minded people. Social media users share a feeling of community as though they are part of something larger than themselves. The Obama campaign used social media tools such as Twitter to win control of the White House. The tools formed a cornerstone of his effort to deliver an unfiltered message to the public at a very low cost. Twitter kept Obama supporters informed and connected to the candidate. While it would be naïve to say that Obama won election to office solely because of his social media presence, Twitter and other social media involvement was part of a broader, winning equation. One area where his Web site and technology presence benefited him tremendously was in fundraising. Twitter helped direct traffic to the campaign Web site where Obama proved to be quite successful in raising significant amounts of money from large numbers of donors making relatively small contributions. Twitter and other social media tools also helped Obama construct an image of being a young, technologically sophisticated leader committed to connecting individual voters to a broader movement of change.

President Obama is using Twitter and other social media tools to deliver his policy messages, to rally support for his initiatives, and to continue connecting people to broader communities of change. In Crenson and Ginsberg's worldview, President Obama takes seriously the importance of organizing and mobilizing constituents now that the election is over. This orientation has become central to his governing strategy. It is an investment in today and it is an investment in tomorrow. Today, the electorate is dominated by "digital immigrants," people who grew up in an analog world and learned to access digital tools later in life.[25] By the time the nation moves into the next presidential election and President Obama begins campaigning for reelection, the electorate will include a greater proportion of "digital natives," people who grew up in the digital world and are native to accessing and understanding the power of these tools. As this transition occurs, President Obama and the Democratic Party are positioned to solidify their foothold within the electorate and to continue controlling the reins of government for some time to come.

NOTES

1. Brian Stelter, "The Facebooker Who Friended Obama," *New York Times*, July 7, 2008, www.nytimes.com/2008/07/07/technology/07hughes.html (26 July 2009).

2. Adam Singer, "Social Media, Web 2.0 and Internet Stats," January 12, 2009, thefuturebuzz.com/2009/01/12/social-media-web-20-internet-numbers-stats (10 July 2009).

3. Thank you, Jason Baer, for framing Facebook's success in these terms in an interaction with the author.

4. Brian Stelter, "The Facebooker Who Friended Obama," *New York Times,* July 7, 2008, www.nytimes.com/2008/07/07/technology/07hughes.html (1 August 2009).

5. Brian Stelter, "The Facebooker Who Friended Obama," *New York Times.*

6. Brian Stelter, "The Facebooker Who Friended Obama," *New York Times.*

7. Ellen McGirt, "How Chris Hughes Helped Launch Facebook and the Barack Obama Campaign." *Fastcompany.com*, March 17, 2009, www.fastcompany.com/magazine/134/boy-wonder.html (7 July 2009).

8. Om Malik, "A Brief History of Twitter," *Gigaom*, February 1, 2009, gigaom.com/2009/02/01/a-brief-history-of-twitter (26 July 2009).

9. "MySpace.com," *Compete.com*, siteanalytics.compete.com/myspace.com (5 July 2009).

10. "Twitter.com," *Compete.com*, siteanalytics.compete.com/twitter.com (5 July 2009).

11. This list of Twitter terms was influenced by a list of terms appearing in "The Digiactive Guide to Twitter for Activism," www.digiactive.org/2009/04/13/twitter_guide (6 July 2009).

12. Helena Deards, "Twitter First Off the Mark with Hudson Plane Crash Coverage," editorsweblog.org, January 19, 2009, www.editorsweblog.org/multimedia/2009/01/twitter_first_off_the_mark_with_hudson_p.php (1 August 2009).

13. "Twitter Used as Fast News Service After Plane Crash," *NRC Handelsblad*, February 26, 2009, www.nrc.nl/international/Features/article2163667.ece/Twitter_used_as_fast_news_service_after_plane_crash (1 August 2009).

14. Ellen Barry, "Protests in Moldova Explode, With Help of Twitter," *New York Times*, April 7, 2009, www.nytimes.com/2009/04/08/world/europe/08moldova.html?_r=1&scp=1&sq=Protests%20in%20Moldova%20Explode,%20With%20Help%20of%20Twitter&st=cse (29 July 2009).

15. Brad Stone and Noam Cohen, "Social Networks Spread Defiance Online," *New York Times*, June 15, 2009, www.nytimes.com/2009/06/16/world/middleeast/16media.html?scp=1&sq=Social%20Networks%20Spread%20Defiance%20Online&st=cse (29 July 2009).

16. Nicholas Kolakowski, "McCain Twitter Interview Draws Buzz," *E-week.com*, March 17, 2009, www.eweek.com/c/a/Messaging-and-Collaboration/McCain-Twitter-Interview-Draws-Buzz-665975 (26 July 2009).

17. Ben Parr, "AT&T Caves to Consumers, Offers $199 iPhone 3G S (For Some)," June 17, 2009, mashable.com/2009/06/17/att-iphone-3gs (26 July 2009).

18. Ari Herzog, "6 Twitter Search Services Compared," April 22, 2009, mashable.com/2009/04/22/twitter-search-services (26 July 2009).

19. "Follow Travel Portland on Twitter," *Travel Portland*, www.travelportland.com/visitors/twitter.html (26 July 2009).

20. "Twitter.com," *Compete.com*, siteanalytics.compete.com/twitter.com (5 July 2009).

21. Philip Elliott, "Obama Launches Grass-Roots Campaign," Associate Press, January 17, 2009, abcnews.go.com/Politics/wireStory?id=6669121 (1 August 2009).

22. Patrick Cooper, "White House Joins Facebook, MySpace, Twitter," *USA Today*, May 1, 2009.

23. Frederic Lardinois, "Obama's Social Media Advantage," ReadWriteWeb, November 5, 2008, www.readwriteweb.com/archives/social_media_obama_mccain_comparison.php (5 July 2009).

24. Matthew Crenson and Benjamin Ginsberg, *Downsizing Democracy: How America Sidelined Its Citizens and Privatized Its Public* (Baltimore, MD: Johns Hopkins University Press, 2002).

25. Marc Prensky, "Digital Natives, Digital Immigrants," *On the Horizon* 9, no. 5 (October 2001).

4

Who Wants to Be My Friend? Obama, Youth, and Social Networks in the 2008 Campaign

Jody C. Baumgartner and Jonathan S. Morris

Without the Internet, Barack Obama would still be the junior senator from Illinois. . . . Obama's online success dwarfed his opponent's, and proved key to his winning the presidency.[1]

Those who see the democratizing potential of the Internet would likely consider the election of 2008 a watershed year. Throughout the campaign citizens made use of any number of interactive Web technologies, including blogging, viral e-mail and video, and social networking Web sites. This is especially true with respect to young people, who seem to adapt well to the rapidly changing Web environment.

In this chapter we examine the role social networking Web sites played in Barack Obama's 2008 presidential campaign, focusing in particular on how these sites seemed to be effective communications channels for mobilizing eighteen- to twenty-four-year-old youth. After discussing the advent and popularization of this form of Internet communication, we discuss how it evolved into a powerful and effective campaign tool. Following this we examine how the Obama campaign used these social networking sites to their advantage, attracting more than 830,000 MySpace "friends" and 2.4 million Facebook "supporters" by late October 2008.[2] In each case Obama boasted almost four times as many supporters than McCain. As the result of the attention he paid to social networking Web sites as well as other Web technologies, Obama has—probably fairly—been called "America's first Internet president."[3] He successfully used these sites "as a vehicle for generating excitement among a vast online community."[4]

Using data from a national survey of college-aged youth, we then look in greater detail at this important age group and how Obama's virtual support manifested itself among them. We show that social networking users reported a much higher level of exposure to information from the Obama campaign than the McCain campaign through their social networking sites. Finally, we discuss how the use of social networking Web sites will affect future campaigns. We conclude that Web 2.0 social networking technologies have become etched in the fabric of American politics, and the successful use of this medium by the Obama campaign ensures that social networks will play a major role in future presidential campaigns.

SOCIAL NETWORKING WEB SITES

Social networking Web sites are designed to allow users "to (1) construct a public or semi-public profile within a bounded system, (2) articulate a list of other users with whom they share a connection, and (3) view and traverse their list of connections and those made by others within the system."[5] To put it simply, these sites allow individuals to construct and maintain connections to others. In its most common form, users create a "profile" of themselves, which they then invite and allow other "friends" to link to. Each person's friends are then displayed, allowing other users to explore and consider adding these friends to *their* friend list. In the end a virtual community is created.

In addition to profile and friend-oriented content (like comments or testimonials from friends), sites also include the option of linking to separate pages with content, picture, message boards, and the like, known as "groups" or "events." These pages, which can be open or closed to membership and are typically run by an administrator, give those with a common interest a virtual meeting place. It is this feature in particular that most political candidates take advantage of.

Facebook and MySpace were not the first social networking Web sites. Precursors to the social networking Web site could be found in the earliest days of mass Internet use—even before the advent of the World Wide Web. For example, if we focus on the idea of connecting people, chat rooms could be considered an early form of the social network. Beyond chat rooms, bulletin boards (technically known as the Bulletin Board System) were also popular in the 1980s. Bulletin boards are text-based online meeting places where users can exchange messages, post questions, answers, and opinions, share files, and more. Unlike social networking Web sites, bulletin boards were primarily the domain of computer hobbyists and enthusiasts, which helps explain why the subject matter of many of the posts was computer-related. Another difference is that most were local in nature, since accessing them meant dialing a telephone number with the computer's modem: long-distance charges applied to those dialing from outside of the area. In spite of these limitations, bulletin boards were quite popular, and a number have survived to this day.[6]

Of course, while chat rooms and bulletin boards did allow users to interact, they were not social networking sites, since they did not to allow people to connect and form communities. Moreover, there was no viral element. The first social networking Web site as such was SixDegrees.com, started in 1997. The name of the site was taken from the trivia game that builds off of the idea that any actor or actress can be linked, through their film roles, to Kevin Bacon within six steps. The site allowed users to create their own profiles, search the profiles of others, invite friends to link to their profiles, and form groups. While at its height membership reached about one million members, overly aggressive marketing turned many away, and the site ceased operation in 2001.[7] Other Web sites experimenting with the social networking model began to emerge around this time, including AsianAvenue, BlackPlanet, Cyworld, and LiveJournal.[8]

The first social networking Web site to gain widespread popularity was Friendster, started in 2002. The site took SixDegrees's notion of degrees of separation and transformed it into what they called the "Circle of Friends." In this iteration of connectivity, links between two people were displayed, allowing others to see where people were connected. Importantly, it also created the perception as well as the reality of a true online community. Within a year the site reportedly had better than three million users and was especially popular among those in their twenties and thirties.[9] Although the site is still in operation, it is currently most popular in Asia.[10]

In 2003, many Friendster users abandoned the site for the newly created MySpace.[11] This was partly a response to a fear that Friendster would begin charging for its services. But beyond this, unlike Friendster, MySpace welcomed the "profiles" of musical bands. Some bands based in San Francisco had been using Friendster to connect with their fan base and promote upcoming engagements. Friendster, however, banned the practice by deleting their profiles.[12] MySpace promoted itself as an alternative to Friendster by allowing this practice, as well as by creating an environment that was geared more toward a younger demographic.[13] The site proved so popular that Rupert Murdoch's News Corporation bought it in July 2005, paying $580 million.[14]

February 2004 saw the launch of Facebook by a Harvard University student. Working from his dormitory room, Mark Zuckerberg started "Thefacebook" with the help of Dustin Moskovitz and Chris Hughes. Zuckerberg had earlier built several other sites working off of the social networking model, including Coursematch, a site that connected Harvard students in the same degree program, and Facemash, which allowed users to rate how attractive their fellow classmates were. "Thefacebook" took off immediately: "1200 students signed up within 24 hours and half the undergraduate student body had opened accounts within a month."[15] The site soon opened its doors to users from other universities, and by year's end, Facebook boasted one million users. In 2005 Facebook expanded further to include students from both international colleges and high schools. The next major expansion came in 2006 when the site opened itself to anyone with a valid e-mail address. The site almost doubled its user base in the following year, from approximately fourteen to twenty-six million users.[16]

By this stage social networking on the Web had become mainstream. One report suggests that by 2008, 75 percent of eighteen- to twenty-four-year-olds had a profile on a social networking Web site, as did 57 percent of twenty-five- to thirty-four-year-olds. The same report suggested that 37 percent of social networking Web site users visited their profile on a daily basis.[17] While statistics measuring Web site usage are sometimes difficult to interpret,[18] MySpace and Facebook consistently rank among the most visited Web sites on the Internet.[19] MySpace was the leading social networking Web site in the United States through 2008, but was overtaken by Facebook in early 2009. One survey reported that Facebook had sixty-eight million unique visitors in January 2009 as opposed to MySpace's fifty-eight million;[20] Facebook claims approximately 150 million members, while MySpace has roughly 110 million.[21] Facebook is the leader worldwide,[22] and seems to be far more popular with the youth demographic.[23] This latter point is important in discussing how the Obama campaign used these sites throughout the campaign.

It was Facebook that first ventured into electoral politics, when in 2006 it independently set up an "Election Pulse" section containing profiles of all candidates for federal or gubernatorial office. The campaigns were given login information in order to manage and update these profiles, add contact information, qualifications for office, and other comments. In all, 32 percent of the candidates for the U.S. Senate updated their profiles on the site, while 50 percent of gubernatorial candidates did so.[24] In a move that foreshadowed the 2008 social network campaign, Facebook also ranked candidates by how many friends they had.

In March 2007 MySpace responded by creating its "Impact Channel," designed to highlight the upcoming presidential campaign.[25] Modeled after similar channels designed to highlight and share music or video, users could read candidate blogs, view pictures and video of the candidates, and importantly, add their favorite candidates to their friends list—where *their* friends could then add the candidate as well. The pages also featured a simple tool to solicit donations which could also be added to individual users' profiles. Another placed candidate ads on the users' pages.[26] In other words, by 2007, the stage was set for social networking Web sites to play an important role in the 2008 presidential campaign.

THE OBAMA CAMPAIGN AND SOCIAL NETWORKING WEB SITES

From the earliest stages of the presidential campaign in 2007 it was apparent that the Web would be an important communication tool. Hillary Clinton, for example, announced her candidacy in a Web video. This said, some candidates seemed to take advantage of the mobilization potential offered by social networking Web sites more than others. Barack Obama was one such candidate. Obama used this newer form of campaign communication and mobilization both aggressively and creatively. This fact was especially important given his popularity among younger voters, the main users of social networks.

While the candidacy of Barack Obama was overall more suited to appeal to social network Web site users, he had another advantage: a head start. Shortly after Obama's election to the U.S. Senate in 2004, an Obama supporter named Joe Anthony set up a MySpace page at "MySpace.com/barackobama." Over the next two-plus years, Anthony improved and maintained the "all things Obama" site, answering e-mails about the senator, pointing people to voter registration sites, and more. By the time Obama announced his presidential candidacy in February 2007 the page had more than thirty thousand friends. The campaign contacted Anthony and began to collaborate with him in keeping the profile updated, although in the end, Anthony retained control of the page. When MySpace started its "Impact Channel," the Obama campaign requested they use Anthony's page. Shortly thereafter the number of friends increased to eighty thousand, and a few weeks after that, MySpace featured Obama on its front page in its "Cool New People" box. Within a week the number of Obama's friends almost doubled.[27]

Sometime in April, however, the relationship between Anthony and the campaign soured, in part because of the amount of work involved in maintaining the page (Anthony was a volunteer). In addition, the campaign team was growing increasingly worried about an outsider controlling an integral component of the campaign effort. After refusing Anthony's request to buy the rights to the page for $39,000, which many observers consider would have been a bargain, the campaign went directly to MySpace administrators, asking them to turn control of the site over to them. They did so, and while the number of friends (who were, technically, Anthony's friends) immediately dropped to twelve thousand, the campaign quickly made up this lost ground. The point is that while many do not think this was the campaign's finest moment, Obama had a large head start on his rivals on the site, and in a viral communications environment, this is important.[28]

In May 2007, Facebook started what they referred to as "Platform," or a way for programmers to build applications (e.g., date books, trivia quizzes, etc.) for Facebook pages. This allowed for greater customization of users' pages compared with MySpace. Within a few weeks the Obama campaign had an application developed that allowed users to see what was happening with the campaign, and importantly, to spread word to others living in early primary (New Hampshire, South Carolina) and caucus (Iowa, Nevada) states.[29] From a political communications perspective, this was "the most impressive aspect of Facebook . . . [because] whenever someone posts an item, joins a group, or tries out a new application, her social network is notified about it."[30] This feature, in other words, added a viral element to the campaign effort.

The advantage Obama had was advance notice as the result of the association of Chris Hughes, one of the four cofounders of Facebook, with the campaign. Hughes had left the company in February to work on Obama's Internet campaign, but importantly, was still associated with Facebook in the capacity of consultant. As it happened, Obama was the only major presidential candidate to develop his own application in the first few weeks after the feature was launched, and some reports suggest that other campaigns were not notified. Whether or not this advantage was fair or unfair is debatable, but it was nevertheless an advantage. Of course, some campaigns were simply slow to recognize the viral potential of this feature. Hillary Clinton, for example, did not have her first application developed until late February 2008.[31]

Overall, it was clear that the Obama campaign took its online activities more seriously than his Republican rival in the general election, John McCain. For example, according to one account he had ten times the number of online staff than McCain.[32] In addition, and unlike most other presidential campaigns, his

> new media department was NOT a part of the campaign's tech team. . . . New media team leader Joe Rospars reported directly to campaign manager David Plouffe, and he was as much a part of the campaign's planning and decision making as they were. . . . [In] many other campaigns and advocacy groups . . . the online staff is buried in a basement and is implicitly expected to know how fix a computer as well as to understand how to use the internet as a modern political mobilization tool . . . while often being excluded from the communications planning process until the last possible moment, rendering the online element an afterthought with a stunted chance at real success.[33]

In other words, Obama created a new organization model for online communications, making it an equal part of the campaign rather than subservient to the rest of the team.

Obama was also well suited to a social network candidacy, in part because of his appeal to the younger demographic. He seemed to be "a natural Facebook politician. . . . The 72-year-old John McCain, by contrast, never managed to connect with the Facebook crowd on the same level. He gave one of his pastimes as fishing and listed *Letters From Iwo Jima* among his favorite movies—not the most popular things among frequent social networking website users."[34]

Obama seemed to inspire support among the social network crowd from the moment he burst onto the national political scene at the 2004 Democratic National Convention. Joe Anthony's MySpace page was evidence of this. But Anthony's page was not necessarily geared to an Obama presidential candidacy, unlike the Facebook group, "Barack Obama for President in 2008," which had over fifty thousand members before Obama had even formally announced his candidacy.[35] Another, "Students for Obama," which started as an online petition to encourage the senator to run for president, had sixty thousand members at eighty different colleges and universities by February 2007.[36] By comparison, when Howard Dean *ended* his presidential campaign in 2004 he had approximately 190,000 supporters on his Meetup.com site.[37]

One of the online groups not affiliated with the campaign that attracted the most attention was formed by Farouk Olu Aregbe, a coordinator of student government services at the University of Missouri. On the day that Obama released a video stating he would explore a run for the presidency ("A Message from Barack," on January 16, 2007), Aregbe created a Facebook group named "One Million Strong for Barack." Within an hour the group attracted one hundred members; within five days, ten thousand; and, by the end of the week, the group had grown to two hundred thousand members.[38] Although there were by this time hundreds of other groups formed in support of Obama and others, none came close to this total. In fact, it should be noted that the overwhelming majority of groups on Facebook throughout the campaign were fairly small, with less than a thousand members.[39]

A good deal of Obama support on social networking sites (as elsewhere) seems to have taken the form of anti-Hillary sentiment. A Facebook group formed opposing Hillary Clinton ("ANTI Hillary Clinton for President '08") had approximately forty-eight thousand members by late February 2007.[40] The first Facebook group to pass the one million member mark (in April 2008) was "One Million Against Hillary Clinton." After Clinton dropped out of the race, Obama's official Facebook page saw a sharp increase in supporters, passing the one million mark on June 17, 2008. At this time the "One Million Strong for Barack" had approximately 565,000 friends. By contrast, John McCain had approximately 146,000 friends at this stage of the campaign.

In the end, there were roughly five hundred unofficial Facebook groups dedicated to support for Obama, and by one estimate, approximately 2.4 million people "friended" the Democratic candidate.[41] Approximately four hundred thousand Facebook friends were gained by Obama in just the last two weeks of the campaign.[42] McCain ended with approximately 620,000 Facebook friends in total. Obama's MySpace campaign followed a similar trajectory relative to McCain's: He counted approximately 830,000 MySpace friends compared with McCain's 217,000.[43]

As further evidence of how seriously Obama took social networking, the Obama campaign spent $643,000 of his $16 million Internet budget to advertise on Facebook.[44] Virtually all of the remainder of that sum was spent advertising on major search engines. In fact, the Obama campaign did not focus their social network effort exclusively on Facebook and MySpace. They maintained profiles on fifteen different social networking sites, many tailored to specific demographics, like BlackPlanet or AsianAvenue. In all they accumulated approximately five million friends on these various sites.[45]

A major component of Obama's social networking effort was the social network established on his own site, "my.barackobama.com" (myBO.com). Unlike other social networks, the site allowed users to post only one picture of themselves and allowed only limited biographical information. However, the site was the hub of an extraordinary amount of activity:

- Over two million profiles were created;
- Two hundred thousand offline events were planned;
- Four hundred thousand blog postings were written;
- Four hundred thousand pro-Obama videos were posted to YouTube through the site;
- Thirty-five thousand volunteer groups were created (over one thousand on the day he announced his candidacy);
- Seventy thousand people raised $30 million on their own fundraising pages;
- Using a virtual phone bank system on the site, three million phone calls were made in the final four days of campaign.[46]

From myBO users were also able to set up MySpace and Facebook profiles, download campaign flyers and videos (with instructions on how to turn them into DVDs), organize campaign events, create their own fundraising sites, form groups of like-minded Obama supporters (e.g., Midcoast Maine for Obama, Educators for Obama, etc.),[47] and "even use a phonebank widget to get call lists and scripts to tele-canvass from home." Behind the scenes the site gathered data from individual users' computers with a "cookie" (a small hidden file that collects information from the user's computer to be used by Web sites) that told the campaign something about the person's browsing habits. This enabled the campaign to target specific ads to that individual in subsequent visits.[48]

In short, Obama was extremely successful in his social networking campaign, both on Facebook and MySpace, as well as his own social networking portal and other niche networks. In part this was due to certain advantages he had in this effort, but in the end his success was due to the fact that he recognized the opportunity to use this new communications channel to augment more traditional campaign strategies and tools. As one observer noted:

> His campaign started from scratch early in 2007 with few resources and little name recognition, but the internet helped him connect to his core supporters in cost-effective ways. Many of his campaign's early efforts were low-overhead strategies that utilised free resources. His nimble use of the internet helped him overcome the huge initial lead of Hillary Clinton in both fundraising and perceived viability. He was able to get more local volunteers on the ground in key states earlier than the Clinton campaign, which was especially important in smaller states and caucus states.[49]

This latter fact was especially important, considering that Obama won every caucus state during the Democratic nomination season, in large part because of his ability, with the help of his online volunteers, to organize in these states. In other words, social networking allowed Obama to go beyond communicating with supporters into actual on-the-ground mobilization of that support.

Of course, Obama's support was especially pronounced among young people, the demographic that is likely to frequent social networking sites. These youth "were attracted to him by his early opposition to the war in Iraq, as well as his personal 'audacity of hope' story, allowing him to mobilize their energy and passion."[50] In the next section we explore the nature of social network users' relationship with the Obama campaign in more detail.

SOCIAL NETWORKING SITES, YOUTH SUPPORT, AND THE OBAMA CAMPAIGN

From December 2007 through November 2008, a series of national Web surveys of eighteen- to twenty-four-year-old college and university students across the country were conducted. The project sought to determine the various ways in which this age group followed the campaign for president and how these methods intersected with their attitudes, beliefs, participation, and more.[51] Included in the survey were various questions about the social networking habits of the participants. Of the 2200 survey respondents, 92 percent said they had a social networking account. Of these, 60 percent were exclusive Facebook-only users and only 3 percent were exclusive MySpace users. A full 37 percent of the respondents claimed they had accounts on both Facebook and MySpace, although 91 percent of these dual-users said they use Facebook with more frequency.

When social network Web site users were examined exclusively, some interesting patterns emerged. Overall, social networking Web site users are not passive in how often they frequent the sites. In total, 69 percent of all social network users visit their Web page at least once a day, and almost half (47 percent) said they visit their site more than once a day. Also, it is clear that social networking Web sites are legitimate sources of news for eighteen- to twenty-four-year-olds. Forty percent of the sample said they received news about the campaign for president from their social networking Web site at least once a week. In terms of frequency of news usage, this percentage rivaled more traditional sources such as CNN (51 percent), Fox News (44 percent), and MSNBC (40 percent).

How often were social networking users exposed to information about the Obama campaign through their online account? Among all social network users in the sample, 27 percent said they received a "fair amount" or a "great deal" of information about the Obama campaign from the social networking Web page. This more than doubles the amount of individuals who reported getting a "fair amount" or a "great deal" of information about the McCain campaign on the social networking account (11 percent). Furthermore, less than half of the social network users in the sample reported that they received no information at all about the Obama campaign on their site (42 percent). However, almost six out of ten users (58 percent) said they had not received any information from McCain.

Individuals who received information about the Obama campaign through their social networking site were more supportive of him than individuals who received no information. In total, 59 percent of those who received at least some information about Obama on the site intended to vote for him, while 51 percent of those who received no information intended to do the same—an eight point difference. This difference, however, is similar when looking at the intended vote for McCain. Thirty-seven percent of those who received some information from the McCain campaign intended to vote for him. Among those who received no information about McCain, only 28 percent said they were going to vote for him.

Based on the above trends, little evidence was found to suggest that the Obama campaign's social networking efforts were any more persuasive than those of his opposition. It is abundantly clear, however, that the Obama campaign had a much larger social networking presence than McCain and that the campaign did a better job of communicating with its supporters.

CONCLUSION

Barack Obama was able to mobilize an enormous amount of support on social networking sites in 2008, especially among youth. This support went beyond attraction to general personality characteristics, and into support for various policies as well. When asked which candidate would do a better job handling various issues, Obama had a clear advantage among social networking users in terms of who would do a better job with education, the economy, the environment, and health care. But this support should perhaps have been expected: "Traffic on the Internet in general tilts toward the young and the more highly educated, demographics which—at least for the time being—are associated with more liberal politics."[52] Indeed, 37 percent of youth social networking users identified themselves as liberals, and 36 percent identified themselves with the Democratic Party. Among those who did not have a social networking account, 33 percent identified themselves as Liberal and 29 percent said they were Democrat.

Whether by design or otherwise, Obama was able to develop a new form of campaign mobilization during his 2008 presidential campaign. While others before him had seen the potential the Web held to mobilize support (John McCain's fundraising in 2000, Howard Dean's "Meetup" support in 2004), social networking technology added new opportunities in 2008. Rather than using Web communication to passively distribute information to those who may come across a page, social networking sites allow candidates to create a modern and viral iteration of grassroots campaigning. It is difficult to imagine how candidates will be able to ignore the potential of the social networking campaign in the future.

Of course, we should temper these conclusions. One truism of political campaigns is that when it is discovered that something works, it becomes standard for all subsequent campaigns. All future campaigns will undoubtedly pay close attention to the social networking possibilities in the future. However, because this campaign tool puts a great deal of control in the hands of users, some campaign teams may be reluctant. The social networking campaign model requires a great deal of trust in the grassroots, and few campaign managers are eager to relinquish control of the message.

Another note of caution is in order. It is not entirely clear that youth mobilization through social networking Web sites (or on the Internet in general) necessarily translates into on-the-ground political activity. In fact, the Baumgartner and Morris findings suggest otherwise. While youth engaged in a variety of online political activities in 2008 (e.g., forwarding a political e-mail), they did not necessarily engage in more traditional political activity like trying to persuade another person to support a particular political candidate or issue, wear a campaign button or put a sticker on their car, attend a political rally or speech, etc.[53] In a closer election this might matter.

Perhaps the real lesson campaigns can learn from the campaign of 2008 is that it is worthwhile to pay close attention to rapidly changing Web technologies and the opportunities they afford to the campaign. It would be foolish to speculate what the landscape of the Web may look like in 2012, but it is a safe bet that a new venue will present itself as it has done in each of the past three or four presidential elections, and that it will look different than it did in 2008. The relatively new phenomenon of Twitter is most likely only the tip of the 2012 iceberg. The candidates who understand the new Web landscape and effectively exploit it will likely benefit in the same way that Obama did in 2008.

NOTES

1. Colin Delany, "Learning from Obama: Lessons for Online Communicators in 2009 and Beyond," *Techpresident.com*, 24 February 2009, techpresident.com/blog-entry/learning-obama-lessons-online-communicators-2009-and-beyond (6 June 2009).

2. Tamara A. Small, "The Facebook Effect? Online Campaigning in the 2008 Canadian and US Elections," *Policy Options*, November 2008, 85–87, www.irpp.org/po//archive/nov08/small.pdf (6 June 2009); Jeremiah Owyang, "Snapshot of Presidential Candidate Social Networking Stats: Nov 3, 2008," 3 November 2008, www.web-strategist.com/blog/2008/11/03/snapshot-of-presidential-candidate-social-networking-stats-nov-2-2008/ (13 June 2009).

3. Samuel Greengard, "The First Internet President," *Communications of the ACM* 52, no. 2 (February 2009): 16–18.

4. Steven Hill, "World Wide Webbed: The Obama Campaign's Masterful Use of the Internet," *Social Europe Journal*, 8 March 2009, www.social-europe.eu/2009/04/world-wide-webbed-the-obama-campaign's-masterful-use-of-the-internet/ (9 June 2009).

5. Danah M. Boyd and Nicole B. Ellison, "Social Network Sites: Definition, History, and Scholarship," *Journal of Computer-Mediated Communication* 13, no. 1 (October 2007), article 11, jcmc.indiana.edu/vol13/issue1/boyd.ellison.html (24 May 2009).

6. Gord Goble, "The History of Social Networking," *Digital Trends*, news.digitaltrends.com/feature/99/the-history-of-social-networking (9 June 2009).

7. Goble, "The History of Social Networking."

8. Mrinal Todi, "Advertising on Social Networking Websites," *ScholarlyCommons@Penn 2008*, repository.upenn.edu/wharton_research_scholars/52/ (28 May 2009).

9. Danah Boyd, "Why Youth (Heart) Social Network Sites: The Role of Networked Publics in Teenage Social Life," in *MacArthur Foundation Series on Digital Learning—Youth, Identity, and Media Volume*, ed. David Buckingham (Cambridge, MA: MIT Press, 2007), 119–42.

10. Goble, "The History of Social Networking."

11. Todi, "Advertising on Social Networking Websites."

12. Boyd, "Why Youth (Heart) Social Network Sites."

13. Goble, "The History of Social Networking."

14. Todi, "Advertising on Social Networking Websites."

15. Todi, "Advertising on Social Networking Websites."

16. Todi, "Advertising on Social Networking Websites."

17. Amanda Lenhart, "Adults and Social Network Websites," *Pew Internet and American Life Project*, 14 January 2009, www.pewinternet.org/PPF/r/272/report_display.asp (2 June 2009).

18. For example, in a given time period should one count users with profiles on social networking Web sites, the total number of visits, the total number of unique visitors, the total number of pages viewed, the number of pages viewed by each visitor, the time each visitor spent on the site, and more. All of these systems would return slightly different site rankings.

19. See ranking at www.alexa.com/topsites.

20. Caroline McCarthy, "Whee! New Numbers on Social Network Usage," *C-Net News*, 10 February 2009, news.cnet.com/8301-17939_109-10160850-2.html (18 May 2009).

21. Monte Lutz, "The Social Pulpit: Barack Obama's Social Media Toolkit," *SVP-Digital Public Affairs, Edelman*, 2009, www.edelman.com/image/insights/content/ Social Pulpit - Barack Obamas Social Media Toolkit 1.09.pdf (26 June 2009).

22. Small, "The Facebook Effect?"

23. Michael Mace, "Online Communities and Their Impact on Business. Part Three: Web Community and Social Life," *Rubicon Consulting*, October 2008, rubicon consulting.com/insight/winmarkets/michael_mace/2008/10/online-communities -and-their-i-4.html (2 June 2009).

24. Jeff Gulati and Christine Williams, "Bentley College Professors Update Data on Candidates' Use of Facebook as Campaign Heads Into Final Days," *AScribe Newswire*, 2 November 2006.

25. Micah L. Sifry, "The Battle to Control Obama's MySpace," *Techpresident .com*, 1 May 2007, techpresident.com/blog-entry/battle-control-obamas-MySpace (6 June 2009).

26. Alex Williams, "The Future President, on Your Friends List," *New York Times*, 18 March 2007, www.nytimes.com/2007/03/18/fashion/18MySpace.html (24 May 2009).

27. Sifry, "The Battle to Control Obama's MySpace."

28. Sifry, "The Battle to Control Obama's MySpace."

29. Joshua Levy and Micah Sifry, "Did Facebook Play Favorites with Obama?" *Techpresident.com*, 4 June 2007, techpresident.com/blog/2396 (6 June 2009).

30. Joshua Levy, "Note to Candidates: There's This Thing Called 'Facebook,'" *Techpresident.com*, 21 June 2007, techpresident.com/blog-entry/note-candidates-theres-thing-called-facebook (6 June 2009).

31. Joshua Levy, "Daily Digest: Too Late for Clinton?" *Personal Democracy Forum*, 27 February 2008, personaldemocracy.com/blog/entry/1791/daily_digest_too_little_too_late_for_clinton (24 May 2009).

32. Lutz, "The Social Pulpit."

33. Colin Delany, "Learning from Obama's Campaign Structure: How to Organize for Success," *e.politics*, 24 February 2009, www.epolitics.com/2009/02/24/learning-from-obamas-campaign-structure-how-to-organize-for-success/ (28 June 2009).

34. Matthew Fraser and Soumitra Dutta, "Barack Obama and the Facebook Election," *US News & World Report*, 19 November 2008, www.usnews.com/articles/opinion/2008/11/19/barack-obama-and-the-facebook-election.html?s_cid=related-links:TOP (13 June 2009).

35. Zachary A. Goldfarb, "Facebook Flexes Political Might," *Washington Post*, 3 February 2007, www.msnbc.msn.com/id/16955489/ (6 June 2009).

36. Jose Antonio Vargas, "Young Voters Find Voice on Facebook," *Washington Post*, 17 February 2007, A01.

37. Joe Trippi, *The Revolution Will Not Be Televised* (New York: HarperCollins, 2004).

38. Vargas, "Young Voters Find Voice on Facebook."

39. Michael Whitney, "Barrack Obama's One Millionth Supporter on Facebook," *Techpresident.com*, 17 June 2008, techpresident.com/blog-entry/barack-obamas-one-millionth-supporter-facebook-updated (6 June 2009).

40. Fred Stutzman, "Understanding Candidate Facebook Groups," *Techpresident.com*, 24 February 2009, techpresident.com/blog-entry/understanding-candidate-facebook-groups (14 May 2009).

41. Small, "The Facebook Effect?"; Jeremiah Owyang, "Snapshot of Presidential Candidate Social Networking Stats."

42. Micah L. Sifry, "Obama Bandwagon Effect on Facebook," *Techpresident.com*, 3 November 2008, techpresident.com/node/6476 (6 June 2009).

43. Small, "The Facebook Effect?"

44. Kate Kaye, "Google Grabbed Most of Obama's $16 Million in 2008," *ClickZ*, 6 January 2009, www.clickz.com/3632263 (6 June 2009).

45. Delany, "Learning from Obama."

46. Delany, "Learning from Obama."

47. Amy Schatz, "BO, U R So Gr8," *Wall Street Journal*, 26 May 2007, A1.

48. Hill, "World Wide Webbed."

49. Hill, "World Wide Webbed."

50. Hill, "World Wide Webbed."

51. Details about the survey are available on request.

52. Nate Silver, "Blogosphere Reality Has a Liberal Bias," *FiveThirtyEight.com*, 18 May 2009, www.fivethirtyeight.com/2009/05/blogosphere-reality-has-liberal-bias.html (14 July 2009).

53. Jody Baumgartner and Jonathan S. Morris, "MyFaceTube Politics: Social Networking Websites and Political Engagement of Young Adults," *Social Science Computer Review* (forthcoming).

5

My Fellow Blogging Americans: Weblogs and the Race for the White House

Nancy Snow

Which came first, the blog or the political campaign? It's the twenty-first-century version of the chicken or the egg dilemma. The race for the White House in 2008 was a clear point from which social media unsavvy presidential candidates need not return. As often as we got the daily horserace numbers on who was up or down in the polls, we heard electronic media stories about John McCain's aversion or inability to send personal e-mail in contrast to Barack Obama's obsessive texting that led to his post-election BlackBerry Withdrawal Syndrome. In July 2008, as Obama was gearing up for his world tour that included stops in Germany, Afghanistan, and Israel, the *New York Times* conducted a lengthy interview with Senator McCain that asked him a series of questions, including an emphasis on his social media skills set. When asked what electronic technology he uses, McCain responded:

> I use the Blackberry, but I don't e-mail. I've never felt the particular need to e-mail. I read e-mails all the time, but the communications that I have with my friends and staff are oral and done with my cell phone. I have the luxury of being in contact with them literally all the time. We now have a phone on the plane that is usable on the plane, so I just never really felt a need to do it. But I do—could I just say, really—I understand the impact of blogs on American politics today and political campaigns. I understand that. And I understand that something appears on one blog, can ricochet all around and get into the evening news, the front page of *The New York Times*. So, I do pay attention to the blogs. And I am not in any way unappreciative of the impact that they have on entire campaigns and world opinion.[1]

McCain said that he read his daughter Megan's blog, among others. It was this admission that McCain did not use e-mail that was seized by the Obama

campaign. In September 2008, the campaign released "Still," a popular You-
Tube video that included 1980s era disco balls, oversized cordless phones,
out-of-date eyeglasses and suits, and a Rubik's Cube. The ad copy referenced
the *Times* interview:

> 1982, John McCain goes to Washington. Things have changed in the last 26
> years, but McCain hasn't. He admits he still doesn't know how to use a com-
> puter, can't send an e-mail, still doesn't understand the economy and favors $200
> billion in tax cuts for corporations, but almost nothing for the middle class. After
> one president who is out of touch, we just can't afford more of the same.[2]

On September 12, 2008, Obama spokesman Dan Pfeiffer told the Associated Press: "Our economy wouldn't survive without the Internet, and cyber-
security continues to represent one of our most serious national security
threats. It's extraordinary that someone who wants to be our president and our
commander in chief doesn't know how to send an e-mail."[3] Another spokesman, Nick Shapiro, defended the ad even further:

> The ad goes directly at the fundamental issue in this race: John McCain is out
> of touch with the American people and unable to address the challenges facing
> the country in the twenty-first century. It delivers the message in a light-hearted,
> humorous way that Americans can relate to. The overwhelming majority of
> Americans of all ages use computers today.[4]

The message was simple: Obama is tech-cool and McCain, war hero or not,
is a computer illiterate who has not updated his suit or his technical knowledge
since the twentieth century. It was part of an aggressive two-month offensive
push by Obama's advisers to put the senior senator on the defensive. "Today is
the first day of the rest of the campaign. We will respond with speed and feroc-
ity to John McCain's attacks and we will take the fight to him, but we will do it
on the big issues that matter to the American people."[5] To Obama's supporters,
this aggressive move in the political chess game was a relief from what some
saw as a too-passive Democratic presidential candidate. To Obama's detrac-
tors, the campaign ad and critical words about technical illiteracy spoken by
Obama spokespeople smacked a bit of ageism, a charge that had not been a
major feature in the presidential race for the White House.
    Within a short time, conservative bloggers like Michelle Malkin's Hot
Air and Jonah Goldberg revealed that McCain did not disdain new media so
much as have a war injury that prevented him from typing, much less raising
his arms. Hot Air's Ed Morrissey posted:

> Making fun of a war hero's severe injuries—smooth move, Team O. Talk about
> computer illiteracy! Doesn't anyone on the Obama campaign know what they're

doing? Didn't it ever occur to them that a man who can't raise his arms above his head might have a physical barrier to using a computer? If this is what happens when they take the gloves off, maybe they should just keep them on in the future.[6]

Jonah Goldberg blogged about McCain's physical limitations, pulling an excerpt from a 2000 *Boston Globe* profile by Mary Leonard.[7] Leonard's lengthy feature revealed a more personal side of the candidate when the Republican senator ran against then Governor George W. Bush of Texas in Campaign 2000.

McCain gets emotional at the mention of military families needing food stamps or veterans lacking health care. The outrage comes from inside: McCain's severe war injuries prevent him from combing his hair, typing on a keyboard, or tying his shoes. Friends marvel at McCain's encyclopedic knowledge of sports. He's an avid fan—Ted Williams is his hero—but he can't raise his arm above his shoulder to throw a baseball.

Forbes magazine also mentioned McCain's limited e-mail ability in 2000:

In certain ways, McCain was a natural Web candidate. Chairman of the Senate Telecommunications Subcommittee and regarded as the U.S. Senate's savviest technologist, McCain is an inveterate devotee of e-mail. His nightly ritual is to read his e-mail together with his wife, Cindy. The injuries he incurred as a Vietnam POW make it painful for McCain to type. Instead, he dictates responses that his wife types on a laptop. "She's a whiz on the keyboard, and I'm so laborious," McCain admits.[8]

If you wanted to be the last one standing in the race for the White House, you had better have nimble thumbs or have hired someone who was long in the information and communications (ICT) technology teeth. Lucky for Obama, not only was he generationally social media savvy at forty-seven, but he understood early on in his candidacy that the Internet universe, including an army of majority liberal bloggers, would be his close ally in getting out his message of just who is this guy.

For years, the old adage when one wanted to run for high office like senator, governor, or president, was "Where are you going to get the money?" Hereafter, the refrain must include, "Who is going to handle your interactive media?" And central to a candidate's interactive media is blogging.

As a blogger for the Huffington Post, it is not always easy to explain this part-time avocation. A blogger is one who keeps and regularly updates a blog, an online commentary site. The activity of blogging is for people who like to comment about either their own lives or about what is going on in the news, post it online, and allow the world to comment on it. The difference between writing it down privately in a journal or diary is that one is logging this Web commentary publicly. While one can sometimes set one's blogs to be closed to comments (a feature offered to Huffington Post bloggers), this is generally frowned upon in the blogosphere (the world of blogging).

Long before blogging became part of our national conversation, there was the online diary. A person would update a Web site with information from his everyday life posted in sequential form or organized by reverse chronology. Many of these online diaries included references to one's daily meals or moods and were intended for friends or family more than a universe of readers. They were not viewed as part of the national conversation or seen as having much of any political influence.

Blogging, a shorthand version of weblog, keeps an online running commentary of one's happenings or events, often with hyperlinked pages to other blogs or Web sites. The term "weblog" is credited, with some debate, to Jorn Barger, who referred to "logging the Web" in December 1997 as opposed to just "surfing the Web" for information. His popular weblog, *Robot Wisdom*, is an eclectic collection of commentary from artificial intelligence to his favorite musicians like Joni Mitchell to writers Thomas Pynchon and James Joyce, about whose *Ulysses* and *Finnegan's Wake* he kept a vast annotated library.[9] A Jeremiah Johnson–looking figure, Barger says that his intent in 1997 was to "make the web as a whole more transparent, via a sort of 'mesh network,' where each weblog amplifies just those signals (or links) its author likes best."[10] Barger's style of blogging is more links-rich one-man band style like Matt Drudge's Drudge Report (circa 1996) as opposed to the graphic and video-rich Huffington Post (circa 2005) that boasts over a thousand bloggers. The Huffington Post's slogan is "The Internet Newspaper: News, Blogs, Video, Community," and unlike Drudge, who spotlights breaking news stories, the Huffington Post emphasizes its political commentary. *Time* magazine named it one of the top twenty-five best blogs of 2009, adding that "[W]hen it comes to political blogs, the Huffington Post is in a class by itself."[11]

The word "blogging" is credited to yet another father, Justin Hall, who was christened "the founding father of personal bloggers" in an article "Your Blog or Mine?" published in the noted newspaper of record, the *New York Times*. Hall began his links.net Web site in 1994 while a student at Swarthmore College. With over a hundred million blogging sites these days, the question of blogging paternity is hampered by a lot of chattering activity on the Internet and little attention to taking credit for whose first post created all this progeny. As CNET News staff writers Declan McCullagh and Anne Broache wrote: "Someone, somewhere created the very first Web log. It's just not quite clear who. . . . Any definition should probably include posts sorted by date, with the newest posts at the top and the rest archived for future use (criteria that would eliminate the Drudge Report, for instance)."[12]

George Washington University professor Jeffrey Rosen, who credited Hall as one of the pioneer bloggers, says that blogging needs to be distinguished from professional journalism:

> There are two obvious differences between bloggers and the traditional press: unlike bloggers, professional journalists have a) editors and b) the need to maintain a professional reputation so that sources will continue to talk to them. I've been a journalist for more than a decade, and on two occasions I asked acquaintances whether I could print information that they had told me in social situations. Both times, they made clear that if I published they would never speak to me again. Without a reputation for trustworthiness, neither friendship nor journalism can be sustained over time.[13]

In the United States, the concept of objectivity—factual and unbiased information—is closely linked to conventional definitions of journalism. Professional journalists are supposed to deliver "the facts" as Sergeant Joe Friday of *Dragnet* implored his female eyewitnesses. In contrast, political blogs have a slant or embedded bias to the way information is packaged and presented. Most blogs are characterized as left-leaning (Daily Kos, Talking Points Memo) or right-leaning (Michelle Malkin, TownHall) but loyal readers of these blogs often find them as reliable as mainstream news media.[14] A Brigham Young study by political scientist Richard Davis found a trend among political blogs that "liberals read almost exclusively liberal blogs, but conservatives tend to read both."[15] Further, liberal views dominate in the blogosphere (Huffington Post) whereas conservative views dominate on talk radio (Rush Limbaugh, Glenn Beck, Bill O'Reilly). Despite the recognized embedded bias in blogging, Richard Davis's research finds that blogs serve as a credible "echo chamber" for traditional news stories: "Blog readers still get most of their news from regular news sources, but they are concerned that they are not getting the whole side of the story there. They suspect habitual bias in the traditional news content."[16]

The terrorist attacks of September 11, 2001, may have helped to fuel an interest in readers to get the other side of the story. In late 2001 and 2002, a number of sites sprouted up that questioned the government's version of the events of 9/11. Liberals who were upset with the Republican control of Congress and the White House were beginning to post their misgivings online, notably Joshua Micah Marshall of Talking Points Memo (talkingpointsmemo .com), who played a key role in pressuring Trent Lott to resign as Senate majority leader. In April 2004, Russ Kick, an Arizona-based blogger, used the Freedom of Information Act to request photos of American military coffins coming back from the Middle East. The Pentagon sent the photos and Kick immediately posted the pictures on his blog, the Memory Hole (thememory hole.org). Within twenty-four hours these photos were on the front pages of newspapers around the world. Bloggers were invited to both political conventions in 2004, and by the end of the year, the Merriam-Webster dictionary identified "blog" as the most searched definitional term. Political blogs came into play mostly for fundraising purposes during the presidential campaign season of 2004.

Democratic presidential contenders Howard Dean and Wesley Clark made use of the activities and endorsements of bloggers to raise their national profiles. Howard Dean's manager, Joe Trippi, attributed much of Dean's popularity and fundraising momentum to the Internet. The tipping point in blogging's influence on mainstream media occurred on September 8, 2004, when Dan Rather of CBS News reported on *60 Minutes Wednesday* a highly damaging story about President George W. Bush's credibility surrounding his National Guard Service during the Vietnam War era. Internet bloggers, especially Power Line and Little Green Footballs, seized on the cornerstone of the Dan Rather piece, a collection of memos that show favorable treatment of Bush. Though Rather dismissed his critics as "partisan political operatives" and referred to the documents as "fake, but accurate," doubts persist that the CBS News–obtained memos were produced using a modern font rather than a 1970s-era typeface. The whole episode was quickly dubbed "Memogate," or "Rathergate."

Time magazine named George W. Bush its "Person of the Year" for having retained his seat as president, but for the first time in its history *Time* named Power Line "2004 Blog of the Year" for the efforts of "three amateur journalists working in a homegrown online medium [who] challenged a network news legend and won."[17] In raising the visibility and credibility of blogs on the media landscape, *Time* explained the growing appeal of blogs to readers.

> If you haven't read one, it's hard to describe what makes blogs so special. There's just something about the rhythm and pace of a blog that feels intuitively right. You don't have to sit through fake-cheerful news-team chitchat or wade through endless column inches. It takes about 20 sec. to read a typical blog post, and when you're finished you've got the basic facts up to the minute plus a dab of analysis and a dash of spin. If you're not satisfied, you can click the link for more. If you are, you can go back to checking your e-mail and jiggering your spreadsheets or whatever you do for a living. This is news Jetsons-style. If it were any neater and quicker, it would come in a pill.

Many conservative bloggers consider the Dan Rather story as a liberal news media organization turning a blind eye to fact checking in its desire to unseat a Republican president. The industry magazine *Broadcasting and*

Cable reported shortly after: "Desire, ambition and haste—and, some would say, the blindness of anti-Bush journalists desperately wanting the story to be true—created the ideal conditions for a network to put its reputation on the line for a story sold with dubious goods."[18] Practically overnight, political blogs earned an immediate credibility in the eyes of many Americans while faith in mainstream media news declined. Today a blog called Rathergate exists to keep "an eye on liberal media bias." Despite the growth in blogs after 9/11 and during the presidential campaign season of 2004, a lot would change between the two campaign seasons. As Michael Kinsley points out, "Way back in 2004, when we last held an election, no one was complaining that there wasn't enough to see or read on the Internet. And that was before YouTube, Politico, Huffington Post, Twitter and Facebook became daily or hourly necessities for millions."[19]

By the conclusion of Election 2008, a quick look back revealed that Obama had an enormous new media advantage to that of McCain. Using data supplied by the online social media statistics firm Trendrr, Frederic Lardinois of ReadWriteWeb reported:

> While overall blog mentions of Obama and McCain varied greatly during the last year (and we can't say if those were positive or negative posts), close to five hundred million blog postings mentioned him since the beginning of the conventions at the end of August. During the same time period, only about 150 million blog posts mentioned McCain (though it would also be interesting to see similar statistics for Governor Palin as well).[20]

This enormous blogging advantage that Obama had over McCain meant that the junior senator from Illinois was no longer an unknown also-ran in the presidential election. It signified that there was excitement—both positive and negative—about seeing Senator Barack Obama elected the forty-fourth president of the United States. These blogging statistics are astonishing when one considers that at the start of 1999 there were less than twenty-five blogs,[21] but by 2008, Technorati had indexed well over one hundred million worldwide.[22] The question remains: Did blogging make the man for the presidency or did the man for the presidency make blogging? That is not an easy question to answer definitively, but let's consider the political landscape that provided the content for the blogosphere.

THE POLITICAL CAMPAIGN

Before we put Obama into the genius campaigner column, let's admit that 2008 was much more likely than not going to be a win for the Democrats. An unpopular war and even more unpopular Republican incumbent whose popularity by the end was barely out of the 20s spells change at the top. The race for the White House 2008 was the Democrats to win or to lose. This gave the eventual Democratic nominee an obvious advantage because the Republican competition—namely the social media disadvantaged John McCain—was not in the position of setting the agenda, but rather defending the indefensible. Add to this mix a Democratic nominee who offered even more change than just party affiliation and you had the recipe for grassroots participatory history making.

From the moment Obama uttered the words "Yes, We Can," he essentially transformed his presidential campaign from his victory to our success. Voters were now in the driver's seat of politics more than at any point in history. Yet how did a relatively obscure politician with the most liberal voting record in Congress unseat "heir apparent" Hillary Clinton and a Republican machine noted for its brilliant political strategizing? Obama emphasized brand management over traditional political strategizing, playing on the candidate's natural personal and very positive appeal. We need not belabor the obvious powers of "Obamasuasion" or the fact that both Hillary Clinton and John McCain lacked comparable charisma and personal charm. Obama had inalienable communicative gifts. No other candidate, Democrat or Republican, had the personal "it" factor of candidate Obama, and Obama soon eclipsed the standard bearer communicator-in-chief of the Democratic Party, Bill Clinton. Further, Obama understood very well—more than Bill Clinton—that personal charisma, like credibility, is not about the sender of a message, but very much about the perceptions of receivers. No message, strategy, or campaign whistle stop was going to make a difference if voters were not buying what he was selling. And what he was selling was magic. He made the election about personal-level transformational politics and the possibility to end ideological stranglehold. Voters who were turned off by politics in general gave Election 2008 a second look because a mid-forties black junior senator with a funny-sounding name believed he could be president. And this served as a brilliant marketing strategy: Try it on for size. See if you like it. It wasn't like a pushy salesperson, but more like someone who says "That's fine" to your "I'm just looking." Not only did voters respond to the man and his message, but also they donated. Of his $639 million raised from individual donors, nearly half were donations of less than $300.

Obama's message was targeted to all, not just likely voters or past voters. In particular, first-time voters and independents were appealed to.[23] Everyone was given a chance to participate and ride the Obama train. No other political campaign had relied on so many millions of supporters, all of whom became fans of their candidate. Once they had buy-in, their loyalty was not only firm but also enthusiastic. This is what a good brand does to build brand loyalty. A person who buys a Toyota for the first time is likely to keep buying that brand for years to come. Obama banked on his novice appeal with a pledge that he would deliver if buyers (voters) would just give his candidacy a test drive. This campaign pledge was "Change you can believe in." It was simple, direct, and consistent throughout his campaign. He did not change anything in his message delivery, be it a new slogan or logo, which further reinforced his consistency and reliability. He never changed his message of hope and redemption (with their obvious Biblical overtones), and he combined these simple positive themes with specific policy details, all available online. He even served himself well in the three main political debates with Senator John McCain. By then, he did well enough that he did not lose any momentum and McCain had given up ground to Obama in the singular issue that became the floundering economy.

At the national level, the campaign strategy was "No drama Obama." Obama relied on a small group of advisers who stayed on message with him. Obama was the face of the entire campaign. Everything was cleared through Obama and Obama was the spokesperson for his campaign more than his campaign advisers like David Axelrod, David Plouffe, Robert Gibbs, and Anita Dunn. Obama relied on his personal biography and powers of oration to inspire people to contribute to his campaign. If he had relied on political operatives to speak on behalf of his campaign, his personal message would have lost cadence. He also capitalized on the enthusiasm of the Democratic voters. While nearly two-thirds of Democrats (61 percent) responded with enthusiasm about the 2008 election, just 35 percent of Republicans felt likewise, all of which translates into a pull up/push down factor in fundraising and volunteer turnout. The *Los Angeles Times* reported in late June 2008 that just 45 percent of McCain's supporters were enthusiastic about their candidate while 81 percent of Barack Obama's supporters were. There was an obvious enthusiasm gap and money gap. The Republican money machine was in need of a major tune-up, but its negative messaging strategy to link Obama to radicals and socialists served only to turn off independents and first-time voters.

A major turning point in Obama's political fortunes occurred at the lowest point in his candidacy. He had everything to lose and nothing to gain if he had followed the advice of his political advisers. But Obama decided that his campaign for the American presidency would be determined by his political instincts more than the advice of his inner circle. After his campaign suffered a beating from the around-the-clock news coverage of his controversial church pastor and spiritual adviser, Reverend Jeremiah Wright, Obama elected to respond to all the criticism with a speech about race in America. His advisers told him not to respond and let the controversy die out. As Steve Kroft said of the inner circle, "Like Obama, they were talented, laid back, and idealistic, with limited exposure on the national stage. But with the candidate's help, the team orchestrated one of the most improbable and effective campaigns in American political history."[24] This was a team that was in a race but did not make race an issue of the campaign. By the time Reverend Wright's speeches were being endlessly looped on television and the Internet, Obama asked his team to create some time in his schedule to give a speech on race. As his adviser David Axelrod recalls Obama saying, "I'm gonna make a speech about race and talk about Jeremiah Wright and the perspective of the larger issue. And either people will accept it or I won't be president of the United States. But at least I'll have said what I think needs to be said."[25] Obama's thirty-eight-minute speech, "A More Perfect Union," which he delivered in Philadelphia on March 18, 2008, has been viewed by millions on YouTube and was received by the major media as a political speech as memorable as the Gettysburg Address. It wasn't until after the November 2008 election that the public realized that Obama's inner circle was not with him on making the speech.

Obama's summer 2008 decision to opt out of public financing was a brilliant strategy in that it had no negative impact on his message of being a change candidate. In fact, electing to raise funds privately did more to underscore his political legitimacy than to question his backpedaling. Obama had originally agreed to public financing but when he saw how much it would restrict his ability to compete nationally, he took a risk, like his race speech, to do something truly extraordinary. He took a chance of being criticized by his campaign finance reformer opponent, John McCain. While McCain did criticize, the public took little notice or at least registered no negative feedback. Obama became the first president since 1976 to pay for his entire presidential campaign with donations and no government subsidy. He went for broke in a fifty-state strategy (somewhat pulled back closer to the election) with the idea that this time voters would go to the polls early. In Colorado alone, which normally leans GOP, he opened fifty-nine campaign offices to McCain's thirteen.

The Internet and social media allowed an individual to make a difference in a state outcome, both in the viral and fiscal strategy. Traditional electoral politics favor the battleground state approach with designated blue "D" and red "R" states where candidates compete. Obama played to a month-long strategy of voter turnout, running his campaign with over a million contributors and volunteers that were unmatched by his opponent. The Republican machine was still mostly a slow-moving RNC ship of state, not the nimble Obama train with its handful of top advisers and millions of "support staff." By Election Day 2008, it was estimated that one-third of all electoral voters

(35–40 percent) had already cast their ballots. This reality made it impossible for McCain to step forward with a message that would alter voter positions.

CAMPAIGN TURNING POINTS

The Media Became the Man

There is no question that the mediasphere was enthusiastic about the Obama candidacy and made a difference in the marketing of Obama's messages. Steve Kroft, a twenty-year veteran of CBS's long-running program, *60 Minutes*, profiled the candidate early on, when it seemed Obama had no chance of winning the nomination. No other candidate was followed so closely as Obama was by *60 Minutes* and after Obama's win, *60 Minutes* was quick to capitalize with a special commemorative edition of Obama's interviews.

Equally important was the merging of the man with social media and online outreach, both fun and user-friendly and serious enough to generate an online Obama universe. Obama Girl's "I Got a Crush on Obama" by satirists Barely Political was one of YouTube's biggest hits in 2007, eventually receiving over six million hits. Not created officially by the Obama campaign, Obama remarked about the video: "It's just one more example of the fertile imagination of the internet. More stuff like this will be popping up all the time."[26]

In early 2008, another turning point came in the form of yet another YouTube sensation. Jon Favreau, Obama's head speechwriter, was then twenty-six and crafted the "Yes, We Can" words that were not in the spirit of a protest song with negative context but were all about the positive. They reinforced Obama's positive messages of hope, reconciliation, and change from the bottom up. Hollywood soon followed. On January 8, 2008, Barack Obama gave a thirteen-minute concession speech. Within a short period, the speech was refashioned to a palatable YouTube-friendly four and a half minutes. The "Yes We Can" video was produced by hip-hop artist Will .i.am and shot by Bob Dylan's son, Jesse. Neil McCormack of the London Telegraph said about the video: "Although made without the Obama campaign's participation, Yes, We Can is an almost perfect piece of political propaganda, aimed at exactly the young voters who might be inclined to support a socially liberal black candidate but are often apathetic when it comes to actually turning up at polling stations."[27] It was shot in a few days and aired before the February 2 primaries. Will.i.am got the idea from the January 29 debate in Los Angeles. He was able to leverage the viral media effect of videos like "Yes We Can" and "I Got a Crush on Obama" without appearing officially tied to either.

On a more serious platform, enter Chris Hughes, creator of my.barackobama
.com, or myBO, a Facebook replicant community for Obama enthusiasts.
Hughes had gone to Harvard with Facebook creators Mark Zuckerberg and
Dustin Moskovitz and had become the Facebook community genius. By the
time Obama announced his candidacy in February 2007 in Springfield, Illinois, my.barackobama.com had announced its presence. Obama's prescient
message, both virtual and literal that day, was that "this campaign can't only
be about me. It must be about us. It must be about what we can do together."
Over two million individual profiles of Obama supporters were created on
the site and more than two hundred thousand organizational events took place
offline. It was 2004's Howard Dean–like meetups on steroids.

From the start of his campaign, Obama wanted a virtual way for his supporters to build community but he did not know how to do it. He relied on the
then twenty-five-year-old Hughes to do his own magic. It just so happened
that by fall 2006, Facebook was allowing candidates to create campaign
profile pages. Obama's rise to national prominence coincided with the rise in
online community. Obama referred to Chris Hughes as "my Internet man."[28]
John McCain and Hillary Clinton had nothing comparable, and Hughes
would later become the online organizer in Iowa. The myBO group spawned
many offspring, including an Obama Rapid Response Group to provide fact-
based responses to negative media stories, particularly during the intense
Reverend Wright period.

Iowa Caucus

Everything about the Obama campaign focused on winning the Iowa caucus
on January 3, 2008. The key strategy with the Iowa win was to score an early
knockout punch to other Democratic nominees and presumptive nominee
Clinton combined with ground strategy to register new voters in recordbreaking numbers. Just two weeks after the Iowa upset, all of Obama's major
competitors had closed down their campaigns.

Testimonials

Though Hillary Clinton would squeak out a win in New Hampshire, she was
lacking a celebrity political endorsement that could slow down the Obama train.
Chicago resident and friend of Obama Oprah Winfrey gave a brand-to-brand
endorsement in 2007, which made him the cooler choice, but he needed some
political heavyweights. Enter some more magic in the form of the Kennedys.
Ted Kennedy compared Barack Obama to his slain brother, John F. Kennedy,
and Caroline Kennedy, not known to seek the spotlight, penned an op-ed published in the *Sunday New York Times* on January 27, 2008. One need not read

beyond the headline. It said simply, "A President Like My Father." Its message was simple, like the logo and the slogan: "I have never had a president who inspired me the way people tell me that my father inspired them. But for the first time, I believe I have found the man who could be that president—not just for me, but for a new generation of Americans." The next day at American University in Washington, DC, Caroline, Ted, and Patrick Kennedy stood together in support of Barack Obama. Ted Kennedy, the liberal elder statesman of the Democratic Party on his fifth decade in the U.S. Senate, was key to Obama's winning over the super delegates since the Kennedy name is of a higher stature than the Clinton name in Democratic Party politics.

Obama v. Clinton

The competition between Obama and Clinton helped Obama because it had a "celebrity death match" appeal to voters. Normally presidential politics are decided in a few months by about 1 percent of the electorate in early primaries and caucuses. Obama's early and unlikely win in the Iowa primary and even his setbacks in Texas and Ohio helped to keep the public interested. As Bill Clinton was able to market himself post–Gennifer Flowers as the "Comeback Kid," so could Obama earn his political stripes as someone with the energy and stamina to last through a grueling fifty-state contest. Voters had something that they often did not get in presidential primaries and caucuses: a real choice between a presumptive Democratic nominee and a challenger.

Look Presidential Before Becoming President

Obama's summer strategy was to keep his presence known, do not let up, and spend, spend, spend. In Virginia alone, another reliably Red state after it went for LBJ in 1964, Obama outspent McCain ten to one. McCain was forced to spend in a state that he thought was a shoo-in. Obama went on his early victory tour to Europe and the Middle East where he gave a particularly memorable speech in Berlin to hundreds of thousands of enthusiastic fans, another testimonial to the power of the candidate to appear like a rock star president before becoming one. Though he had already secured his nomination in June, by August there was a very public reconciliation with his Democratic opponent Hillary Clinton. It was she, the formidable opponent to Obama, who put his nomination forward from the convention floor of the Democratic Convention in Denver.

MOVING FORWARD, ONE BLOG AT A TIME

Today many Obama-themed blogs continue to flourish in the first year after the historic presidential election. They include This Week with Barack Obama

(thisweekwithbarackobama.blogspot.com), Reflecting Obama (reflectingobama
.blogspot.com), Art of Obama (www.artofobama.com), and Literary Obama
(literayobama.com), about creative works associated with the Obama family.
There is even a blog about the Obama dog, Bo, a gift from Senator Edward M.
Kennedy (www.obama-dog.com). An American president who continues to
embrace all social media is meeting these sites halfway. Obama's White House
is open for public viewing and participating through sites such as the president-
elect Web site that appeared on election night, Change.gov (www.change.gov),
and White House blog (www.whitehouse.gov/blog). At these sites, citizens can
share both their stories and their goals for government and the nation.

This interactive online conversation may have kicked off when Obama
filed papers for the presidency with the Federal Elections Commission in
January 2007, but winning the election is clearly just the beginning of this
story. Way back in 2004 *Time* magazine predicted great things for the blogosphere as a result of the Power Line blog's ability to undermine the power of
mainstream media giants like *60 Minutes* and correspondent Dan Rather:

> A phenomenon like "The 61st Minute" is the result of the journalistic equivalent
> of massively parallel processing. The Internet is a two-way superhighway, and
> every Power Line reader is also a Power Line writer, stringer, ombudsman and
> editor at large. There are 100,000 cooks in the kitchen, and more are showing up
> all the time. Call it the Power Line effect. Conventional media may have more
> readers than blogs do, but conventional media can't leverage those readers the
> way blogs can. Want a glimpse of the future of blogs? The more popular blogs
> are, the stronger they get. And they're not getting any less popular.[29]

A popular candidate who won the White House in 2008 knows that his
continued popularity with the public rests with his ability to be not only
heard from but also interested in what his fellow Americans have to say to
him. We may reach a time in this Obama presidency—perhaps we already
have—where blogging is as important as any primetime news conference to
doing the nation's business. What's certain is that no presidential candidate
worth his or her political weight will ever consider making a run for the White
House without fully embracing online connectivity that informs, engages,
influences, and listens to the citizenry.

NOTES

1. Adam Nagourney and Michael Cooper, Transcript, "The Times Interviews John
McCain," *New York Times*, 13 July 2008, www.nytimes.com/2008/07/13/us/politics/
13text-mccain.html?_r=1 (15 July 2009).

2. Andrew Malcolm, "Oops, Obama ad mocks McCain's inability to send e-mail. Trouble is, he can't due to tortured fingers," Top of the Ticket, *Los Angeles Times*, 13 September 2008, latimesblogs.latimes.com/washington/2008/09/obama-ad-email .html (15 July 2009).

3. Nedra Pickler, "Obama mocks McCain as computer illiterate," Associated Press, 12 September 2008.

4. Jim Puzzanghera, "Obama ad slams McCain for being computer illiterate," Technology: The Business and Culture of our Digital Lives from the LA Times, *Los Angeles Times*, 12 September 2008, latimesblogs.latimes.com/technology/2008/09/ obama-slams-mcc.html (15 July 2009).

5. Jim Puzzanghera, *Los Angeles Times*.

6. Ed Morrissey, "Why can't McCain e-mail? Boston Globe explained it in 2000," Hot Air, 12 September 2008, hotair.com/archives/2008/09/12/why-cant-mc cain-email/ (15 July 2009).

7. Jonah Golberg, "Wondering No More," *The Corner on National Review Online*, September 12, 2008, corner.nationalreview.com/post/?q=OTliMTNiZjg5ZDEw ZWNiZDYwZWFjN2JlNjNjNjkxZmM= (15 July 2009).

8. Richard Rapaport, "Net vs. Norm," *Forbes*, 29 May 2000, www.forbes.com/ asap/2000/0529/053_print.html (15 July 2009).

9. Julian Dibbell, "Portrait of the Blogger as a Young Man," *Idee Fixe*, 10 May 2000, web.archive.org/web/20000510161001/www.feedmag.com/feature/cx329 .shtml (15 July 2009).

10. Jorn Barger, "Top 10 Tips for New Bloggers from Original Blogger Jorn Barger," *Wired*, 15 December 2007, www.wired.com/print/culture/lifestyle/ news/2007/12/blog_advice (15 July 2009).

11. *Time* magazine, "25 Best Blogs of 2009," www.time.com/time/specials/ packages/article/0,28804,1879276_1879279_1879212,00.html (15 July 2009).

12. Declan McCullagh and Anne Broache, "Blogs turn 10—who's the father?" *CNET News*, 20 March 2007, news.cnet.com/2100-1025_3-6168681.html (15 July 2009).

13. Jeffrey Rosen, "Your Blog or Mine?" *New York Times Magazine*, 19 December 2004.

14. Jeremy Hsu, "People Choose News that Fits Their Views," *U.S. News and World Report*, 7 June 2009, www.usnews.com/articles/science/culture/2009/06/07/ people-choose-news-that-fits-their-views.html (15 July 2009).

15. Hsu, "People Choose News That Fits Their Views," 2009.

16. Brigham Young University News Release, "Political blogs more accurate than newspapers, say those who read both; Plus: Political reporters aware of blogs on the right but follow blogs on the left," 13 May 2009, byunews.byu.edu/archive09-May -blogs.aspx (15 July 2009).

17. "Time Person of the Year: Blogs Have Their Day," December 2004, www .time.com/time/subscriber/personoftheyear/2004/poyblogger.html (15 July 2009).

18. Mark Lasswell, "Truth and Consequences," *Broadcasting and Cable*, 27 September 2004.

19. Michael Kinsley, "How Many Blogs Does the World Need?" *Time*, 20 November 2008, www.time.com/time/magazine/article/0,9171,1860888,00.html (15 July 2009).

20. Frederic Ladinois, "Obama's Social Media Advantage," *ReadWriteWeb*, 5 November 2008, www.readwriteweb.com/archives/social_media_obama_mccain_comparison.php

21. Garance Franke-Ruta, "Blogged Down," *The American Prospect*, 4 March 2005, Web only, www.prospect.org/cs/articles?articleId=9292 (15 July 2009).

22. "State of the Blogosphere," *Technorati*, 2008, technorati.com/blogging/state-of-the-blogosphere/ (15 July 2009).

23. David Plouffe on "Obama Campaign Strategy," *Obama Magazine*, 27 June 2008, www.obamamagazine.com/latest-news/david-plouffe-on-obama-campaign-strategy/ (15 July 2009).

24. Steve Kroft, correspondent, "Obama's Inner Circle Shares Inside Story," *60 Minutes*, 9 November 2008, www.cbsnews.com/stories/2008/11/07/60minutes/main4584507.shtml (15 July 2009).

25. Steve Kroft, "Obama's Inner Circle," 2008.

26. Jason Clayworth, "Obama responds to 'crush,'" *Des Moines Register*, 18 June 2007.

27. Neil McCormack, *London Telegraph*, 14 February 2008, www.telegraph.co.uk/culture/music/3671190/Barack-Obamas-Yes-We-Can-video.html (15 July 2009).

28. Ellen McGirt, "How Chris Hughes Helped Launch Facebook and the Barack Obama Campaign," *Fast Company*, 17 March 2009.

29. Lev Grossman, "Blogs Have Their Day," *Time*, 19 December 2004, www.time.com/time/subscriber/personoftheyear/2004/poyblogger.html (15 July 2009).

6

Obama and Obama Girl: YouTube, Viral Videos, and the 2008 Presidential Campaign

Larry Powell

On June 13, 2007, the BarelyPolitical.com Web site posted a video on YouTube. Their independent production, "I've Got a Crush . . . On Obama," featured actress/model Amber Lee Ettinger lip-synching to a song while dancing in a bikini. One shot had Ettinger pole-dancing in the subway. Another featured her pining about her admiration for the Democratic presidential candidate while gazing at his photo—one that pictured him on a beach and wearing no shirt.

Ettinger quickly became an Internet star known as "Obama Girl." Her video became an Internet sensation, triggering more than three million views in the first two months. Before the campaign was over, it had tallied more than thirteen million views—double the best total of any of the Obama campaign's official videos.[1] The original posting was followed by a number of sequels featuring the same actress and character.[2]

The video was the opening salvo in an unofficial online campaign—unofficial because it had no direct connection to the Obama campaign. Importantly, it also signals a change in presidential campaigning. Television—the medium long considered the king of campaign communication—was now challenged by an online entry that had the potential to become a major channel for communicating with voters,[3] particularly young voters.[4]

How big was the use of the Internet in politics? Alessandra Stanley described the 2008 election as one "that changed the way we watch and drew new audiences . . . including younger people who mostly ignore the news and download their entertainment from the Internet."[5] Joe McGinniss[6] noted that while the Internet was drawing only a small percentage of advertising dollars, it was still having an impact—particularly among young voters. As Democratic consultant Will Robinson noted, "if you're under twenty-five you don't

83

watch television that much. You're just as likely to be on YouTube, making videos, or text messaging friends as doing anything else."[7]

That conclusion was supported by academic studies that found Internet media were effective in reaching young voters,[8] particularly for young African American voters.[9] Further, not only were young voters seeking political information on the Internet, but they were also using the Internet to pass along videos of Barack Obama's speeches to their friends. As Stelter noted, "younger voters tend to be not just consumers of news and current events but conduits as well—sending out e-mailed links and videos to friends and their social networks."[10] Such behavior caused Joe McGinniss to ask, "Can it be that political ads don't influence us the way they once did?"[11] The first online presidential campaign was about to break open.

INTRODUCING A NEW TECHNOLOGY

YouTube had no impact on the 2004 presidential election for an obvious reason—it wasn't even around. The Web site was created in February 2005—three months after the 2004 election—with its headquarters in San Mateo, California. Chad Hurley, Steve Chen, and Jawed Karim—three former employees at PayPal, an Internet payment agency—created the site to provide people with a way to display videos.

One of the founders made the first video for the site. Karim uploaded "Me at the Zoo" on April 23, 2005, with footage showing him at the San Diego Zoo. A preliminary beta version of the site was made available to the public in May, in part financed with an $11.5 million investment from Sequoia Capital.[12] In November 2005, YouTube was officially opened to the public[13] and quickly became popular. The initial investment financed the site through April 2006, keeping it viable while word of the site spread.

That word spread quickly. The site was soon so popular that, less than one year after its official launch date, YouTube became a target for other investors. In October, Google, Inc., paid more than $1.65 billion to acquire the site and move its base of operation to San Bruno, California. By July 2006, Internet users were uploading more than sixty-five thousand new videos a day, while the site was recording one hundred million viewers daily. Most users were individuals, people putting up home videos of themselves, their families, and pets. But some media companies—including CBS and the BBC—also became registered users and provided video footage.[14] Anybody can watch a YouTube video, but only registered viewers are allowed to upload videos. Each registered user has their own "channel" where their videos are posted. Thus, viewers who find something they like can easily return to the same "channel" for similar materials.

The Obama Girl video, for example, was produced by Barely Political, a Web content producer that specialized in producing online video. The release of "I Got a Crush on Obama," the first Obama Girl video, was followed by a series of other Obama Girl releases—all on the same YouTube channel. That series culminated in "Red States, Blue States," released on Inauguration Day in 2009.

"Obama Girl" represented a step forward in the role of the Internet in political campaigns, one that was not fully foreseen by the 2006 elections—YouTube's first foray into politics. Still, in 2006, YouTube was mostly a channel for "gotcha" journalism, a place where users could post videos of politicians saying or doing embarrassing things. Its role as an outlet for made-for-the-Internet videos was still ahead.

YOUTUBE AND "GOTCHA" JOURNALISM

At the beginning of the 2006 U.S. Congressional elections, Senator George Allen confidently campaigned for reelection to his senate seat in Virginia. Allen's election seemed so certain that the cowboy-boots-wearing U.S. senator had been mentioned as a possible presidential candidate for the Republican Party in the 2008 cycle. One observer described him as "a paragon of Sunbelt conservatism with national ambitions."[15] All of that started to crumble, however, on August 11, 2006.[16]

The day began innocently enough, with Allen making typical campaign stops and delivering typical campaign speeches. At one of those rallies, Allen pointed out a college student in the crowd, somebody who had been following him around and recording his speeches. The student, a twenty-year-old man of Indian descent, was a worker for the Democratic Party. His recording duties are a typical activity that both parties use—hoping to catch their opponent saying something that will be politically unpopular.

On August 11, 2006, at a rally in Breaks, Virginia, the student hit pay dirt, even if he had to be the target of the resulting sound-bite. Allen pointed out the young man to the crowd and said, "This fellow here, over here with the yellow shirt, Macaca, or whatever his name is, he's with my opponent. He's following us around everywhere. And it's just great."[17] Innocent enough, perhaps, except for the use of the word "Macaca"—an obscure racial slur aimed at people with Indian heritage. Even then, it likely would have been merely a minor incident had it occurred in earlier campaigns. This time, though, Allen was captured on video making the statement. And the video was posted on YouTube. That started an uproar that changed the campaign. As one reporter noted, "August, usually the sleepiest month in politics, has suddenly become raucous, thanks in part to YouTube, the vast video sharing Web site."[18]

Senator Allen first dismissed the uproar as unimportant, saying he meant no disrespect by the remark, but the controversy continued. Eventually Allen called the student, S. R. Sidarth, and personally apologized. By then, though, the mistake had "complicated his re-election campaign and raised doubts about his potential as a Republican presidential contender in 2008."[19]

As Allen's campaign faltered under the resulting media coverage, that of his opponent gained momentum.[20] Pundits felt that Democrat Jim Webb, a decorated Vietnam veteran and former secretary of the Navy, still faced "an uphill battle,"[21] but he was closing the gap. Eventually, Allen's campaign got buried by the YouTube video and its resulting publicity. As the election neared, one pundit noted that "If Jim Webb . . . wins in Virginia, technology will get credit,"[22] while another noted that Allen's gaffe made the campaign competitive.[23]

On election night, Webb won by a thin margin and claimed victory the next day.[24] Allen formally conceded one day later. The win provided the Democrats with the margin they needed to take control of the U.S. Senate.[25] Post-election analysis of the win credited YouTube with being the deciding factor.[26] While Allen was the poster child for the YouTube Effect, he wasn't its only victim. Conrad Burns, the incumbent Republican senator from Montana, was seen in videos which showed him sleeping through meetings and joking about serious topics such as terrorism.[27] That prompted President Bush to visit Montana in an attempt to save the seat for Republicans.[28]

By the end of the 2006 campaign, candidates had become aware of YouTube's influence on campaigns and fearful that they might be the next victim of the "candid camera" moment.[29] David Karph labeled the phenomenon as "Macaca moments," which he defined as "high profile candidate gaffes that are captured on YouTube and receive a cascade of citizen viewing, leading to substantial political impacts."[30] The threat was that amateur reporters might capture unscripted moments that caught the politician "off message" with a comment or behavior that could damage the campaign. In past elections, such mistakes were often minor problems that did no lasting damage to their campaign. Conrad Burns, for example, had a reputation for being "gaffe-prone" in previous campaigns, but none had been captured on video before.[31] YouTube had suddenly transformed those gaffes into major mistakes. As Steven Levy noted, "This new technology brings radical transparency to the Internet, where information is available immediately and anyone could end up an unwilling figure of shame and ridicule."[32]

THE TECHNOLOGY MATURES: YOUTUBE IN THE 2008 ELECTION

After the dramatic impact of YouTube on Senator George Allen's campaign, most observers waited to see how the technology would influence the 2008 election. Most campaigns tried to use the Web site to their own advantage. The number of congressional and Senate campaigns using YouTube doubled compared to the 2006 election.[33] Similarly, most of the presidential campaigns assumed there was value in an online presence.[34] At the outset, Democrats seemed to have an edge over Republicans.[35] Democrat John Edwards shifted his entire campaign approach to adjust to the Internet presence.[36] Senators Hillary Clinton and Barack Obama announced their campaigns simultaneously on both TV and YouTube.[37]

The Republicans, meanwhile, lagged behind. In the first quarter of 2007, the top three Republican candidates—Senator John McCain, Mayor Rudy Giuliani, and Governor Mitt Romney—did not release their expenditures on Internet expenses "because the amounts were embarrassingly small."[38] But some caught up. By December 2007, Governor Mike Huckabee's Web site became the most popular of all Republican candidates.[39] Still, not all campaigns fully embraced online campaigning. As Jill Lawrence noted, the general attitude for most campaigns was that the Internet was needed to compete, but "it's not a substitute for politics as usual."[40]

The Obama campaign was an exception; it viewed an online presence as critical to its campaign efforts. At least one observer described the Internet as a primary communication vehicle for Obama.[41] Obama's campaign created its own YouTube channel to raise funds and to provide supporters a place to post their own videos.[42] The campaign posted more than 1,800 videos of the candidate's speeches on the site, encouraging comments and responses from supporters.[43] Obama's speech on race triggered more than 1.6 million views on YouTube within twenty-four hours of its posting, with pastors of some churches recommending that their congregation view the speech online.[44] It was part of an overall Internet presence that was twice as large as that of John McCain's.[45]

The John Edwards campaign had another problem, one triggered by a posting from a university student. The student posted a report—a class assignment—that was critical of the Edwards campaign for basing its local campaign headquarters in an affluent section of the city, while the campaign focused on poverty as its major issue.[46] The resulting discussions between the campaign and the student's journalism professor became heated, with the professor eventually claiming that the campaign demanded that the report be removed from YouTube.

Meanwhile, the voting public was increasingly using the Internet as a source of information. Political Web sites such as MoveOn.org experienced triple-digit increases in site visits.[47] YouTube became a major channel of information during the Democratic convention. Katharine Seelye called the Chicago convention the first "batonical" convention, with coverage passed to voters via blogs and YouTube. The Democrats, Seelye wrote, were "relying heavily on new media to pass on enormous amounts of information about Mr. Obama to friends inside the hall and out, who will in turn pass it to more friends, mostly by way of YouTube."[48] One amateur reporter, Mike Stark, made a name for himself by getting into venues of conservative speakers (e.g., Rush Limbaugh and Bill O'Reilly) and asking embarrassing questions—with the exchanges posted online.[49]

Regardless, the "gotcha" journalism of YouTube continued, starting in the primaries. In some cases, campaigns used YouTube in an effort to take advantage of their opponents' gaffes. On the Republican side, John McCain's campaign tried to discredit Mitt Romney's shift on the abortion issue (moving to a strong anti-abortion position) by posting a video on YouTube that showed Romney in a 2005 appearance saying he was "absolutely committed" to a pro-choice position.[50] After conservative commentator Ann Coulter called John Edwards a "faggot," Romney called the remarks offensive—only to have his reaction nullified by a video showing him and Coulter laughing backstage.[51]

McCain, though, had problems when videos emerged of Reverend John Hagee, an evangelical preacher who had endorsed him, attacking the Catholic church as "the Great Whore."[52] McCain eventually had to disavow the endorsement, causing Hagee to disavow his support of McCain.[53] One of the most devastating gotcha videos came at the expense of Democratic contender Hillary Clinton. The problem was a statement that she made several times during March 2008 about being threatened by sniper fire in a visit to Bosnia. Once CBS made video of the event available, though, it showed Clinton calmly exiting from her aircraft and being greeted by local VIPs. That turned Clinton's remark into fodder for late-night comedians. One conservative Web site, The Drudge Report, provided a link to the YouTube video that became popular with conservative audiences. As *New York Times* columnist Frank Rich wrote:

> The Drudge Report's link to the YouTube iteration of the CBS News piece transformed it into a cultural phenomenon reaching far beyond a third-place network news program's nightly audience. It had more YouTube views than the inflammatory Wright sermons, more than even the promotional video of Britney Spears making her latest "comeback" on a TV sitcom.[54]

Another comment was aimed at Clinton, but also said something about this new campaign medium. As Rich concluded, "YouTube videos of a candidate in full tilt or full humiliation, we're learning, can outdraw videos of a candidate's fire-breathing pastor."[55]

John McCain became an ironic victim of an Internet video posted by a newspaper. In his interview with the editorial board of the *Des Moines (Iowa)*

Register, McCain apparently gave some "sarcastic, and sometimes testy, responses" that the newspaper videotaped and posted online.[56] Obama also became one of the "gotcha" victims. In April 2008, prior to the Pennsylvania primary, Obama flew to San Francisco for a private fundraising event—one in which he assumed that those attending were all his supporters. While speaking to the crowd, the candidate said that many small-town Pennsylvania voters were bitter over their economic circumstances and "cling to guns or religion or antipathy to people who aren't like them."[57] Those remarks were audiotaped and subsequently posted on the Huffington Post Web site. The statement was quickly criticized by Democratic opponent Hillary Clinton, who said she was "taken aback by the demeaning remarks Senator Obama made about people in small-town America. (And) . . . Senator Obama's remarks are elitist and they are out of touch."[58] Obama apologized, saying he meant no insult in the comment. "No, I didn't say it as well as I should have," he said. "But what is absolutely true is that people don't feel like they are being listened to."[59] That response merely triggered criticism from the Republicans. McCain spokesperson Tucker Bounds chimed in, saying, "Instead of apologizing to small-town Americans for dismissing their values, Barack Obama arrogantly tried to spin his way out of his outrageous San Francisco remarks. . . . You can't be more out of touch than that."[60]

The online tape became Obama's first major crisis in the primary campaign. The criticism it engendered was summarized by conservative *New York Times* columnist William Kristol, who said the comments were important because it showed that Obama was "disdainful of small-town America. . . . He's usually good at disguising this. But in San Francisco the mask slipped. And it's not so easy to get elected by a citizenry you patronize."[61]

The incident seemed to make Obama more cautious in his campaign rhetoric. *New York Times* columnist Maureen Dowd noted that in a subsequent appearance before the media, "He gives the impression of someone who would like to kid around with reporters for a minute, but knows he's going to be peppered with on-the-record minutiae designed to feed the insatiable maw of blogs and Internet news."[62] But Obama weathered the storm. Clinton won the Pennsylvania primary by enough of a margin to keep the contest going, despite growing concerns within the party that her continuing campaign might hurt the party's effort in the general election.[63] Further, she did nothing to sway the superdelegates that she needed at that point in the campaign to be truly competitive.[64]

By the time the nominees for both parties were decided, Republican vice presidential nominee Governor Sarah Palin had become a national sensation. After the initial GOP euphoria subsided, Palin also became the target of YouTube videos. The first came from a woman, Lisa Donovan, who did imitations of Palin on YouTube.[65] The most devastating came from CBS, which had its own channel on the site. During an interview with CBS's Katie Couric, Palin gave rambling and evasive answers to simple questions. She spoke fast, seemed unprepared to answer serious questions, and even dodged questions about her reading habits. As Alessandra Stanley noted, "That exchange was so startling it ricocheted across the Internet several hours before it appeared on CBS."[66] It was a devastating interview that quickly received more than 1.4 million views via YouTube, while the *Saturday Night Live* parody of the interview received more than four million hits.[67]

But YouTube users were not content to limit the Web site's impact to unscripted videos. One major change in the 2008 election was that the site became an outlet for displaying videos produced for the campaigns. Rudy Giuliani, short on campaign funds, put his ads on YouTube before any appeared on cable or broadcast outlets.[68] And the campaign's first attack ads premiered online. Mitt Romney released an Internet ad attacking John McCain on the immigration issue, while McCain released one that described Romney as a "phony."[69] On the Democratic side, Barack Obama released an Internet ad touting his 2002 opposition to the Iraq war.[70] Hillary Clinton's campaign's early attempts at YouTube were ineffective, but the campaign got better at the medium as the campaign progressed.[71] When she was criticized for a primary debate performance, she posted a video to refute the charges—the fastest way to address the issue.[72] One consistent factor in these videos, though, is that many conformed to the standard thirty- or sixty-second length of broadcast ads, even though Internet videos are not bound by such time constraints.[73] Some of the traditional media producers, it seemed, had still not adapted to the new technologies. Further, the effectiveness of these campaign efforts were dependent upon the ability of the campaigns to present the candidates as a candidate identity that included a willingness to establish a personal bond with others.[74]

Independent groups also got involved, with most of them also using the standard ad formats. Health Care for America spent $40 million on a cable and online ad promoting comprehensive health care.[75] The AFL-CIO and Service Employees joined forces for an online video called "McCain's Mansions: The Real Elitist" that featured McCain's homes and condos in a manner that tried to portray the Republican as elitist and out of touch.[76] Another conservative group, "Vets for Freedom," released two Internet ads attacking Obama for his position on the Iraq war; those ads led to Senators Joe Lieberman and Lindsey Graham resigning their membership in the group. The McCain campaign subsequently released a new conflict-of-interest policy that prohibited McCain campaign workers from participating in 527s or other independent groups.[77]

YouTube became a favorite vehicle for attacking the opposition. YouTube videos were used as part of a coordinated effort by some Republicans to attack Mitt Romney.[78] On the Democratic side, John Edwards was the target of "I Feel Pretty," a video that depicted the candidate admiring himself in the mirror.[79] Edwards, in particular, was feeling the wrath of YouTube's ability to parody a candidate.[80]

The incident that best illustrated the value of campaign ads on YouTube came when Republican Mike Huckabee held a news conference to show an ad that his campaign had decided not to air. The spot was a negative commercial attacking Romney. Huckabee showed the ad to reporters and then announced he was not planning to use it. *New York Times* reporter Katherine Seelye described it as "a bizarre bit of political theater" in which he got free publicity for the message while maintain a position of "high moral ground."[81] And Seelye added, "The circumstances of the commercial and the nature of free media, particularly now with YouTube, make it likely that the advertisement will be viewed far more often than if it had simply run."[82]

The YouTube Debate

Perhaps the most unusual involvement from YouTube in the presidential election was its participation in a presidential debate. On July 23, 2007, the Web site became a channel for trying a new way to pose questions to the candidates.[83] The debate, cosponsored by YouTube and CNN, was held in Charleston, South Carolina, was anchored by CNN's Anderson Cooper, and featured all eight Democratic primary candidates.[84] Voters could use the Web site to upload a video that asked a question for one of the Democratic primary candidates. Internet junkies and politicos alike awaited the event. As Ken Dilanian wrote, "Now political junkies are eager to learn whether the Web's most popular homemade video forum can spice up the presidential debates."[85] The debate even started with a nontraditional introduction, thanks to YouTube. The forum was opened by a homemade video of a man who encouraged the candidates to answer each question directly and not "beat around the Bush."[86]

More than two thousand people submitted videos for consideration.[87] The results were mixed, at best. Supporters praised it for providing a means "for the American populace to become engaged in national political discussion."[88] Critics noted that some questioners were apparently selected on the basis of the creative presentation of their questions rather than the informational value of the potential answers. There were concerns that the YouTube approach had succeeded only in demeaning the debate process. As a result, some Republican candidates were reluctant to participate when it came their time to take the Internet questions. Mitt Romney, in particular, was concerned about a video of an animated snowman asking a question about global warming.[89] Within a week of the Democratic debate, Romney announced that he would not participate in the Republican version scheduled for September 17, 2007, while Rudy Giuliani said he was considering not participating too.[90] As Nagourney wrote, "The Republicans are . . . a little more tentative about the new media world. CNN and YouTube are struggling to get the Republican field to agree to a similar debate. . . . For now, the Republican field seems content to stay on the traditional road."[91]

Other Republicans, concerned that such decisions painted a negative image of the party's understanding of the Internet, urged the candidates to reconsider.[92] Concerns about the frivolity of the approach may have been alleviated when Democrat John Edwards participated in an online forum cosponsored by MySpace and MTV in September. As Julie Bosman noted, the participants in that forum "stuck stubbornly to questions on policy issues."[93] Romney finally agreed to participate in the YouTube version, but the event was delayed until November. Even then, questions about the demeaning impact of the Internet continued. That concern caused Seelye to write, "A news snowman video has been submitted for the Republicans. Will it be shown?"[94] Meanwhile, observers were waiting to see if the GOP would be successful in this new medium. Thus Katharine Seelye wrote, "Voters, especially young ones, will be watching to see if the candidates can show them that this is not their fathers' Republican Party."[95]

INDEPENDENT VIDEOS

The YouTube debate was a major addition to the campaign playing field. So were the "gotcha" videos that started appearing on the site. Still, perhaps the biggest change was the introduction of freelance videos from individuals who were not connected with campaigns. Suddenly, individuals outside of the normal campaign teams were having an impact on the election. As Jim Rutenberg noted, "in the 2008 race . . . the most attention-grabbing attacks are increasingly coming from people outside the political world. In some cases they are amateurs operating with nothing but passion, a computer, and a YouTube account; in other cases sophisticated media types with more elaborate resources but no campaign experience."[96] Inexpensive video cameras and editing programs made YouTube a fertile ground for amateurs. One anti-Obama ad got national exposure while costing only about $50 to produce.[97]

The professionals had their day too. Comedian Sara Silverman headed up a group that produced "The Great Schlep," a video aimed at getting Democratic

primary support among Jewish grandparents for Obama.[98] Media producer
Robert Greenwald provided a number of videos on behalf of Obama.[99] Two—
"Xanadu" and "The Burning Bed"—took statements about Islam from one of
McCain's religious supporters [Rob Parsley] and juxtaposed them with statements from McCain praising the preacher; McCain eventually rejected the
endorsement of Parsley. Greenwald also posted a number of McCain videos,
with most presenting him making contradictory statements before different
audiences. One of the most popular videos was "Yes We Can," a pro-Obama
music video that became one of the most viewed items on the Internet, aided
by encouragement from the Obama campaign.[100]

OBAMA GIRL

Considering YouTube's broad role in the 2008 election, pundits might have
had a hard time picking its most visible component. That, however, turned out
to be easy. A YouTube video named "Obama Girl" was the site's runaway hit
during the primary season.

The three-minute, eighteen-second spot, "I Got a Crush . . . on Obama,"
as noted, was produced by an independent company called Barely Political
and posted on YouTube in June 2007. The ad abandoned the thirty-second
ad approach of most campaign videos, opting instead for a format and length
more akin to a music video. The creative genius behind the ad was ad executive Ben Relles, who cowrote the script with Leah Kauffman. Kauffman
also wrote and provided the vocals for the song featured in the spot. "Obama
Girl" featured a provocatively clad model pining in song about Obama while
pole-dancing on the subway and caressing pictures of her presidential hero.
Kate Phillips described it as "an incredibly racy, well, steamy new video."[101]

The first response from the traditional media and from the campaign was
skepticism. The *New York Times* described it as an "amateur video" that had
"a campy appeal."[102] Even the Obama campaign seemed unsure of how to
respond, with the candidate merely complaining about the use of photos from
his Hawaiian vacation and the resulting focus on his bare chest.[103] Was this
parody a part of a coordinated campaign by Obama's opponents? No. It was
a new entity of the Internet age—a truly independent production—something
campaign election laws had tried to get for years but never fully achieved
(consider, for example, the instances of the so-called independent 527 groups,
which seem to always have a campaign agenda). Indeed, the independent
nature of the video was part of its appeal.

Regardless, the video quickly became a viral hit. Obama Girl triggered
four video responses and was named Web video of the year by a variety of

publications, including the Associated Press, *Newsweek*, *People* magazine, and AOL. Some of the clothing used in the spot was sold on eBay, with the proceeds going to charity. Actress Amber Lee Ettinger, who portrayed the lovesick Obama girl, made television appearances with Geraldo Rivera and Fox's Bill O'Reilly. MSNBC named her character one of the top ten influential women of 2007. E! named her the "#1 Hottest Woman on the Web." The Obama campaign even recruited her to make automated "robo" calls for the campaign.

Ettinger, meanwhile, was also making more Obama Girl sequels. One of the first was "Giuliani Girls," which pitted Obama Girl against attractive supporters of Republican Rudy Giuliani.[104] Ettinger continued to pursue the role through the 2008 primary and general election campaigns. In January 2008, she returned in a video that featured her with superhuman powers. The following March, she starred in an anti-Clinton video called "Hillary! Stop the attacks! Love, Obama Girl."

Further, the parodies of Barely Political were not limited to assisting the Obama campaign. In May 2008, the company posted another video on YouTube that promoted the campaign of Libertarian Party candidate, Mike Gravel. The video, "Mike Gravel Lobbies for the Obama Girl Vote," depicts Gavel trying to persuade Obama Girl to support him instead of Obama. She agrees to consider it. Later in the campaign—in September—Obama Girl promoted the candidacy of independent Ralph Nader. The video presented Nader's argument that he should be included in the presidential debates. There was even speculation (untrue) that Obama Girl might ask a question in the campaign's YouTube debate.[105] And, once the campaign was over, Obama Girl continued to star in new features that parodied politics, technology, and an "inauguration dance party" video.[106]

But the tie-ins to other candidates were merely window dressing. Obama Girl's biggest impact was on the Obama campaign. One way it did so was by addressing image factors that the campaign itself avoided. As Katharine Seelye noted, "the video plays on the sex appeal of the candidate, a terrain considered off limits by political campaigns in their own commercials."[107]

The bigger issue, though, was the broader impact of YouTube on voters and its potential for the future. Vassia Gueorguieva analyzed the 2006 elections and accurately described the impact of sites such as YouTube and MySpace for the 2008 campaigns:

These social networking sites, which are used by a substantial segment of the U.S. voting age population, represent the next Internet generation, which is primarily user driven. They have created benefits such as increasing the potential for candidate exposure at a low cost or no cost, providing lesser known candidates with a viable outlet to divulge their message, and allowing campaigns to raise contributions and recruit volunteers online. In conjunction with these benefits, YouTube and *MySpace* have also posed a new set of challenges to campaign staff, the most important of which is the reduced level of control that campaigns have over the image and message of the candidate, which is of critical importance to election outcomes.[108]

There were critics of this new campaign medium. Elizabeth Edwards, wife of unsuccessful candidate John Edwards, came down hard on the press for what she perceived as a trend toward allowing the Internet to set the news agenda. In an op-ed article for the *New York Times*, she wrote:

> The vigorous press that was deemed an essential part of democracy at our country's inception is now consigned to smaller venues, to the Internet and, in the mainstream media, to occasional articles. . . . [E]very analysis that is shortened, every corner that is cut, moves us further away from the truth until what is left is the Cliffs Notes of the news, or what I call strobe-light journalism, in which the outlines are accurate enough that we cannot really see the whole picture.[109]

Similarly, research on the 2008 election indicates that YouTube is more effective at focusing on candidates' character rather than their policies, while it tends to trigger only passive (not active) political involvement.[110] To what extent can such a limited basis of information serve as a basis for objective voting decisions?

Implications for Future Elections

The 2008 presidential election changed the way campaigns will be conducted in the future. Perhaps emblematic of this change, in November at the Jefferson-Jackson dinner in Iowa—a prelude to the Iowa caucuses, Hillary Clinton gave one of her most impassioned speeches at the dinner, but Obama gave a more subdued call for change. Obama, of course, eventually won the Iowa caucus, the Democratic nomination, and the presidency. *New York Times* columnist David Brooks foresaw that potential in Obama's speech, calling it "a defining moment" in which "Obama found his voice."[111] More importantly, the speech addressed a different medium. As Brooks wrote, "For young people who have grown up on Facebook, YouTube, open-source software and an array of decentralized networks, this [Obama's approach] is a compelling theory of how change happens."[112]

By the time the election was over, YouTube and the Internet had become barometers of public opinion that was measured by the number of hits and popularity of videos on a topic. *New York Times* columnist Frank Rich, for example, noted that a group called the National Organization for Marriage spent $1.5 million to post a sixty-second video that argued that homosexuality was "a national threat second only to terrorism."[113] The video received few views itself but triggered a number of parodies and was ridiculed by comedian Stephen Colbert, leading Rich to argue that public opposition to homosexual marriage was dissipating.[114]

YouTube also changed the journalistic process.[115] Before the 2008 election had started, reporters were using e-mail to gather information and scouring the Internet for information to use in their stories. With the 2008 campaign, videos on YouTube became fodder for the mainstream media.[116] Political stories were now available to some reporters without the necessity of leaving the newsroom.

YouTube and other Internet sites also served to combine politics with a social function that demonstrated a potential for political involvement. Such sites provide an additional means for individuals to interact with their friends, thus indirectly spreading political information.[117] It was particularly effective among young people, of all ethnic backgrounds, who spend a significant portion of their daily time online.[118] As Hillary Savoie argued, "While this election does not owe its outcome entirely to new media, new media provided platforms upon which portions of the election played out . . . [the medium] represents an effort toward the establishment of commonality between individuals who might otherwise never interact."[119] Charlene Li and Josh Bernoff argue that the sites have moved into a second stage of utility that goes beyond the first step of just getting people connected.[120] The second stage involves using those connections in a new wave of communication and human networks. In that mode, YouTube and social networking sites are becoming new tools for grassroots campaigning, replacing or supplementing traditional community organizational techniques.[121]

Additionally, YouTube provided a means for individual voters to influence the election. As Judy Bacharach noted, the best videos on the Internet were not made by the campaigns, but by voters and independent producers.[122] The Internet offered a channel by which individuals could post material that could reach thousands—even millions—of voters through a viral process of viewing and chain distribution via e-mail, to "allow individuals to become part of the larger political process just by using their laptop or personal digital assistant."[123] Still, the potential impact of amateurs on the process may be overstated. The better videos—including Obama Girl—were produced by professionals. As Virginia Heffernan wrote, "Playing well online is not simply a function of offline charisma. Unlike playing well on cable or on late-night talk shows, it takes not only performance skills but also an extensive personal production team."[124]

Obama's presidency may hasten a transition to the Internet as a major means of communicating with voters. Several pundits predicted that the

Obama administration would raise the Internet and the presidency to new levels of activity.[125] Democratic consultant Joe Trippi said he expected the Obama presidency's use of the Internet would influence government administrations and businesses, changing the way that the nation conducted business.[126]

Not everyone considered this a positive change. Lee Siegel, for example, argued that it had a negative effect on the nation's culture and the individuals' perceptions of themselves in that it engendered a false sense of connectivity because people were still largely sitting alone at their computers while supposedly engaged with others.[127] Similarly, Moises Naim argued that such Web sites make it harder to identify whether the item being presented is real or fake.[128] Along this line, Virginia Heffernan was concerned about potential voter confusion between reality and fantasy, noting that "In the eclectic YouTube interface, all videos—the parodies and the propaganda alike—can simply look like news."[129]

Further, the likelihood that a video will impact the campaign increases if it approaches or crosses some undefined threshold of truthfulness and taste. "YouTube really rewards risk takers," said John Lapp of the Democratic Congressional Campaign Committee, "the edgier the ad, the more likely it is to be viewed, forwarded and echoed throughout the Internet and into the mainstream media."[130]

Morley Winograd and Michael Hais called the 2008 election a "millennial makeover" that offered an opportunity for the Democratic Party "to become the majority party for at least four more decades."[131] Their logic, however, was based upon the election as reflecting a generational shift. Typically, history has shown that no party can maintain dominance for more than ten to twenty years, so Winograd and Hais's prediction is likely an overly optimistic projection for the Democrats, and the Republicans are likely to close the technological gap. But if the ideological shifts may be transitory, the media shifts may last longer. Along this line, Heffernan wrote, "millions of people now behold, scrutinize and evaluate public figures chiefly in online video clips."[132]

Regardless, the new technology has altered the public's media environment.[133] But it still has plenty of room to grow. The 2008 campaign, for example, saw most candidates embracing the new technology of the Internet, particularly in terms of social networks and viral video sites; but there was relatively little online advertising by those same campaigns.[134] Future campaigns are likely to see an increase in Internet advertising.

Campaigns will also have to learn to use and respond to YouTube more effectively. Lim and Ki,[135] for example, analyzed YouTube parodies from 2006 and found that voters could be inoculated against their impact if provided with an advance message about the parody. Still, for the 2008 election, YouTube caught most campaigns by surprise. There was no opportunity for advance inoculation. As YouTube becomes more ingrained in the campaign process, perhaps some campaigns will anticipate postings from oppositions and beat them to the punch by posting their inoculation messages before the attacks arrive.

Thus the new medium will have to mature. There are still copyright issues to resolve,[136] and lines between reality and fiction will have to be better defined. Can it mature into a more complete source of information? Regardless, YouTube has shown that the Internet will have a major role in future political campaigns.

NOTES

1. Brian Stelter, "Some Media Companies Choose to Profit from Pirated You-Tube Clips," *New York Times*, 16 August 2008, 1(C).

2. Lisa Tozzi, "Online: 'Obama Girl,' the Sequel," *New York Times*, 17 July 2007, 19(A).

3. Maria Puente, "Election Interest Goes Viral," *USA Today*, 2 April 2008, 1–2(A); Brian Stelter and Richard Perez-Pena, "Voting with Their Eyeballs," *New York Times*, 4 August 2008, 1(C), 6(C).

4. Laura Donnelly-Smith, "Political Engagement in the Age of Facebook: Student Voices," *Peer Review* 10, no. 2/3 (2008), 37–39.

5. Alessandra Stanley, "No Debate: It's Great TV," *New York Times*, 8 June 2008, 1(MT), 6(MT).

6. Joe McGinniss, "The Selling of a President," *Parade*, 27 April 2008, 12–14.

7. Quoted by Garrett M. Graff, *The First Campaign: Globalization, the Web & the Race for the White House* (New York: Farrar, Straus and Giroux, 2007), 262.

8. Robin Blom, "Reaching the Young and Uninvolved" (paper presented at the conference on YouTube and the 2008 Election Cycle in the United States, University of Massachusetts, Amherst, April 2009); Matthew Kushin, "Exploring YouTube: Civic Engagement and Perceptions about the Role of the Internet in Civic Engagement among College Students" (paper presented at the conference on YouTube and the 2008 Election Cycle in the United States, University of Massachusetts, Amherst, April 2009).

9. Yosem Companys, Alicia DeSantola, Carlos Rodriguez-Lluesma, and Miguel Unzueta, "Racist or Race-Neutral? How the Social Context of YouTube Political Speeches Affects Voter Attitudes" (paper presented at the conference on YouTube and the 2008 Election Cycle in the United States, University of Massachusetts, Amherst, April 2009).

10. Brian Stelter, "Finding Political News Online, Young Viewers Pass it Along," *New York Times*, 27 March 2008, 1(A).

11. McGinnis, "Selling," 12.

12. Miguel Helft and Matt Richtel, "Start-up Meets Search Engine: Venture Firm Shares a Jackpot," *New York Times*, 10 October 2006, 1(A).

13. Jefferson Graham, "Video Websites Pop Up, Invite Postings," *USA Today*, 21 November 2005, 3(B).

14. Stelter, "Finding Political News," 1(A).

15. Robin Toner, "As Senator Falters, a Democrat Rises in Virginia," *New York Times*, 18 September 2006, 1(A).

16. Mike Allen, "On Candid Camera," *Time* 168, no. 9 (28 August 2006), 17.

17. Quoted by David Stout, "Senator Says He Meant No Insult by Remark," *New York Times*, 16 August 2006, 14(A).

18. Ryan Lizza, "Candidly Speaking: The YouTube Election," *New York Times*, 20 August 2006, 1(A).

19. Carl Hulse and David D. Kirkpatrick, "Senator Apologizes to Student for Remark," *New York Times*, 24 August 2006, 20(A).

20. Fred Barnes, "Is There Life After 'Macaca'?" *Wall Street Journal*, 28 September 2006, 17(A).

21. Toner, "Senator Falters," 1(A).

22. Anne E. Kornblut, "6 Ways to Watch the Election: The Influence of the Internet," *New York Times*, 5 November 2006, 4(A).

23. Bill Marsh, "6 Ways to Watch the Election: The Impact of Gaffes on the Stump," *New York Times*, 5 November 2006, 4(A).

24. John M. Broder and Ian Urbina, "Senate Is at Stake," *New York Times*, 8 November 2006, 1(A).

25. John M. Broder, Holli Chmela, David D. Kirkpatrick, and Rachel L. Swarns, "Democrats Take Senate," *New York Times*, 10 November 2006, 1(A).

26. Waldo Jaquith, "Two Years Makes a Big Difference," *Campaigns & Elections* 28, no. 1 (2007), 58.

27. Amy Schatz, "In Clips on YouTube, Politicians Reveal Their Unscripted Side," *Wall Street Journal*, 9 October 2006, 1(A), 14(A).

28. Carl Hulse and Anne E. Kornblut, "Bush Shores up his Base as Democrats Spot Opening," *New York Times*, 3 November 2006, 22(A).

29. Allen, "On Candid Camera," 17.

30. David Karpf, "Macaca Moments Reconsidered: YouTube Effects or Netroots Effects?" (paper presented at the conference on YouTube and the 2008 Election Cycle in the United States, University of Massachusetts, Amherst, April 2009), 1.

31. Schatz, "Clips on YouTube," 1(A).

32. Steven Levy, "Smile! You're an Unwitting Net Star," *Newsweek* 148, no. 24 (11 December 2006), 17.

33. Christine Williams and Jeff Gulati, "Congressional Use of YouTube in 2008: Its Frequency and Rationale" (paper presented at the conference on YouTube and the 2008 Election Cycle in the United States, University of Massachusetts, Amherst, April 2009); Jonathan Godfrey, "Congressional Communication via YouTube" (paper presented at the conference on YouTube and the 2008 Election Cycle in the United States, University of Massachusetts, Amherst, April 2009).

34. Sarah Wheaton, "Buying into Web Presence," *New York Times*, 10 July 2007, 16(A); Michiko Kakutani, "Campaign Song 2008? Strike up the Broadband," *New York Times*, 18 December 2007, 9(A).

35. Aaron Dalton, "The Digital Road to the White House," *PC Magazine* 26, no. 9 (24 April 2007), 19–20.

36. Adam Nagourney, "Edwards Overhauls His Campaign to Harness Internet," *New York Times*, 1 August 2007, 12(A).

37. Dalton, "Digital Road," 19–20.

38. Graff, *The First Campaign*, 258.

39. Farhana Hossain, "Huckabee Takes the Lead Online," *New York Times*, 12 December 2007, 28(A).

40. Jill Lawrence, "As a Campaign Tool, Web Has Its Uses and Limits," *USA Today*, 14 June 2007, 10(A).

41. Chris Stallings-Carpenter, "The Obamachine: Techno-Politics 2.0" (paper presented at the conference on YouTube and the 2008 Election Cycle in the United States, University of Massachusetts, Amherst, April 2009).

42. Max Harper, "Uploading Hope: An Inside View of Obama's HQ New Media Video Team" (paper presented at the conference on YouTube and the 2008 Election Cycle in the United States, University of Massachusetts, Amherst, April 2009).

43. Virginia Heffernan, "The YouTube Presidency," *New York Times Magazine*, 12 April 2009, 15.

44. Larry Rohter and Michael Luo, "Groups Respond to Obama's Call for National Discussion about Race," *New York Times*, 20 March 2008, 17(A).

45. Carole Coleman, *The Battle for the White House . . . and the Soul of America* (Dublin, Ireland: The Liffey Press, 2008).

46. Jim Rutenberg, "Student Paper Upsets the Edwards Camp," *New York Times*, 27 October 2007, 13(A).

47. Sarah Wheaton, "Sites Drawing More Eyeballs," *New York Times*, 19 June 2007, 16(A).

48. Katharine Seelye, "New Words and Tools for Covering the Conventions," *New York Times*, 28 August 2008, 20(A).

49. Noam Cohen, "A Political Agitator Finds a Double-edged Weapon," *New York Times*, 6 July 2008, 18(A).

50. Mark Memmott, "McCain, Romney Trade Barbs over Abortion," *USA Today*, 14 June 2009, 11(A).

51. Graff, *The First Campaign*.

52. Frank Rich, "The All-White Elephant in the Room," *New York Times*, 4 May 2008, 12(WK).

53. Neela Banerjee and Michael Luo, "McCain Chides Pastor over Sermon on Holocaust," *New York Times*, 23 May 2008, 15–16(A).

54. Frank Rich, "Hillary's St. Patrick's Day Massacre," *New York Times*, 30 March 2008, 13(WK).

55. Rich, "Hillary's St. Patrick's Day Massacre," 13(WK).

56. Sarah Wheaton, "The Republican Nominee: A Primer on Testiness," *New York Times*, 2 October 2008, 24(A).

57. Jeff Zeleny, "Obama Works to Limit Fallout over Remark on 'Bitter' Working Class," *New York Times*, 13 April 2008, 20(A).

58. Quoted by Zeleny, "Obama Works," A20.

59. Quoted by Zeleny, "Obama Works," A20.

60. Quoted by Zeleny, "Obama Works," A20.

61. William Kristol, "The Mask Slips," *New York Times*, 14 April 2008, 27(A).

62. Maureen Dowd, "The Wrong Stuff," *New York Times*, 2 July 2008, 19(A).

63. Patrick Healy, "Clinton Takes Duel with Obama in Pennsylvania," *New York Times*, 23 April 2008, 1(A), 17(A); Adam Nagourney, "The Bruising Will Go on for the Party, Too," *New York Times*, 23 April 2008, 1(A).

64. Patrick Healy, "Superdelegates Unswayed by Clinton's Attacks," *New York Times*, 18 April 2008, 1(A), 14(A).

65. Amanda M. Fairbanks, "Finding Her Inner Palin," *New York Times*, 16 September 2008, 21(A).

66. Alessandra Stanley, "A Question Reprised in a Third Palin Interview, but the Words Come No More Easily," *New York Times*, 26 September 2008, 20(A).

67. Bill Carter, "Palin Effect on Ratings Only Modest for CBS," *New York Times*, 1 October 2008, 1(B), 8(B).

68. Jim Rutenberg, "Still No Giuliani TV Ads, but He's Ready for the Web," *New York Times*, 5 November 2007, 17(A).

69. Julie Bosman and Michael Luo, "Edwards Evokes Nation at Risk; McCain and Romney Wage Ad War," *New York Times*, 29 December 2007, 12(A).

70. Jim Rutenberg, "Finding Archives Lacking, Obama Returns to 2002," *New York Times*, 13 October 2007, 16(A).

71. Amber Davisson, "'I'm in!': Hillary Clinton's 2008 Democratic Primary Campaign on YouTube" (paper presented at the conference on YouTube and the 2008 Election Cycle in the United States, University of Massachusetts, Amherst, April 2009).

72. Kate Phillips, "The Internet Factor: Can Voters Hear a Rally If It's Held in Cyberspace?" *New York Times*, 4 November 2007, 25(A).

73. Robert Klotz, "The Sidetracked 2008 YouTube Senate Campaign" (paper presented at the conference on YouTube and the 2008 Election Cycle in the United States, University of Massachusetts, Amherst, April 2009).

74. Steve Duman and Miriam A. Locher, "'So Let's Talk. Let's Chat. Let's Start a Dialog': An Analysis of the Conversation Metaphor Employed in Clinton's and Obama's YouTube Campaign Clips," *Multilingua* 27, no. 3 (2008), 193–230.

75. Julie Bosman, "New Group to Spend $40 Million," *New York Times*, 3 July 2008, 16(A).

76. Steven Greenhouse, "Hitting McCain Where He Lives," *New York Times*, 19 August 2008, 14(A).

77. Michael Luo, "2 Senators for McCain Leave Group after Ads," *New York Times*, 29 May 2008, 20(A).

78. Adam Nagourney and Michael Luo, "Rivals and Voters Push Romney on Conservative Credentials," *New York Times*, 10 August 2007, 14(A).

79. Graff, *The First Campaign*.

80. Chuck Tryon, "Pop Politics: Online Parody Videos, Intertextuality, and Political Participation," *Popular Communication* 6, no. 4 (2008), 209–13.

81. Katharine Q. Seelye, "Huckabee Shows Negative Spot after Pulling it from Television," *New York Times*, 1 January 2008, 11(A).

82. Seelye, 2008, 11(A).

83. Ken Dilanian, "YouTube Makes Leap into Politics," *USA Today*, 23 July 2007, 5(A); Katharine Q. Seelye, "Presidential Debates Are about to Enter the World of Web Videos," *New York Times*, 14 June 2007, 22(A); Katharine Q. Seelye, "Debates to Connect Candidates and Voters Online," *New York Times*, 23 July 2007, 14(A).

84. Seelye, "Presidential Debates," 22(A).

85. Dilanian, "YouTube Makes Leap," 5(A).

86. Patrick Healy and Jeff Zeleny, "An Unusual Debate with Some Traditional Trappings," *New York Times*, 24 July 2007, 18(A).

87. Dilanian, "YouTube Makes Leap," 5(A).

88. LaChrystal Ricke, "A New Opportunity for Democratic Engagement: The CNN-YouTube Presidential Candidate" (paper presented at the conference on YouTube and the 2008 Election Cycle in the United States, University of Massachusetts, Amherst, April 2009), 1.

89. Katharine Q. Seelye, "The Cyber Race," *New York Times*, 2 September 2007, 17(YT).

90. Seelye, "Debates to Connect," 14(A).

91. Adam Nagourney, "As Democrats Face Bloggers, G.O.P. Wants Its Old TV," *New York Times*, 31 July 2007, 13(A).

92. Katharine Q. Seelye, "2 Republicans Demur on a YouTube Debate," *New York Times*, 28 July 2007, 11(A); Katharine Q. Seelye, "Allies Urge Republicans to Join YouTube Debate," *New York Times*, 2 August 2007, 12(A).

93. Julie Bosman, "For Edwards MTV Turn Takes Twist to Serious," *New York Times*, 28 September 2007, 22(A).

94. Katharine Q. Seelye, "YouTube and the G.O.P. and, Perhaps, Him," *New York Times*, 27 November 2007, 27(A).

95. Seelye, "The Cyber Race," 17(YT).

96. Jim Rutenberg, "Independent YouTube Videos Replace the Attack Ads of Old," *New York Times*, 29 June 2008, 1(A).

97. Rutenberg, "Independent YouTube," 1(A), 17(A).

98. Julie Bosman, "Seeking the Bubbe Vote," *New York Times*, 27 September 2008, 12(A).

99. Rutenberg, "Independent YouTube," 1(A), 17(A).

100. Kevin Wallstein, "'Yes We Can': How Online Viewership, Blog Discussion, Campaign Statements and Mainstream Media Coverage Produced a Viral Video Phenomenon" (paper presented at the conference on YouTube and the 2008 Election Cycle in the United States, University of Massachusetts, Amherst, April 2009).

101. Kate Phillips, "Obama Girl and More," thecaucus.blogs.nytimes.com/2007/06/13/2008-obama-girl-and-more (13 June 2007).

102. Katharine Q. Seelye, "Net Watch: A Hit Shows Big Interest in Racy Material—and Obama," *New York Times*, 15 June 2007, 22(A).

103. Phillips, "Obama Girl and More."

104. Tozzi, "Online: 'Obama Girl,'" 19(A); Dilanian, "YouTube Makes Leap," 5(A).

105. Phillips, "Obama Girl and More."

106. Brian Stelter, "'Obama Girl' Team Retools for Tech Satire," *New York Times*, 26 January 2009, 6(A).

107. Seelye, "Net Watch," 22(A).

108. Vassia Gueorguieva, "Voters, MySpace, and YouTube: The Impact of Alternative Communication Channels on the 2006 Election Cycle and Beyond," *Social Science Computer Review* 26, no. 3 (2008), 288.

109. Elizabeth Edwards, "Bowling 1, Health Care 0," *New York Times*, 27 April 2008, 12(WK).

110. Scott Church, "YouTube Politics: YouChoose and Leadership Rhetoric during the 2008 Election" (paper presented at the conference on YouTube and the 2008 Election Cycle in the United States, University of Massachusetts, Amherst, April 2009).

111. David Brooks, "A Defining Moment," *New York Times*, 4 March 2008, 25(A).

112. Brooks, 2008, 25(A).

113. Frank Rich, "The Bigots' Last Hurrah," *New York Times*, 19 April 2009, 10(WK).

114. Rich, 2009, 10(WK).

115. Amelie Hössjer and Kerstin Eklundh, "Making Space for a New Medium: On the Use of Electronic Mail in a Newspaper Newsroom," *Computer Supported Cooperative Work: The Journal of Collaborative Computing* 18, no. 1 (2009), 1–46.

116. Graff, *The First Campaign*.

117. Craig Ross, Emily S. Orr, Mia Sisic, Jamie M. Arseneault, Mary G. Simmering, and R. Robert Orr, "Personality and Motivations Associated with Facebook Use," *Computers in Human Behavior* 25 (2009), 578–86.

118. John Raacke and Jennifer Bonds-Raacke, "MySpace and Facebook: Applying the Uses and Gratifications Theory to Exploring Friend-Networking Sites," *Cyber-Psychology & Behavior* 11, no. 2 (2008), 169–74.

119. Hillary Savoie, "YouTube, Community, and Me: The New Media Balance Between Self and Community" (paper presented at the conference on YouTube and the 2008 Election Cycle in the United States, University of Massachusetts, Amherst, April 2009), 1.

120. Charlene Li and Josh Bernoff, *Groundswell: Winning in a World Transformed by Social Technologies* (Boston: Harvard Business School Press, 2008).

121. Jerome Armstrong and Markso Moulitsas, *Crashing the Gate: Grassroots and the Rise of People-Powered Politics* (White River Junction, VT: Chelsea Green Publishing, 2006).

122. Judy Bachrach, "The 'Low-Tech' Election Year," *Current* 500 (February 2008), 5–6.

123. "Beyond 'Boxers or Briefs?' New Media Brings Youth to Politics like Never Before," *Phi Kappa Phi Forum* 88, no. 2 (2008), 14.

124. Heffernan, "The YouTube Presidency," 15.

125. Jim Rutenberg and Adam Nagourney, "Melding Obama's Web to a YouTube Presidency," *New York Times*, 25 January 2009, 1(A); Heffernan, "The YouTube Presidency."

126. Quoted by Mitch Wagner, "Dawn of the Internet Presidency," *Information Week* 1210 (10 November 2008), 17.

127. Lee Siegel, *Against the Machine: How the Web Is Reshaping Culture and Commerce—and Why it Matters* (New York: Spiegel & Grau, 2009).

128. Moises Naím, "The YouTube Effect," *Foreign Policy* 158 (2007), 104–5.

129. Heffernan, "The YouTube Presidency," 15.

130. Quoted by Graff, *The First Campaign*, 259.

131. Morley Winograd and Michael D. Hais, *Millennial Makeover: MySpace, YouTube, and the Future of American Politics* (Trenton, NJ: Rutgers University Press, 2008).

132. Heffernan, "The YouTube Presidency," 15.

133. Lynn Spigel, "My TV Studies . . . Now Playing on a YouTube Site Near You," *Television & New Media* 10, no. 1 (2009), 149–53.

134. Ira Teinowitz, "Note to Politicians: It's Not the Spending, Stupid," *Advertising Age* 79, no. 11 (17 March 2008*)*, 17.

135. Joo Soo Lim and Eyun-Jung Ki, "Resistance to Ethically Suspicious Parody Video on YouTube: A Test of Inoculation Theory," *Journalism & Mass Communication Quarterly* 84, no. 4 (2007), 713–28.

136. Fred Von Lohmann, "Fair Use, Film, and the Advantages of Internet Distribution," *Cinema Journal* 46, no. 2 (2007), 128–33.

7

E-mail and Electoral Fortunes:
Obama's Campaign Internet Insurgency

Brandon C. Waite

FROM E-MAIL TO THE INTERNET

Electronic mail, or e-mail, has come to play a crucial role in American political campaigns. It allows candidates to target their messages to specific kinds of voters in order to recruit volunteers, solicit donations, and urge supporters to go to the polls. However, with new opportunities come new challenges. This chapter examines the rise of e-mail as a campaign tool and its use by candidates in the 2008 presidential election.

The origins of e-mail can be traced back to 1965, when it began as a simple file directory. Two users on the same computer could communicate with each other by putting messages into each other's directory. When one user logged on they would see the message left by the other user. This technology enabled computer users at their work desks to access and send messages to one another on one mainframe computer. As technology evolved, computers began talking to each other over networks. As a result, messages needed to be directed to the correct user at the correct computer. In 1972, a contractor for the Pentagon's Advanced Research Projects Agency Network (ARPA-NET) named Ray Tomlinson came up with an address system for e-mail. He simply used the @ symbol to denote sending messages from one computer to another. This set the standard for addressing electronic mail to name-of-the-user@name-of-the-computer. By the end of the decade, electronic mail, or e-mail (as it came to be known), made up 75 percent of all ARPANET traffic. This internetworking among computers became the driving force behind the development of the Internet throughout the 1980s. In 1990, trials for the World Wide Web began and by 1992 more than two dozen preliminary Web sites had appeared. In 1994, the first Web browser was developed and soon Web interface providers such as Yahoo and Hotmail began offering free e-mail accounts.[1] As Internet access spread, hundreds of millions of people began communicating via e-mail. By the end of the decade, politicians and their strategists began experimenting with e-mail as a campaign tool.

POLITICS MOVES ONLINE

Senator John McCain's bid for the presidency in 2000 was the first national political campaign to attempt to harness the power of the Internet. The Mc-Cain campaign, with the help of Webmaster Max Fose, developed a strategy that depended heavily on an integrated Web site/e-mail campaign package from a company called VirtualSprockets. The ability to communicate directly with several different constituencies is critical to both fundraising and voter turnout. The VirtualSprockets software enabled McCain to target anywhere from one to hundreds of thousands of voters, sending different e-mail messages to specific types of recipients.[2]

McCain used his e-mail list to organize more than 140,000 volunteers and distribute petitions for supporters to sign in order to get the candidate on states' ballots during the primary season. Following his surprise victory in the New Hampshire primary, the Internet helped McCain raise $6.4 million by enabling individuals to give small donations ($10–$25) in chunks until they reached the $250 individual limit allowed for candidates receiving matching federal funds. Despite the success of these groundbreaking campaign tactics, McCain lost the nomination to Texas Governor George W. Bush. Regardless, McCain's bid in the 2000 presidential election began the practice of interactive Internet campaigning.

Joe Trippi, a technology consultant and veteran Democratic campaign director, watched McCain's bid for the presidency closely. Trippi had been envisioning a bottom-up, Internet-based political campaign for some time, but had not gotten the opportunity to try it.[3] His chance came in 2002, shortly after the governor of Vermont, Howard Dean, began his bid for the 2004 presidency.

Dean was trailing a pack of candidates that included Senators John Edwards, Joe Lieberman, and John Kerry, and Representative Richard Gephardt. These candidates' campaigns were running like well-oiled machines raising money and gathering supporters. Having taken over the Vermont governorship after the death of Richard Snelling, and then handily winning reelection four more times, Dean had never been seriously challenged in an election. He was a populist candidate in a crowded field with a tiny grassroots political organization and no money; his presidential hopes were falling fast. Despite having just finished a knock-down, drag-out congressional election in Pennsylvania, Trippi agreed to join the flailing "Dean for America" campaign.[4]

Lacking resources, Dean needed to find a way to decentralize the campaign and let the momentum come from his supporters. Trippi could see that using the Internet was their only hope but had to convince the governor, who was a self-described "technophobe" and had only been using e-mail since 2001. It wasn't until Dean for America put a link to the popular social networking site Meetup.com on their campaign Web site, and saw thousands of supporters sign up to meet each other offline, that the candidate was convinced. Soon, Trippi took over as campaign director and focused their strategy and tactics around the Internet. As he explains in his memoir of the campaign, "I was always on the lookout for more help, and now, when these young people would straggle in from the road, my first question to them was whether they had any experience with Web sites, blogs, or emails."[5]

The campaign, dismissed by mainstream media, began actively courting voters on the Internet. Dean began sending members of Meetup.com e-mails letting them know he would be stopping by their "meetups" when he passed through their city, causing the number of people joining Web site and attending the offline gatherings to skyrocket. One Meetup.com member began an e-mail campaign asking other members of the site to add a penny to their donation to signal that it was, indeed, from a Meetup.com member. This e-mail campaign generated nearly $400,000 by the end of the fundraising quarter.[6] After seeing the groundswell of support for Dean's campaign, particularly the amount of money being raised online, the other contenders for the 2004 presidency began to follow suit and strengthen their Internet operations.

After struggling in the Iowa caucuses, Dean eventually lost the nomination to Senator Kerry. Mainstream media had been slow to acknowledge Dean's online support, but by the time he dropped out of the race it was apparent that Dean had fundamentally changed the way campaigning takes place in the twenty-first century. A handful of activists who worked on the Dean campaign formed a company specializing in online campaigning called Blue State Digital and continued to work for Dean when he became chairman of the Democratic National Committee the following year.

OBAMA'S E-MAIL INNOVATIONS

A young African American senator from Illinois named Barack Hussein Obama gave the keynote address at the 2004 Democratic National Convention. The speech was the highlight of the convention and immediately elevated the senator's status as a star in the Democratic Party. By 2006, the pressure was on for Obama to make a run for the White House. On February 10, 2007, Obama announced his candidacy for president of the United States, joining a crowded field with the likes of Senators Hillary Clinton, John Edwards, Joe Biden, and Chris Dodd.

Obama assembled an experienced team to manage his online campaign. Julius Genachowski, who would eventually be Obama's choice to head the Federal Communications Commission, was hired as the campaign's chief technology advisor. Genachowski brought in Blue State Digital's cofounder, Joe Rospars, as director of new media and gave him an office next to the research and communications departments. Having spent three years working on the Dean campaign, Rospars was able to quickly establish Obama's online presence and organize his support network.

It was clear from the beginning that e-mail would be a central component to Obama's campaign. Before the primaries even began, the candidate set up e-mail lists in each state. The lists grew exponentially as the campaign gathered the e-mail addresses of those who attended the candidate's public rallies. Visitors to Obama's Web site could easily subscribe to receive the candidate's e-mail messages and could even sign up their friends and family members.

The Obama campaign took groundbreaking steps to make everyone on their e-mail list feel like a valued asset, and reward them as such. On August 10, 2008, the campaign sent out an e-mail promising that Obama would announce his running mate via e-mail and text message. "You have helped build this movement from the bottom up," it said, "and Barack wants you to be the first to know his choice."[7] Individuals were required to subscribe to Obama's e-mail list to receive the announcement. By promoting an event happening in the future, at some unspecified time, the campaign dovetailed e-mail and text messaging. The message urged recipients to forward the e-mail to their friends, family, and coworkers so that they could sign up to receive the alert. With Clinton out of the race, there was much speculation about who would join Obama on the ticket. He used the stunt to elicit hundreds of thousands of e-mail addresses, particularly those of former Clinton supporters, and galvanize his support two weeks before the Democratic National Convention.

By Election Day, Obama's e-mail list was estimated to contain upward of thirteen million addresses. During the course of the campaign, over seven thousand different messages were sent, landing in more than one billion inboxes.[8] Having collected data on most of their e-mail recipients, the Obama campaign had unbridled segmentation to specifically tailor their messages based on the recipient's interests, demographic characteristics, and donor level. Using an analytics team to track what e-mails got opened most the Obama campaign developed an e-mail marketing strategy capable of generating campaign donations, driving the candidate's message, and mobilizing his supporters.

Obama had watched Dean use the Internet to generate large sums of cash, much of it in increments of $100 or less. Building on this strategy, Obama placed a bright red donate button within nearly every Internet ad, blog post, Web page, and e-mail under the campaign's control. The campaign opened up the political process to ordinary Americans by allowing individuals to donate small amounts of as little as $20 or less. It also gave people the option of making recurring payments. Rather than write a single check for $2,300, the limit placed on individual contributions, supporters could contribute $200 a month or less. Over time, small donors became large donors. Obama raised half a billion dollars from three million donors online during the twenty-one months he campaigned for the White House. Out of 6.5 million online donations, six million were in increments of $100 or less.

Obama set a new standard for political fundraising, in large part, by sending a torrent of e-mails to potential donors that consistently reinforced the campaign's core themes. During an election candidates and their supporters do everything they can to stay on message (and force their opponents to go off message). The director of e-mail and online fundraising, Stephen Geer, made sure that the campaign followed strict messaging discipline by maintaining consistent long-term and short-term themes. In support of those themes, e-mail was used to drive home the points made by the candidate that day or that week.

Maintaining message discipline on the Internet is an enormous challenge. In the chaos of a presidential race with a large decentralized staff it is easy for a campaign to send mixed and conflicting messages. Obama and his advisers were faced with the task of coordinating messaging strategies with a large staff in charge of an information-rich e-mail list and the candidate's presence on online social networks, YouTube, a Web site, and a blog. The campaign used each of these mediums to reinforce the candidate's long-term and short-term themes on a daily basis. To attract individuals to as many of these technologies as possible, each had to present the candidate's message in slightly different ways. Otherwise, potential voters would resort to one technology or begin to tune out the mind-numbing repetition altogether. Taking a cue from the Dean campaign that preceded them, messages targeted to specific audiences were written by an e-mail team rather than speechwriters in order to keep the discourse as organic as possible. The subject lines of Obama's e-mails were oftentimes personalized to the recipient and asked them to become involved with the campaign. Examples include "It's in your hands, Brandon" and "Will you join me on election night?" Most importantly, messages from the Obama campaign were clear and concise. This put them in stark contrast to e-mails from McCain's online team, which often contained more than five hundred words and only one discreet link at the bottom of the message.[9]

Along with driving the message, e-mail was critical to driving action. Obama saw technology as a means of transferring traditional community organizing to a national level. He used e-mail to reinforce the three-word mantra at the heart of his grassroots campaign: respect, empower and include.[10] As a result, ordinary members of the public became big-time players in the campaign. Rather than simply ask individuals to click on a button to donate money, the campaign asked them to become actively engaged by knocking on doors, handing out pamphlets, and expressing their support to their peers. Once individuals volunteered they were asked to escalate their involvement, by hosting a phone bank or a debate watch party. Supporters were also asked to create their own events wherein they could recruit their friends to support Obama. This strategy continued right up to election day when e-mails contained not only a get-out-the-vote message, but also the names of five people in one's neighborhood who were targeted as likely to vote for Obama.

During her acceptance speech at the Republican National Convention, vice presidential candidate Sarah Palin mocked Obama's experience as a community organizer. "I guess a small town mayor is like a 'community organizer,'" she said, "except that you have actual responsibilities." The next day the Obama campaign sent out an e-mail to their supporters accusing Palin of belittling ordinary Americans who organize for the benefit of their communities and country. The e-mail, which asked individuals to give a small donation to the campaign to show their opposition to Palin's remarks, helped set a new record for the single biggest day of fundraising in the history of politics. Obama raised $10 million in twenty-four hours.

THE UGLY SIDE OF E-MAIL

In an interview with the *New York Times*, McCain admitted that he didn't use e-mail: "I don't e-mail, I've never felt the particular need to e-mail. I read e-mails all the time, but the communications that I have with my friends and staff are oral and done with my cell phone. I have the luxury of being in contact with them literally all the time. We now have a phone on the plane that is usable on the plane, so I just never really felt a need to do it."[11] Presumably, McCain preferred not to rely on e-mail for communication because of injuries sustained in the Vietnam War that prevented him from combing his hair, tying his shoes, or typing on his keyboard. McCain explained that when he wanted to send an e-mail, and he certainly knew how to do so, his wife would transcribe the message for him.

Obama, jumping at the chance to portray the seventy-two-year-old McCain as out of touch, ran an ad tinged with ageism. Featuring outdated pictures of McCain, a disco ball, and a Rubik's Cube, a voice in the ad said: "1982, John McCain goes to Washington. Things have changed in the last 26 years, but McCain hasn't. He admits he doesn't know how to use a computer; can't send an e-mail." This line of attack was repeated by Obama spokesman Dan Pfeiffer, who said, "Our economy wouldn't survive without the Internet, and cyber-security continues to represent one of our most serious national security threats. It's extraordinary that someone who wants to be our president and our commander in chief doesn't know how to send an e-mail."[12] It reinforced the image of McCain as a geriatric unfit for the presidency, despite the fact that McCain was the first presidential candidate to use the Internet for campaigning. It was one of many untruths circulated during the campaign.

Rumors and politics have always gone hand in hand. Now that politics has moved online, rumors and rebuttals can be distributed widely, instantly, and at no cost by simply clicking the "forward" button in one's e-mail. During the 2008 election, hundreds of different e-mail chain letters were circulated on the Internet making it, without a doubt, the most effective rumor mill in the history of politics. Obama was the target of the most outlandish of these rumors, which tended to focus on three overlapping themes: race, religion, and patriotism. The e-mail chain letters were malicious and, bolstered by blogs that thrive on speculation and hearsay, eventually made it into the discourse of the Washington press corps. While not condoning the online attacks, the Republican ticket used parallel themes to reinforce their plausibility.

Barack Obama's unusual background made him a one-of-a-kind candidate open to unique lines of attack. His mother, a white woman from Wichita, Kansas, met his father, a black Muslim from Kenya, while they attended college in Hawaii. She gave birth to Barack Hussein Obama, Jr., on August 4, 1961, in Honolulu. Obama's parents divorced when he was only two years old. His mother then married an Indonesian student and relocated to Jakarta, Indonesia, where Obama spent time enrolled in both Muslim and Catholic schools. Nearly five years later, Obama returned to Hawaii to be raised by his maternal grandmother.

Obama's opponents used his unusual background to make him appear un-American, oftentimes using messages with racial overtones. E-mails circulated claiming that Obama was born in Africa, and thus constitutionally prohibited from becoming president of the United States. Several contained conspiracy theories regarding Obama's birth certificate, or lack thereof. These e-mails were set to a backdrop of talking heads on television using terms such as "exotic" and "foreign" to describe his pedigree. The Republican ticket built their strategy around characterizing Obama as an outsider who could not be trusted.

Making matters more difficult for Obama was Dr. Jeremiah Wright, his pastor at the Trinity United Church of Christ in Chicago. Reverend Wright, who had baptized Obama in the early 1990s, had a history of making salacious and sensational remarks about white Americans. Numerous e-mails containing YouTube clips of Wright's rants against whites circulated on the Internet. Questions were raised regarding Obama's adherence to Wright's ideas. Eventually Obama responded by severing his ties to the Trinity United Church of Christ and giving a nationally televised speech about race, titled "A More Perfect Union," in which he talked openly about his background and condemned Wright's comments. Unfortunately the speech, widely regarded as one of his best, did not put an end to the e-mail rumor mill.

GOP leaders played upon the fears many whites had of Obama. At a campaign stop in North Carolina the state's junior senator, Richard Burr, introduced Palin, saying "A lot of you feel like you know Sarah Palin. And you do, because she's one of us."[13] It was the same line used by the late Sen. Jesse Helms when Nick Galifianakis, a Greek American whose support came from the urban Piedmont Triad, challenged him in 1972. Although skin color was never mentioned, observers could not help but contrast Palin's speeches about "small-town values" against Obama's cosmopolitan background. The "Us vs. Them" narrative carried racial undertones that did not go unnoticed.

E-mail attacks that focused on Obama's religious affiliation and patriotism tended to be more explicit. A number of e-mail rumors alleged that Obama was really a radical Muslim lying about his religious background, including his claim to being a devout Christian. These e-mails claimed, among other things, that Obama had been educated at a radical Muslim madrassa and remained a subversive terrorist. "The Muslims have said they plan on destroying the U.S. from the inside out," claimed one widely circulated e-mail, titled "Who is Barack Obama?" "What better way to start than at the highest level?"[14] This allegation was one of many Internet rumors eventually aired by Fox News, prompting other cable news stations to respond. The Republican ticket politely condemned the e-mail, but reinforced the theme as it fell behind in the polls. At several speaking events, Palin accused Obama of "palling around with terrorists," a reference to 1960s radical Dr. William Ayers whom, after denouncing his past, sat with Obama on a charity board in 1990s. The politics of personal destruction continued right up to the inauguration when e-mails were circulated claiming that Obama placed his hand on the Qur'an, rather than the Bible, when being sworn into office.

Internet rumors became so prevalent that the Obama campaign established a task force dedicated to debunking them. The task force set up two Web pages, Factcheck.barackobama.com and Fightthesmears.com, to address the persistent myths about the senator. They walked a fine line defending their candidate without appearing defensive. Despite lacking any credibility, Internet rumors enabled many white voters to pretend there were too many "unknowns" about Obama to justify supporting him. The sheer abundance of these e-mails confirmed their suspicions, regardless of whether or not the facts supported the allegations.

E-MAIL'S POTENTIAL PITFALLS

The Internet offered unheard of opportunities for all of the candidates in the 2008 election, but it also presented some unique pitfalls. Hackers broke into Palin's e-mail and took screen shots of her inbox, contact list, a couple of e-mails, and some family photos. The hacker posted the screen shots on a Web site that hosts anonymously leaked government and corporate documents.[15] Palin, who opposes abortion even in cases of rape and incest, was also at the center of an e-mail pitch that asked individuals to donate to Planned Parenthood in her name. According to the e-mail, for every donation made in her name Planned Parenthood sent a thank you note to Palin. Planned Parenthood was not behind the effort, but the e-mail generated more than $1 million for the organization.[16]

Others used the candidates' names for nefarious purposes. Spam containing their names in the subject line was used to sell everything from pornography to pharmaceuticals, as well as install information-stealing code for identity theft schemes. For instance, during the campaign an e-mail circulated purporting to have a video clip of Obama having sex with several young Ukrainian girls. If recipients played the fourteen-second video, which of course did not contain the candidate performing sex, malicious applications were installed on their computer compromising their personal data.[17]

Other problems were of the campaign's own doing. Not everyone who received messages from the Obama campaign signed up for them. At campaign events, attendees were encouraged to sign up their friends with simple incentives, like free bumper stickers. Not surprisingly, some of these "friends" complained when they began to receive unsolicited e-mails from the candidate—particularly those without meaningful content that simply asked the recipient to contribute money to the campaign.

Individuals who wanted to receive e-mails from Obama could simply visit his Web site and fill out an open subscription form asking for their first and last names, e-mail address, and zip code. However, the campaign did not send a confirmation message to new registrants requiring them to respond in order to be added to the file. Thus, unwitting individuals could be fraudulently signed up under false names like "Stupid Jerk," or worse. This unleashed a barrage of e-mails from the campaign to the prank's victim that began "Dear Stupid."[18] This is certainly not how a candidate wants to be addressing potential voters.

Other problems were the result of confusion. Some expected to receive e-mails from the campaign that were relevant to their region and were annoyed when they received e-mails about rallies taking place fifteen thousand miles away. When Obama announced that his running mate would be revealed to the public via text message and e-mail, thousands of people signed up to receive the alert. During this time, his Web site focused almost exclusively on the "Be the First to Know" concept so it appeared clear what one was signing up for. However, immediately upon signing up subscribers began receiving *all* of the campaign's e-mail messages—everything *except* what they signed up for. While the huge number of additional subscribers likely justified being vague about the nature of the sign-up, the campaign may have left a bad impression on some who felt bombarded with unwanted e-mail. Making matters worse, someone in the Obama campaign leaked the candidate's choice for vice president to the *LA Times* hours before the official text message and e-mail were sent.[19]

Obama also confused voters by engaging in "sender roulette," the practice of sending out e-mails under the names of different people within the campaign, but retaining a central e-mail address.[20] Subscribers to Obama's e-mail list received messages not only from the candidate, but also his wife, David Plouffe, David Axelrod, and Jon Carson, among others. Presumably, this was done to make recipients feel like they were a part of Obama's inside circle. Not knowing who these individuals in the inner circle were, however, they may have been more inclined to delete the messages or mark them as spam.

Other complaints centered on the sheer amount of e-mails coming from the candidates. During the run-up to the election, recipients on Obama's list often times got up to three e-mails per day from the campaign. Many subscribers complained that the e-mails did not stop coming once the race was over. Leading up to the inauguration, Obama used his e-mail list to tout limited edition merchandise like T-shirts, coffee mugs, and calendars. Once in the White House, Obama used his e-mail list to build support for policies. The amount, and ongoing nature, of these e-mails prompted some to accuse Obama of being a spammer. In some places, ISPs began to block certain e-mails from the Obama campaign due to customer complaints.[21]

The Controlling the Assault of Non-Solicited Pornography and Marketing Act of 2003 (CAN SPAM), signed into law by President George W. Bush, established national standards for sending commercial e-mail. Politicians and nonprofits, however, are not subject to the legislation for fear that such restraints might hinder political speech and public debate. Campaigns often compile their own voter registration data by obtaining public records from local governments and then take advantage of services that match, or append, e-mail addresses to the data. This allows candidates, political action committees, and advocacy groups to target their messages to specific types of voters based on their demographic characteristics, partisanship, location, etc. While Obama might have engaged in ethically dubious e-mail practices, he did not meet the legal definition of a spammer.

E-MAIL FROM THE BULLY PULPIT

Before the election had even taken place, pundits and political strategists across the country focused on how Obama could use his enormous list of e-mail addresses, complete with demographic information and policy preferences of the recipients, once he was in the White House. Shortly after taking office, the new president changed the name of his campaign organization from "Obama for America" to "Organizing for America" and placed it under the control of the Democratic National Committee. Building on the grassroots movement started during the campaign, Organizing for America promised to connect citizens to debates taking place in Washington as well as their own communities.

To use his e-mail list effectively, Obama had to know *who* was on the list and *why* they were on it. With only sixty-one days to go before the inauguration, the campaign sent out an e-mail with a subject line that read: "Where do we go from here?" In it, they asked their supporters to fill out a four-page survey asking how the Obama administration should move forward.[22] The survey included information about their location, demographics, policy interests, and willingness to volunteer in their communities. Armed with this information, Organize for America became a permanent, nation-wide lobbying organization dedicated to promoting Obama's political agenda and overall discipline within the Democratic Party. With the click of a button the president could ask citizens to call their elected representatives, write letters to the editorial boards of their local papers, and support one candidate over another. The e-mail list could be particularly effective in pressuring leaders in conservative strongholds, including Blue Dog Democrats, to support the president's agenda.

Less than three months into office the president put Organizing for America, whose offices are located only two blocks from the White House, to work in an attempt to push a $3.55 trillion economic stimulus package through Congress. He began by targeting his most active supporters with e-mails that provided a state-by-state analysis of the plan and official talking points in support of the stimulus. He requested they act on their own by hosting "economic recovery" meetings in their homes and going door-to-door to urge their neighbors to sign a pledge in support of his budget plan.

Organizing for America was unapologetically propagandistic, but the president also requested feedback from the public. In an e-mail titled "Open for Questions," Obama invited recipients to submit their own questions or ideas about the economy for the president to answer via streaming video in an online town hall the following day. The administration was taken by surprise when a large portion of the 33,477 responses pointed to marijuana legalization and taxation as a viable solution to the economic crisis. The president casually dismissed the idea with a deprecating joke about the nature of his online audience.[23] The small audience in attendance got a good chuckle out of the president's joke, but the online audience was not laughing.

The incident highlighted one of the potential pitfalls associated with using Organizing for America's e-mail list to generate public policy ideas and support. A large portion of Obama's base of support comes from young adults who voted in recordbreaking numbers in 2008. He gained the support of this demographic by promising to empower their voices. By asking his online audience to submit their suggestions for reform, and then dismissing an idea that came from a large portion of respondents as preposterous, Obama ran the risk of alienating a number of his most ardent supporters. By dismissing the idea as foolishness, instead of explaining why it would not work, the president sent a broader message that his request for ideas was insincere.

Moderate Democrats presented the greatest obstacle to passing the president's budget. Hoping to flood their offices with calls from constituents, the president sent an e-mail to everyone on his list asking them to call their members of Congress in support of the stimulus. Absent from the e-mails, however, were the specifics of the president's plan. Obama's propaganda machine infuriated the base of the Republican Party. The economic stimulus passed both chambers of Congress, but without the bipartisan support the president was seeking.

Organizing for America came to life again during Obama's push for healthcare reform using its e-mail list to organize events in all fifty states. In one series of events, tens of thousands of attendees across the country watched a video address from the president and then engaged in a public dialogue about healthcare reform. In another, thousands of volunteers gathered to take part in a National Health Care Day of Service in farmers' markets, rehab clinics, parks, and libraries nationwide to drum up support for the president's reform proposals. Along with calling on individuals to bombard their congressmen with phone calls and their local newspapers with letters to the editor, the organization asked its e-mail recipients to post first-person accounts of their healthcare tribulations online in blogs and YouTube videos. Organizing for America used the videos in e-mails and television ads targeting Democratic senators who were reluctant to support the president's proposals. The organization's activities appeared to anger lawmakers involved in the delicate negotiations. Senate Majority Leader Harry Reid told reporters, "It's a waste of time. . . . It's a waste of money to have Democrats swinging against Democrats."[24]

E-MAIL STUMPING

In the months leading up to midterm elections, presidents traditionally crisscross the country stumping for their party's candidate in key races. These campaign obligations have the potential to distract the president and limit the amount of time they can spend working with Congress to pass their agenda. This is where Obama's e-mail list is likely to come in handy. For example, without leaving the White House President Obama sent an e-mail to voters in New York's 20th Congressional District urging them to vote for businessman Scott Murphy in the upcoming special election.[25] Likewise, he penned an e-mail from the Oval Office to Virginia voters on behalf of Democratic gubernatorial candidate Creigh Deeds. By supplementing his campaign stops with e-mails in which he expresses support for Democratic candidates, Obama has the opportunity to spend more time in Washington than his predecessors.

Despite making it easier for the president to stump from the White House, e-mail has not eliminated the risks associated with presidential meddling in statewide elections. "I really don't understand why President Obama got involved in our primary," Representative Charles Rangel told the *New York Daily News*. "I don't want to use the word 'wrong,' but it doesn't seem like the astute political thing to do."[26] The president's e-mail list is a valuable political tool, but it has the potential to promote resentment and infighting among members of his own party.

CONCLUSION

Prior to 2004, an online audience that was largely computer illiterate skipped to and from static Web sites and sent e-mail to friends and family using slow Internet connections. Coinciding with Dean's bid for the White House, fundamental changes were beginning to take place online. Internet connection speeds were increasing exponentially and Web site content was becoming decentralized and created from the bottom-up. Dean's campaign produced a glimpse, albeit a short one, of what was to come. The campaign was driven by a candidate who was willing to relinquish control of his candidacy to a seamless network of e-mail users, bloggers, and Web site contributors. Rather than organize these individuals from the top-down, Dean empowered supporters to organize themselves from the bottom-up and used their ingenuity and energy to drive his campaign. By the time Dean's insurgent bid for the White House ended, the Internet was shifting from Web 1.0 to Web 2.0, ushering in a new phase in the development of online technologies.

What separates Web 1.0 from Web 2.0 is the latter's emphasis on online applications that empower users to communicate and collaborate. It is the vision of the Web as a platform upon which user-generated content provides the substance of the Internet. Just as Dean's campaign was coming to an end, a host of new media technologies like profile-based social networking sites and viral videos were being introduced to the online public that embodied Web 2.0 principles. By the time Obama announced his intention to run for the presidency tens of millions of Internet users had integrated Web applications like MySpace, Facebook, Twitter, and YouTube into their daily lives alongside more traditional forms of online communication like Web pages, blogs, and e-mail. With a background in community organizing, Obama was poised to take online campaigning to a new level by using these applications to empower citizens in the political process.

Obama's greatest campaign asset was his enormous list of e-mail addresses. He relied on the list to generate contributions to his campaign, communicate his vision to voters, and mobilize his supporters. He took risks and experimented with e-mail by dovetailing it with text messaging, embedding videos in his messages, and soliciting questions for online town hall meetings. He made e-mail a central component of his campaign because it is the most common medium of online communication, enabling content from the newest Web applications to be shared with tens of millions of people. Political strategists all over the world watched Obama transform the country's political landscape using e-mail and new media technologies in ways they had never imagined.

Researchers at the Pew Internet and American Life Project have tracked the role of the Internet and e-mail in people's lives since 2000. According to their research on the 2008 election, three-quarters of Internet users in the United States went online to collect and disseminate information about the campaign. This represents more than half (55 percent) of the entire adult population, a first for the Pew study.[27] Obama's victory is likely to change the way politicians campaign to an American public that is increasingly comfortable with gathering and disseminating information on the Internet. He was far more successful than his competitor at using the Internet, and e-mail in particular, to empower citizens by promoting the free flow of information and providing the resources needed to organize themselves. Along with participating in a wide range of online political activities, Obama supporters took the lead in using e-mail as a form of political communication. The Pew study found that 48 percent of Obama voters, compared to only 38 percent of McCain voters, received e-mail directly from a political party or candidate for office. Likewise, 12 percent of Obama voters signed up for e-mail news alerts, compared to only 8 percent of McCain voters.[28] If the president continues to reach out to the online community these numbers could spell trouble for Republicans down the road.

However, the challenge of adapting to politics online is not a uniquely partisan one. Candidates in both parties must adapt to the changing nature of online campaigning. This can be tough for those who have been entrenched in Washington politics for some time. Incumbents typically overestimate their own proclivity for making wise strategic moves in a campaign, and tend to rationalize their setbacks as a result of circumstances out of their control. Likewise, incumbents are more likely to follow strategies that have worked before, whereas challengers are more likely to innovate.

The 2008 campaign established a new era of online politics. E-mail is no longer a campaign novelty; it is a necessity being used in novel ways. Questions remain about the long-term viability of Obama's online presence and his ability to use e-mail and other emerging media technologies to govern. However, it is undeniable that American society is being transformed by online technologies that empower citizens. The months and years ahead will be exciting as our political system adapts to its changing environment.

NOTES

1. Ian Peter, "Ian Peter's History of the Internet," *Net History* 2003, www.nethistory.info/ (8 June 2009).

2. Richard Rapaport, "Net vs. Norm," *Best of the Web* 2000, www.forbes.com/asap/2000/0529/053_print.html (8 June 2009).

3. Joe Trippi, *The Revolution Will Not Be Televised* (New York: HarperCollins, 2008), 59.

4. Trippi, *Revolution*, 76–81.

5. Trippi, *Revolution*, 90.

6. Trippi, *Revolution*, 106.

7. Andrew Malcolm, "Obama's VP Choice Imminent via Website, Email, Text Message," *LA Times* 2008, latimesblogs.latimes.com/washington/2008/08/obama-vp.html (8 June 2009).

8. Jose Antonio Vargas, "Obama Raised Half a Billion Online," *Washington Post* 2008, voices.washingtonpost.com/44/2008/11/20/obama_raised_half_a_billion_on.html (8 June 2009).

9. Michael Whitney, "The McCain Campaign's 'Reckless' Email Strategy," *Tech-President* 20 May 2008, techpresident.com/blog-entry/mccain-campaigns-reckless-email-strategy (18 June 2009).

10. Stephen Geer, "Email and Politics: Case Study of the Obama Campaign" (Keynote address presented at MediaPost's Email Insider Summit, Park City, Utah, December 2008).

11. Adam Nagourney and Michael Cooper, "The *Times* Interviews John McCain," *New York Times* 2008, www.nytimes.com/2008/07/13/us/politics/13text-mccain.html?_r=2&oref=slogin&pagewanted=print (1 July 2009).

12. Nedra Pickler, "Obama Mocks McCain as Computer Illiterate," Associated Press 2008, abcnews.go.com/Politics/wireStory?id=5785969 (1 July 2009).

13. Jordan Green, "Palin Speech Stresses Familiarity and Small Town Values," *Yes Weekly* 2008, www.yesweekly.com/article-920-palin-speech-stresses-familiarity-and-small-town-values.html (1 July 2009).

14. Ben Smith and Jonathan Martin, "Untraceable e-mails Spread Obama Rumor," *Politico* 2007, www.politico.com/news/stories/1007/6314.html (1 July 2009).

15. Anonymous, "VP Contender Sarah Palin Hacked," *Wikileaks* 2008, wikileaks.org/wiki/Sarah_Palin_Yahoo_inbox_2008 (6 July 2009).

16. Pat Morrison, "Governor Palin, Planned Parenthood and I Thank You," *Huffington Post* 2008, www.huffingtonpost.com/patt-morrison/governor-palin-planned-pa_b_127352.html (9 July 2009).

17. David Kravets, "Malware Lurks Behind Obama Sex Video Spam," *Wired* 2008, www.wired.com/threatlevel/2008/09/barack-obama-se/ (14 July 2008).

18. Ken Magill, "You Ask for Garbage, You Get It," *Direct* 2008, directmag.com/disciplines/email/0902-obama-biden-mail-followup/ (6 July 2009).

19. Andrew Malcom, "Breaking: Obama Selects Joe Biden as his VP Running Mate," *LA Times* 2008, latimesblogs.latimes.com/washington/2008/08/obama-biden-vp.html (15 July 2009).

20. John Caldwell, "Don't Play Email Sender Roulette," *Red Pill Email* 2009, redpillemail.com/blog/2009/dont-play-email-sender-roulette.html (12 July 2009).

21. Gene Davis, "Suffocation via Emails?" *Denver Daily News* 2008, www.thedenverdailynews.com/article.php?aID=2211 (11 July 2009).

22. "Supporter Survey," *Obama for America* 2008, my.barackobama.com/page/s/pesurvpage1 (15 July 2009).

23. Sam Stein, "Obama Takes Pot Legalization Question During Town Hall," *Huffington Post* 2009, www.huffingtonpost.com/2009/03/26/obama-takes-pot-legalizat_n_179563.html (16 July 2009).

24. Susan Ferrechio, "Reid Says DNC Ads 'A Waste of Money,'" *Washington Examiner* 2009, www.washingtonexaminer.com/opinion/blogs/beltway-confidential/Rids-says-DNC-health-ads-a-waste-of-money-50956547.html (18 July 2009).

25. Mike Allen, "Obama Hits E-Campaign Trail," *Politico* 2009, www.politico.com/news/stories/0309/20692.html (18 July 2009).

26. Michael Saul, "Rangel Defends Maloney's Bid for Gillibrand Senate Seat; Criticizes Obama for Butting into Primary," *New York Daily News* 2009, www .nydailynews.com/news/politics/2009/07/03/2009-07-03_rangel_defends_maloneys_ bid_for_gillibrand_senate_seat_criticizes_obama_for_butt.html#ixzz0MTbXwJQw (20 July 2009).

27. Aaron Smith, "The Internet's Role in Campaign 2008," *Pew Internet and American Life Project* 2009, www.pewinternet.org/Reports/2009/6--The-Internets -Role-in-Campaign-2008.aspx (July 20, 2009).

28. Smith, "Internet's Role."

8

Game ON: Video Games and Obama's Race to the White House

Eric E. Otenyo

One of the most visible features of Barack Obama's campaign was the employment of a wide array of technologies to reach a larger section of voters than had previously been reached in presidential campaigns. Computer-based technologies had dramatic effects on various aspects of e-participation; the most striking effect was the revolutionary new ways technology was used to mobilize supporters and distribute information about the candidates via the Internet. The 2008 presidential election campaign featured innovative and untried forms of political communication. Specifically, the Obama campaign found innovative uses of Internet and new media technologies to popularize and spread Obama's message.

The Obama campaign had learned from previous successful utilization of Internet e-campaign strategies in previous political races at national and state-wide levels. In 1998, for example, Jesse Ventura, a former professional wrestler, known as "The Body," had harnessed technology to mobilize supporters via the Internet to win the gubernatorial election in Minnesota.[1] Likewise, Governor Howard Dean, in 2000, and Senator John Kerry, in 2004, were also highly successful in recruiting hundreds of campaign volunteers through Internet media.[2] In recent years, the Internet, therefore, served the causes of democratic participation in a more profound way than radio, television, and other previous communication technologies.

These new technologies, for the most part, have been very effective at image making beyond the reach of traditional media. Internet technologies offer a cheaper and unmediated means to communicate to a wider audience than traditional media. The success of e-campaigns drew immediate attention from the scholarly community, notably in the area of information awareness and recruitment efforts.[3][4][5][6][7][8] Although the majority of those observations and commentary focused on the presidential election, there was examination of potential use of e-campaign strategies at the state legislative level along with its interactive capabilities.[9] [10] [11]

Something new happened during the 2008 presidential election that was not captured in the aforementioned set of literature. Obama's presidential campaign became the first to apply the immense potential of advertising in the gaming world, interfaced through the Internet to engage a large section of potential and previously untapped voters. This chapter describes and analyzes Obama's groundbreaking campaign strategy that took advantage of the intersection between gaming and politics to successfully capture the Oval Office.

Like no other candidate in modern history, Obama's persona and campaign, to quote presidential adviser David Gergen, was "connected with culture."[12] Today more than ever, political marketing is essential for American democracy.[13] Therefore, Obama's ability to engage the electorate through popular culture during and after the election was part of the reason he "spawned an ancillary marketing operation befitting a mega budget blockbuster, with vendors plastering his face on action figures, water bottles, DVDs, and of course, commemorative plates, among scads of other products."[14]

His campaign message in online video games is the subject of this chapter and it is organized into three sections. The first section introduces the concept of video gaming. The second section provides an analysis of how Obama used video games in the race for the White House. And the final section discusses and describes the future implications of this strategy for politicians running for office in local, state, and national elections.

THE VIDEO GAME IDEA AND MARKET

A video game is a two-dimensional game in which there is an interaction with a user interface which is fed into a video device. The idea of video was originally drawn from a raster display device but in today's language refers to any display type. Video games can be played on a variety of electronic systems including computers, handheld communication devices, and television sets. Ironically, video games were an offshoot from engineers seeking to build interactive television sets. Engineers in the 1940s and 1950s sought to develop a product for consumers to utilize for game playing. There are several disputed accounts as to who invented video games and it is safe to point out that multiple inventers, some of whom did not patent their work, shared the laurels.

Several sources indicate that the first games were played on cathode ray tube (CRT) television devices. The first patented video games, employing eight vacuum tubes, emerged in 1948. These first-generation video games did not generate video signals for display as seen on computer monitors or television screens. Later, the devices mushroomed rapidly into more sophisticated forms that included electronically drawn graphics. The pivotal year seemed to be 1952, when British scientist Alexander S. Douglas advanced the idea of human-computer interaction through a well-developed cathode ray tube platform on which he played, for illustration, a graphic tic-tac-toe game.[15]

Years later, other engineers linked analog computers to oscilloscopes for display. By 1966, the first modern video game prototype had all the major features of today's platforms. These devices were very successful and eventually morphed into other devices, some employing vector graphics that could simulate games ranging from target shooting sprees to ordinary sports like chase, basketball, football, soccer, bowling, and tennis, among others.

By 1972, the electronic company Magnavox had released the video game system Odyssey. Arguably, it is the first commercially successful home video game system in the world. Soon afterward, Atari built their successful PONG arcade game. New industries continued evolving, often merging into huge corporations.[16] As the industry continued to evolve, several American, Japanese, and European manufacturers including the giant software corporations Microsoft Game Studios, Nintendo, and Sony began building and selling sophisticated low-cost chips. This allowed video gaming to flourish into a multibillion dollar industry. By the time the PC industry had perfected what Alan Stone called the "marriage made in heaven" between computers and communications, possibilities for online gaming were virtually unlimited.[17]

Software applications capable of converting speech to data and back, from data to visual images at very low costs enabled engineers to merge video gaming to computer networks. Thus, the possibility of sending data, at high speeds, over telephone lines and through wireless broadband systems, made video gaming an attractive business proposition. By all measures, advertisers now recognized that in-game advertising was a prime way to target specific demographics, especially younger groups who were increasingly moving away from television and instead favoring computers and video games. The first online game ads were developed in 2006 but had been confined to clients such as the Air Force, Twentieth Century Fox, Axe, BP America Inc., Coca Cola, Ford Motors, Dodge, and other corporate brands.

Business potential was enormous for both general video game sales and for advertising. For example, according to data based on aggregates from the NPD Group (formerly the National Purchase Diary), which is the leading global provider of consumer and retail market research information for a wide range of industries, along with data from the Entertainment Software Association (ESA), Motion Picture Association of America (MPAA), Records Industry

Association of America (RIAA), and the International Federation of the Pho-
nographic Industry (IFPI), in the United States alone, video games earned more
than $18.5 billion in hardware, accessories, and game sales in 2007. Of that,
approximately 267.8 million games were sold across all platforms—PC games,
portable devices, and consoles.[18] Once the Wii gaming system was introduced,
two new groups emerged as gaming consumers in 2007 that included people
aged thirty-five and over and more women playing video games. Also, the
older groups were uncharacteristically attracted to the Wii Nintendo console.
The latter features motion detection controls, which enables users to simulate
actual activities such as playing guitar as in the bestselling game *Guitar Hero*
and for the older players, bowling. Wii also actively targets older users by
simulating games such as yoga, Pilates, and other rehabilitation exercises.

These groups joined the traditional eighteen- to thirty-five-year-old male
demographic to boost video game sales to record highs. This was not unex-
pected, according to the Entertainment Software Association's (ESA) Web
page as the average game player is thirty-five years old.[19] [20] Twenty-five
percent are under eighteen years of age, 49 percent are eighteen to forty-nine
years old, and 26 percent are fifty years old and above. In terms of gender,
56 percent of online game players are male. Also, women age eighteen years
old and above represent a greater portion of the game-playing population (33
percent) than male minors aged seventeen and under (18 percent). Additional
data from Abt SRBI Inc., a global research and strategy organization, suggests that a little more than a quarter of Americans, age twelve to fifty-five
years old, report playing online (27 percent) and video (27 percent) games.
Remarkably, since 2004, there has been a marked increase in online gaming.
Many more Americans now play video games on wireless devices such as
cell phones and PDAs. Growth in video game sales surpassed both the movie
and music industries in 2007.

Clearly, political entrepreneurs saw the now family-friendly video game
entertainment industry as an ideal market for seeking votes and communicating with the electorate during the 2008 election cycle. By purchasing
advertising in online games, the campaign mainly targeted the eighteen- to
thirty-four-year-old male demographic, the mainstream demographic for the
hard-core gamer. This group was considered by media analysts "hard to get
to because they don't watch much TV and they don't read a lot."[21]

The convergence of interests between video gaming and political forces
took full advantage of the association with online communities that now incorporated social activity into the gaming experience. Business entrepreneurs
began developing software that permitted charging a monthly fee for users
or receiving revenue from site sponsors who allowed users to play for free
at beginning levels. A vast array of online video games included those that

offered real-time strategy games, cross-platform online play, and numerous multiplayer games. Multiplayer online role-playing games, a creation of the 1990s, permit a large number of individuals to interact with each other in the virtual world and were an excellent avenue for commercial brand advertising generally. But it was the Obama campaign that established a precedent by opening the door for political marketing through these uncharted avenues.

HOW OBAMA USED ONLINE
VIDEO GAMES IN THE 2008 CAMPAIGN

For the Obama campaign, the game was on. The decision to use video games in political campaigns was based upon two reasons; first, to attract the typical online game players who were considered young and uncommitted voters, and second, to build a loyalty among the same voters. The Obama campaign made a strategic decision to market their candidate, increase his public profile, and publicize his policies in a simplistic but effective way. The campaign recognized that voters needed images of a candidate who would identify with them and their interests. In the video games, Obama marketed himself as a new and different candidate who was most likely positioned to change Washington, DC. The Internet community, one would assume, shared distaste for top-down advertisements and was ready to warm up to the candidate who was ready to meet them in the virtual game venues.

From a historical sociocultural perspective, Obama's relative youthfulness and penchant for computer-based communications served him well. He easily adapted to the new technologies. Unlike other contenders, he had talked about how he used a Webcam and BlackBerry to stay in touch with his family as he campaigned across the country. He was clearly computer savvy and comfortable using the full potential of computer mediated technologies and major broadcast networks, which included his own dedicated satellite channels to communicate with the voters. For instance, Obama's embrace of the nonconventional media by using social networks such as Facebook, MySpace, Twitter, and YouTube to reach out to his supporters had been an essential and integral part of his mobilization strategy. After all, he had started as an underdog with very few resources and the Internet opportunities made all the difference in his bid to raise campaign funds and to become a serious contender for the White House. Therefore, while my.barackobama .com combined constant updates including his choice of running mate, videos, photos, ringtones, and events that gave his supporters a reason to stay excited, the extension of his campaign message over online gaming platforms was a narrow and targeted strategy.

And just how did he do it? For starters, there are two different types of in-game advertising which include "dynamic advertising" and "static advertising." Dynamic advertisements are generally placed in the game via an ad server. As Steve Gorman noted, "Such ads can be directed to particular geographical areas through the Internet Protocol addresses registered with Internet service providers when players' Xbox 360 consoles go online."[22] In addition, placing ads online allows the advertiser to choose a specific time slot during the campaign. Dynamic ads provided Obama's campaign staff with the ideal opportunity to incorporate billboard ads.[23] This was due to the complexity of campaign messages, perhaps occasioned by the campaign's need to present Obama's image and message in the most favorable way. The second variant, the static ads, were not the campaign's favored avenue. Static ads are placed directly into the games during the development phase of game production. Generally speaking, it is harder to replace the static ads but changes are possible through online updates and patches. Interestingly though, advertisers and developers have greater leverage at integrating the ads.

The campaign purchased advertisement space in several Internet-enabled video games operating through Microsoft's Xbox 360 console. Incidentally, Xbox online gamers, when polled for preferences among presidential candidates, overwhelmingly leaned toward candidate Obama.[24] Perhaps, one may speculate, the decision to use this avenue was based on a variety of advantages and practicalities of gaming hardware and not polling results. Nonetheless, the mechanics were simple enough. To be a part of the political process, Xbox 360 users first connected to the Internet—in order to be updated at frequent intervals with new features via online downloads. Each advertisement's screen time was brief and was rotated with those from other sponsors, mostly commercial ventures such as Burger King, Ford, and other regular merchandise. The campaign's core message remained static and focused on games that were suitable for general family entertainment, in terms of the Entertainment Software Rating Board (ESRB) content rating system. Several popular games including those published by Electronic Arts such as *Burnout Paradise* and *Madden NFL 09* were selected based on ratings and their potential to reach out to the widest possible voting blocks (see Table 8.1). Reports noted that the Obama campaign restricted the advertisements to users residing in ten battleground states including Iowa, Ohio, Florida, Indiana, Montana, North Carolina, Nevada, New Mexico, Colorado, and Wisconsin. The advertisements were aired in October 2008 through November 3, 2008, and with minor variations in duration of exposure. In smaller states, the advertisements were displayed throughout the month while in the larger states the duration was much shorter.[25]

The in-game ads were displayed as billboards that said "Early Voting has begun/VoteForChange.com."[26] The ads essentially displayed Obama's picture and directed potential voters to the campaign's early voting site, VoteForChange.com, a Web site that had more than 5 million visitors by October 2008.[27] An Obama campaign spokesperson epitomized the phenomena: "These ads will help us expand the reach of VoteForChange.com, so that more people can use this easy tool to find their early vote location and make sure their voice is heard."[28] [29] The Obama campaign had made the decision to expand both the process and electorate.

The strategy of pushing for early voting was, in part, a response to the nationwide expansion of early voting provisions and fewer restrictions on absentee voting. It had been estimated that about a third of the electorate would vote early and using video games for outreach purposes was considered one of the most efficient means to counter the perceived advantages that Republicans enjoyed during previous elections. Nationally, the Republican Party had developed an extensive database of voter information that the party relied on for its "get-out-the-vote operations."[30] Voting early meant avoiding long lines on Election Day, which was an attractive proposition for many of the young groups that Obama's campaign targeted. This demographic, commentators widely agreed, is not known to participate in the electoral process on Election Day.

OTHER CANDIDATES AND INTERNET TECHNOLOGIES

In many ways, Obama's campaign outperformed all his rivals in both the primary and national presidential elections. During the Democratic Party presidential primary, Obama's Internet fundraising greatly outpaced his main opponent, Senator Hillary Clinton. As the race to the White House progressed, the Clinton campaign suffered funding shortages and lapses in strategic organization. Perhaps for the campaigns with limited funding, embracing new media technologies was not a priority and advertising in online games was not considered at that stage of the race to be financially feasible.

The post-primary stage provided political entrepreneurs an opportunity to use the full resources available online. However, only Obama seized the moment. His campaign set the precedent during the primaries, by performing better than most in efforts to mobilize supporters and raise money online. It is fitting to point out that Obama's opponent, Senator John McCain, did not take advantage of the online video game platform for political advertisement although it was offered to his campaign team as an option by the video gaming industry. While commentators had already recognized that the Internet

Table 8.1.   Selected Popular Games Used in the 2008 Campaign Ads

Video Game	ESRB Content Rating	General Sales 2008 Avg. Ratio %
Madden NFL 09	E	85
NBA Live 08	E	68.5
Burnout Paradise	E 10+	88.3
Nascar 09	E	65.3
Need For Speed Carbon	E 10+	73
Need For Speed Pro Street	E 10+	67.8
NFL on Tour	E	49.5
NHL 09	E 10+	88.7
Skate	T	86.4
Guitar Hero 3	T	85.6
The Incredible Hulk	T	83.8

Source: News 4 Gamers (N4G)

was now a mainstream of political life in the United States, there was very clearly a deep digital divide between Senators McCain and Obama.[31] [32]

Although McCain had been a previous chairman of the U.S. Senate Committee on Commerce, Science, and Technology, at a personal level, he did not embrace technology to the extent that Obama did and was perceived by the youth as being "too old." Although during the campaign he outlined a range of e-government initiatives, McCain's political philosophy of "less intrusive government" seemed to be at odds with his goals of expanding the momentum to avail broadband technologies more widely. McCain made it worse for himself by admitting to the *New York Times* that he depended on his wife and staff to show him Web sites. He was quoted as stating that, "I am learning to get online myself. . . . And I will have that down fairly soon—getting on myself. I don't have to be a great communicator. I don't expect to set up my own blog, but becoming computer literate to the point where I can get the information that I need."[33] His campaign failed to turn around his image as "computer illiterate" thereby, perhaps, lessening his appeal among groups that frequented online gaming.

FUTURE IMPLICATIONS FOR
POLITICIANS AND POLITICAL CAMPAIGNS

Although Obama's campaign was the first to incorporate online video games in a presidential election, the implication for future political recruitment at local and state levels is clear. Political advertising through the medium of online video games is no longer a future possibility, it is already here! Access to the online gaming infrastructure will continue to be controlled by the vast array of telecommunications and entertainment corporate giants. The immediate outcome of the successful nature of Obama's campaign will, of course, mean the entry of additional corporate players in the emerging nexus between game publishers and political parties as well as interest groups and candidates for public office. Major publishers such as Electronic Arts, which published *Burnout Paradise* and the bulk of the games in which Obama placed ads, will be joined by American and international competitors. Although Electronic Arts did not endorse Candidate Obama, it welcomed the opportunity to be a part of this new business model.[34]

The top video game publishers are Nintendo, Activision, Ubisoft, Sony Computer Entertainment, Take-two Interactive, Sega Sammy Holdings, THQ, Microsoft Game Studios, Square Enix, Konami, Vivendi Games, Capcom, Namco Bandai Games, Disney Interactive Studios, Lucas Arts, Codemasters, Eidos Interactive, and Midway Games, among others. It is safe to argue that new players from among this list will enter the market in some form or another. It is possible that future campaigns will purchase ads in platforms other than Xbox 360—which was Obama's preferred outlet.[35] Potential entrants will include Sony and Nintendo. However, it is most unlikely that the new players in online video game campaign advertising will change the structure of cyber-democracy. The new features supplement existing political communication tools and those players who dominated in the past are better positioned to provide future leadership, at least in the short run.

Political ads of any kind are not cheap. Obama's campaign had an enormous advantage in terms of financial resources. The Campaign Media Analysis Group (CMAG), a service that monitors political advertising, noted that just before the election, between September 12, 2008, and October 11, 2008, Obama's campaign spent $71 million on approximately 130,000 ads compared to $32 million on about seventy thousand ads by John McCain, the Republican candidate.[36] Political interests seeking to advertise in the new media will have to contend with the high advertising costs associated with this venture. According to Massive, Inc., a subsidiary of Microsoft, advertising prices can range from $10,000 for brief product placement to six figures for large-scale ads. Video advertisements also varied and were approximately fifteen to sixty seconds, which was sufficient time for most viewers to notice. According to the Videogame Advertising Engagement Study led by Sandra Marshall and collaborators from the Cognitive Ergonomics Research Facility at San Diego State University, three-quarters of gamers notice ads while playing online games.[37] One may reasonably assume, therefore, that in the near future, acceptance of political ads in these games will be on condition that the ads do not interrupt the flow of the game and interfere with playing time. Thus, online game advertising

is just one of the new efficient technological means candidates may use to
better communicate with younger voters.

Double Fusion's pioneering research on advertising effectiveness validated
what many had assumed but never proven—that gamers not only noticed ads
in games but were impacted by them positively. The results of the study had
direct relevance to political advertising, asserting increasing ads in online
gaming would be effective at reaching out to targeted undecided voters. Another finding with direct relevance to political online campaigning was that
"not all ads are created equal—dynamic billboards, around-game interstitials,
sponsorships, and interactive product placements all offer different levels of
user engagement and pervasiveness in the game."[38]

Pundits regarded the strategy as targeting the "couch vote: online gamers."[39] Although the strategy to reach out to potential voters via online gaming
was an innovative campaign move, critics noted that some issues were un-
resolved or problematic. For example, influential blogger Dennis McCauley,
the editor of GamePolitics.com, a Web site that posts articles about the nexus
between politics and gaming, pondered why the Obama campaign got to
choose the games in which their ads appeared. It is possible that in the future
the appearance of ads from opposing candidates would lead to mudslinging.
Other critics preferred not to mix games with politics.[40 41]

Another line of criticism popularized in the electronic and print media was
that Obama himself had on several different occasions derided parents for
allowing their children too much time to play video games. While campaigning in a predominantly African American neighborhood, in Beaumont, Texas,
Obama urged parents to take an active role in helping their children with
homework and giving them less time to play video games. Obama stated,
"It's not good enough for you to say to your child, 'Do good in school.' And
then when that child comes home, you got the TV set on, you got the radio
on, you don't check their homework, there is not a book in the house, you've
got the video game playing." Again, in Gary, Indiana, while on the campaign
trail, Obama told the audience, "You've got to turn off the television set in
your house once in a while; you've got to put the video game away once in a
while."[42] In other words, for Senator Obama, video games were a metaphor
for underachievement in school and were part of the problem of declining
achievement levels in American schools.

The use of the same media that Obama was quick to criticize created a
paradox. The Obama campaign not only identified online gaming as an outlet
for placing political ads, but recognized video games as a way to reach out
to and communicate to a very specific demographic with very specific interests. For example, in Riverside, California, at its Market Street headquarters,
ordinary video gaming was used by the Obama campaign strategists to rally

younger voters. During the presidential primaries, Obama's campaign sponsored a "video-game night" to gather young people to make calls and to prepare for a get-out-the-vote rally the next day.[43] Perhaps, this argument is only mildly relevant to the issue at hand. What is important is that the campaign saw video games as an intrinsic part of American culture and that gaming provided important opportunities for political communication.

From a market standpoint, the simplistic argument is that the Obama campaign reached out to video game suppliers to take advantage of the opportunity to "sell the candidate's message" and popularize his party. On their part, video game publishers were in the business of making money and accepted political advertising in video online games in the same way as radio, television, and print media outlets. However, Obama's exhortation of parents to limit children's use of video gaming was taken out of context, and still, made some rounds in the media and blogosphere.

Probably a more serious problem is the fact that while Obama's campaign rhetoric derided pettiness and trivialization of politics, the very art of embracing embedding political messages within entertainment games undermined the strength of his message of change. It is fair to say that while Obama's campaign was a defining moment in using online video games for political advertising, there is the possibility of the reification of the risky notion that politics is a simple game and therefore adding to the now well-documented cynicism in American politics.[44] [45] [46] [47]

Although political video games in general can be an entertainment enterprise, there are potential risks to civic engagement. This is particularly the case in situations where important policy issues are trivialized. Therefore, the possible consequence of injecting trivia is to lower levels of civic participation in certain groups. The matter seems to have gained further currency due to such political events as Muntader al Zeidi, an Iraqi journalist, throwing shoes at then visiting American president George W. Bush. The event was quickly engineered into online video games for entertainment purposes. The incident took place on December 14, 2008, at the end of President Bush's eight years in office and was widely shown on the Internet and television stations around the world. Essentially, the game involved simulating throwing virtual shoes at the president's head to see how many times he could be hit. One of the games, *Sock and Awe*, reportedly received 1.4 million hits on the Web site www.sockandawe.com. Similarly, another game produced in Norway attracted 2.69 million online viewers at the Web site www.kroma.no/2008/bushgame.[48]

There are other examples of the trivialization of the presidency communicated in video images embedded within video games. For instance, the French company VerSim released a game titled *Commander-in-Chief* and it was an "Obama administration simulator."[49] Other recent games with political content include *President Forever, Democracy, Darfur is Dying*, and *The Political Machine 2008. President Forever*, developed for the 2004 election cycle by Canadian software company, TheorySpark, used real-life poll numbers to simulate presidential elections in a fun and interesting way. In this game, players take control of all aspects of the campaign in an effort to reach voters across the nation. Likewise, *The Political Machine*, created by Stardock, was an election-themed game, rated for teens. In this game, a simulation of the election between John Kerry and George W. Bush (interchangeable with other candidates of individual preference), provided an opportunity for players to be a part of the political process, watching the making of history as a candidate assumes the highest office in the land. While some of the activities in simulated political video games are not campaign activities, they do serve to reinforce the notion that politics, especially presidential recruitment, is a game of trivia and subject to the same entertainment properties as all other games.

The scenario seems an unintended consequence of the pending expansion of placing ads in online games. In this case, it is a convergence of e-business with e-governance at its best. As Associated Press writer Devlin Barrett pointed out, the Obama ads were mainly juxtaposed in games involving NASCAR, NBA, NHL, and skateboarding, "meaning EA Sports motto: it's in the game, now applies to presidential politics as well."[50] It is possible to interpret the aforementioned assertion loosely to imply that presidential politics is much like a game or a popularity contest as one would observe in popular culture. Arguably, therefore, the juxtaposition of important political and policy messages in video games undermines possibilities of using new media to strengthen the quality of political discourse and processes in subsequent elections. Hopefully, the fact that campaign ads in online games were only aired briefly may mitigate against such possibilities but that is to be empirically tested in future studies.

CONCLUSION

It can be speculated that being perceived as the most pop culturally "clued-in" presidential candidate in the 2008 presidential campaign helped Obama forge a special bond with not only younger voters but with all consumers of video games. None of the other candidates from any parties used this medium in their campaigns. From the start of his race for the White House, Obama's "electronic campaign optics" served him well. His campaign learned from the experiences of past e-campaign strategies and looked for opportunities to outperform other campaigns. The very possibility of adding billboards to online video games, an invention that only came to fruition after 2006, was the niche market the campaign yearned for and actually received. Therefore, the application of the novelty of online video game ads in battleground states perhaps boosted his broad strategy to win some of the traditional Republican "red" states and the White House. Communication in video games was visually powerful and, perhaps, made it easy for his campaign to take advantage of the candidate's immensely exciting and mythological story. It was possible to get to know Obama, a relatively new figure in national politics, in a more relaxed manner via a simple video game. It was as if Obama's campaign was inviting the public to join in and play a game with him!

From a philosophical standpoint, technologies of the future will continue to be available for candidates running for public office. Humans, as Aristotle had insinuated, are political animals and humans, as we all know, like to play. Video games have been a part of the arsenals of entertainment and, for some ages, the most important free-time activity. Video game manufacturers did not lose sight of this fact. In fact, over the years, they developed several election-themed games, often simulating candidates or parties, not infrequently represented as the party mascot of the Democrat's donkey and the Republican's elephant. But political game simulations were not the same thing as placing political ads in video games. In this chapter, it has been articulated that video games can serve as both an instrument of culture which frequently communicates indirect political messages and a means to make appeals for political support and to develop party loyalty. The campaign took politics to a popular leisure outlet and expanded market opportunities for the online gaming industry. From a political communication standpoint, the Obama campaign has made it possible to make a transition from extrapolating political messages from video presentations presented in the form of entertainment scripts to a more direct instrument for political recruitment.

NOTES

1. Douglas Holmes, *eGov: eBusiness Strategies for Government* (London: Nicholas Brealey Publishing, 2001), 207.

2. Matthew Hindman, "The Real Lessons of Howard Dean: Reflections on the First Digital Campaign," *Perspectives on Politics* 3, no. 1 (2005): 121–28.

3. Bruce Bimber and Richard Davis, *Campaigning Online: The Internet in U.S. Elections* (New York: Cambridge University Press, 2003).

4. David A. Dulio, Donald L. Groff, and James A. Thurber, "Untangled Web: Internet Use During the 1998 Election," *PS: Political Science and Politics* 32, no.1 (1999): 53–58.

5. Paul S. Herrnson, *Congressional Elections: Campaigning at Home and in Washington* (Washington, DC: CQ Press, 2004).

6. David C. King. "Catching Voters in the Web in the Elections of 1998," in *Democracy.com: Governance in a Networked World*, ed. Elaine Ciulla Karmack and Joseph S. Nye, Jr. (Hollis, NH: Hollis Publishing, 1999), 99–123.

7. Sonia T. Puopolo, "The Web and U.S. Senate Campaigns 2000," *American Behavioral Scientist* 44, no. 12 (2001): 2030–47.

8. Daniel M. Shea and Michael J. Burton, *Campaign Craft: The Strategies, Tactics, and Art of Political Campaign Management* (Westport, CT: Praeger, 2001).

9. Paul S. Herrnson, Atiya Kai Stokes-Brown, and Matthew Hindman, "Campaign Politics and the Digital Divide: Constituency Characteristic Considerations, and Candidate Internet Use in State Legislative Elections," *Political Research Quarterly* 60, no.1 (March 2007): 31–42.

10. Wayne Rash, Jr., *Politics on the Nets: Wiring the Political Process* (New York: W. H. Freeman, 1997).

11. Jennifer Stromer-Galley, "On-line Interaction and Why Candidates Avoid It," *Journal of Communication* 50, no. 4 (2000): 111–32.

12. Benjamin Svetkey, "Barack Obama: President Rock Star," *Entertainment Weekly*, www.ew.com/ew/article/0,,20254654,00.html (16 June 2009).

13. John A. Quelch and Katherine E. Jocz, *Greater Good: How Good Marketing Makes for Better Democracy* (Cambridge, MA: Harvard Business School Press, 2008).

14. Svetkey, *Entertainment Weekly*, 22–26.

15. Alexander Shafto Douglas, *Computers and Society: An Inaugural Lecture.* Delivered on 27 April 1972, London School of Economics, 1973.

16. *Economist*, "Video-Games Industry: A Big Merger in the Video Games Industry," London, www.economist.com/daily/news/displaystory.cfm?story_id=10238617 (4 December 2007).

17. Alan Stone, *How America Got On-Line: Politics, Markets, and the Revolution in Telecommunications* (London: M. E. Sharpe, 1997).

18. Eric Bangeman, "Growth of Gaming in 2007 Far Outpaces Movies, Music," *Ars Technica*, arstechnica.com/hgaming/news/2008/ (24 January 2008).

19. Karen Brooks, "Obama Campaign Buys Ads Inside Online Video Games in Battleground States," *The Dallas Morning News*, www.dallasnews.com (17 October 2008).

20. Entertainment Software Association (ESA), "Essential Facts About The Computer and Video Game Industry," www.theesa.com/facts/pdfs/ESA_EF_2008.pdf (23 March 2009).

21. Steve Gorman, "Obama Buys First Video Game Campaign Ads," *Reuters*, reuters.com/article/technology (15 October 2008).

22. Steve Gorman, *Reuters*.

23. Karen Brooks, *The Dallas Morning News*.

24. Karen Brooks, *The Dallas Morning News*.

25. Devlin Barrett, "Video Games Feature Ads for Obama's Campaign," *Breitbart.com*, Associated Press, breitbart.com (14 October 2008).

26. Chris Dannen, "Tech Watch: Obama Launches Video Game Campaign," *FAST COMPANY.com*, www.fastcompany.com/news (15 October 2008).

27. Steve Gorman, *Reuters*.

28. Karen Brooks, *The Dallas Morning News*.

29. Steve Gorman, *Reuters*.

30. Stephen Ohlemacher, "Democrats Bank Early Votes in Battleground States," Associated Press, www.electiononline.org (21 October 2008).

31. David Kestenbaum, "The Digital Divide Between McCain and Obama, NPR," www.npr.org (3 April 2008).

32. Steve Schifferes, "Internet Key to Obama Victories," *BBC News*, www.bbc .co.uk (12 June 2008).

33. David Kestenbaum, *NPR*.

34. Misha Davenport, "Obama Will Be the First Candidate to Advertise in Video Games: GAME ON—Even Video Game Players Can't Avoid Political Ads," *Chicago Sun Times*, www.suntimes.com/entertainment (15 October 2008).

35. Dave Itzkoff, "Obama Ads Appear in Video Game," *New York Times*, 15 October 2008.

36. Christina Bellantoni, "Cash-Flush Obama Steamrolls McCain in Ads; $150 Million More Raised in September," *The Washington Post*, 20 October 20008, A6.

37. Double Fusion, "Double Fusion Releases Landmark Research on Videogame Advertising Effectiveness; Multi-Title, Multi-Advertiser Study Establishes Key Factors That Influence and Attract Gamers, Business Publications," *Business Wire*, find articles.com/p/articles/mi_m0EIN/is_2007_July_23/ai_n19378379 (23 July 2007).

38. Double Fusion, *Business Wire*.

39. Karen Brooks, *The Dallas Morning News*.

40. Karen Brooks, *The Dallas Morning News*.

41. "Game Politics.com: Where Politics and Video Games Collide," www.game politics.com/2008/10/09/report-obama-ads-burnout-paradise (9 October 2008).

42. Winnie Forster, *The Encyclopedia of Game Machines: Consoles, Handhelds & Home Computers 1972–2005* (New York: Hagen Schmid, 2005).

43. Jim Miller, "Candidates Court Young Voters," *The Press Enterprise* (Riverside, CA), 27 January 2008, A1.

44. David H. Kamens and Charles Cappell, "Confidence and Cynicism in American Institutions: Consequences for Political Participation," Paper presented at the Cultural Turn Conference: Institutions and Institution Building, Santa Barbara, California, March 7–8, 2003.

45. Demetrios Caraley, "Elections and Dilemma of American Democratic Governance: Reflections," *Political Science Quarterly* 104, no. 1 (Spring, 1989): 19–40.

46. Mari Boor Tonn and Valerie A. Endress, "Looking Under the Hood and Tinkering with Voter Cynicism: Ross Perot and 'Perspective by Incongruity,'" *Rhetoric & Public Affairs* 4, no. 2 (Summer 2001): 281–308.

47. Priscilla L. Southwell and Kevin D. Pirch, "Political Cynicism and Mobilization of Black Voters," *Social Science Quarterly* 84, no. 1 (December 2003): 906–17.

48. Egan Orion, "'Throw Shoes at Bush Games Appear Online' Therapeutic and Great Fun," *The Inquirer*, www.theinquirer.net/inquirer/news/086/1050086/-throw -shoes-at-bush-games-appear-online (17 December 2008).

49. Dennis McCauley, "The Power Up: Unsatisfying Simulator of Obama Administration," *Philadelphia Inquirer*, 6 February 2009, www.philly.com/inquirer/ columnists/dennis_mccauley/20090206_Power_Up__Unsatisfying_simulator_of_ Obama_administration.html.

50. Devlin Barrett, Associated Press, breitbart.com (14 October 2008).

9

Political Campaigns in the Twenty-First Century: Implications of New Media Technology

Melissa M. Smith

2008 CHANGED POLITICS AS USUAL

The extensive use of new media in the 2008 presidential campaign caught many by surprise, but a few people saw the shift in politics coming. Micah Sifry was one who looked into his crystal ball and predicted a rise in the use of social networking media and voter-generated content.[1] That prompted him to cofound techPresident.com, a blog established to analyze how candidates were using the Web. It featured the comments of political professionals, many of whom were involved in 2008 political races.

Sifry and his fellow bloggers had a lot to talk about during the 2008 election. This was the first election in which more than half of all Americans used the Internet to find out more about candidates, share their own thoughts about campaigns and issues, and work to mobilize others.[2] Sifry's conclusion, even before the 2008 campaign was fully under way, was that the days of top-down campaigns are over. Instead, if you viewed campaign organization as a 3-D object, it would look less like an inverted triangle and more like a mowed-over Gumby—flat, but with lateral connections. While this reduces campaign organizations to a somewhat simplistic metaphor, it does dramatize how the new media approaches taken by the 2008 presidential candidates have changed the face of campaign messaging and management and turned political campaigns on their heads.

POWER TO THE PEOPLE

The 2008 presidential race utilized several different types of new media, many of which were not even available during the 2004 election. Campaigns made use of social networking via Facebook, MySpace, and Twitter, encouraged supporters to start blogs and post creations to YouTube, and published the most technically sophisticated candidate Web sites that have ever been used by presidential candidates. While these are all very different types of media platforms, they do share a few common characteristics: they provide a way for the average American to generate his or her own content regarding political campaigns; they provide an avenue for feedback to candidates, campaigns, and news providers; and they allow candidates and campaigns to collect huge amounts of personal data. This flattening of campaign organization and message delivery allowed average Americans to participate in the primaries and general election in ways never before possible.

According to the Pew Internet and American Life Project, 60 percent of Internet users went online for news about politics or campaigns in the 2008 election. These people were searching out information about campaigns online from the campaigns themselves, news sources, blogs, or other outlets. The survey also found that 59 percent of Internet users shared or received campaign information via one or more of these tools: e-mail, instant messaging, text messages, or Twitter.[3] It is clear that Americans were taking advantage of the opportunity to follow—and comment on or engage in—the campaigns using these new media platforms.

For the campaigns this quest to conquer new media leads to two things: votes and the collection of data. Winning the election is the short-term goal, and it is the one that is most visible to the public. But the long-term goal, especially for parties, is the collection of information about potential voters. For many years, both the Republican and Democratic national parties kept lists of voters and likely voters. State parties also maintained lists, which often contained the names of those participating in both primary and general elections. But as campaigns began to bump against the inability of traditional media to disseminate targeted messages, they started looking for innovative ways to collect more information about voters that would allow them to produce more finely targeted messages. In 2004, for instance, microtargeting allowed President George W. Bush's reelection team to find lapsed Republicans watching the Golf Channel and listening to country music radio stations. President Barack Obama's campaign went far beyond that, tracking the social networks built by individuals within a campaign site, keeping detailed records of how individuals responded to various campaign messages, and even tracking which e-mail messages prompted individuals to open a particular link.[4] According to Jonathan Karush, a political consultant, "The online voter files are becoming more comprehensive each cycle, with massive amounts of individual data available to campaigns. Soon campaigns will be able to massively target and approach potential voters on a very personal level."[5] In today's society, information is power, and the Obama campaign used a savvy new media strategy to win the power battle in 2008. That strategy placed the Internet and new media squarely in the middle of the campaign, rather than relegating it to a defacto parallel campaign. New media was the engine that drove the campaign, and that engine pumped both energy and money into Obama's election effort.

Using new media to locate and interact with potential voters and supporters allowed the Obama campaign to interact with people in ways that had never been used in campaigns before. This served to energize young people—who are often the first adopters of new technology—and led to the inversion of the typical campaign management. "The ability to connect via the Internet to groups, segments, and individuals changes everything. It flattens the process and creates a bottom-up approach to participation," noted Joe Trippi, who headed up Howard Dean's campaign in 2004.[6] The top-down strategy that had been used in most previous elections—and had succeeded in 2004—failed in 2008, acknowledged David All, a Republican political strategist.[7] He said the Internet has forever changed not only presidential politics, but also the entire electoral process.

Communication scholars have pondered what affect the Internet would have on democracy and political campaigns. Few predicted that it would so quickly change the structure of campaign organization and supporter participation in campaigns. In 2000 Norris theorized that the Internet's influence on politics would either be mobilization or reinforcement.[8] Mobilization refers to a new degree of empowerment in a digital world, while reinforcement refers to the Internet strengthening existing patterns of political participation. Obama's success in 2008 using the Internet seems to point in the direction of mobilization, as his campaign was able to move a significant number of people from being passive onlookers to active participants in his campaign for the White House.

Obama was clearly the leader in using new media to his campaign's advantage, as his supporters were more likely to take part in a wider range of online political activities, as well as text messaging.[9] His online supporters were also more likely to create content through online social networks, share video sites, use Twitter, and use blogs. His campaign was able to strike a balance "between top-down control and anarchy."[10]

Obama was also extraordinarily successful at online fundraising, bringing in more than a half billion dollars online.[11] In September 2008, he raised $100 million online, most of it from donors giving less than $100 each. He collected more than thirteen million e-mail addresses and sent more than seven thousand different messages via e-mail during the course of the campaign.[12] Many of those messages were targeted to specific donation levels. In comparison,

Senator John F. Kerry collected only three million e-mail addresses in his 2004 presidential campaign. Obama had a million people signed up to receive his text messages, and more than seven million people supported him through social networking sites. For some on Obama's campaign, the Internet provided the opportunity to draw individuals into the political process who might never have participated before, or who might have previously felt left out of the process. According to one Obama staffer, "Even before I joined the campaign, the fundamental premise was to help put the political process into people's own hands."[13]

FUTURE CAMPAIGNS AND NEW MEDIA

Few will argue with Obama's success, but the question remains—will his use of new media mark the beginning of a different way of running election campaigns? Most political consultants agree that the ground rules have changed, but say that it will be impossible for most candidates to replicate Obama's success—mainly because they are not Barack Obama. He is seen as a one-in-a-million candidate—the one perceived as leading a movement, not just running for president. His uniqueness, ability to organize people, and unparalleled fundraising lifted him above the average presidential candidate in terms of voter campaign involvement. But many of the resources for that involvement were delivered through his campaign Web site, and other candidates can follow his example in that area.

Web Sites Are the Foundation

Just a few months after the presidential election, one consultant said he already had clients asking how they could have a Web presence like Obama's.[14] However, he doesn't see that as realistic. Jonathan Karush described Obama as a "transformational political figure" who would have been successful online even without the talent he assembled in his online team.[15] However, Karush noted that Obama built on a technology foundation laid by previous presidential candidates: "The Obama campaign simply took the next evolutionary step in the development of the Web as a powerful campaign medium."[16]

Karush indicated future candidates can benefit from a solid online strategy, but it requires devoting the necessary resources to build a good, strong Web site.[17] He said one of Obama's campaign strengths was that his Web site empowered regional and neighborhood leaders through online organizational tools. For instance, the Obama campaign made available downloadable campaign materials, provided guidance for hosting fundraisers, allowed volunteers to upload information about coffees and debate watches they hosted, and even allowed volunteers to personalize Obama's campaign materials. This is a tactic that can be implemented by other candidates, but it will require allocating the necessary resources to build and maintain the site, plus require staffing to oversee the site as the campaign progresses.

Others agree that the Web is key, but they differ in how they think it might be used in the future. For instance, some political media strategists see a merging of the Web and television. Instead of watching a political event on television and using a laptop computer or cell phone to surf and provide feedback, they see the day coming when it will all be linked together as a stand-alone medium. The Web provides a depth of information that one consultant said is not possible on television because of the limits based on airtime, commercial breaks, and channel surfing.[18] Having an all-in-one device will simplify the process and make it easier for individuals to follow political events and information. Before this day arrives, however, candidates must develop strategies that locate volunteers wherever they are in cyberspace: whether that is surfing Web sites from a computer, checking e-mail from a cell phone, following Twitter feeds, or hanging out on Facebook.

Right now, everyone agrees that candidates must devote more money to building their sites, and they should make wise choices regarding who is designing this all-important part of the campaign. Mindy Finn, a Republican new media strategist, acknowledged many campaign Web sites are actually worse than they were four years ago. She attributed this to campaigns that hire designers who are straight out of college. These Web designers have taken all the classes, understand the basics of the software, and can build nice-looking sites, but their Web sites do not always offer the functionality needed by a campaign.[19]

This point is echoed by other consultants and campaign professionals, who say that campaigns should not look for the cheapest option when it comes to Web sites. Instead of looking for bargains, they should be looking for people who understand how political campaigns work—and who can translate that to an online site.

It is not cheap to build and maintain a good site. However, it is vital for candidates to understand that the new frontier of campaigning lies not in simply sending messages, but in empowering volunteers and supporters. Jonathan Karush said the smartest move Obama made was empowering regional and neighborhood leaders: "He created a tiered community-based online approach that put the burden of organizing on key community individuals that never had to be physically connected to any campaign personnel."[20] This was not only organizationally effective, but it was less expensive than the traditional method of establishing field teams and community leaders through the use of campaign personnel.

Future candidates will have to decide how much of their budgets should be dedicated to new media. One strategist suggested that "what we need to do moving forward is look at the breakout of budgets between phones, direct mail and TV, and allocate proportionally based on where the eyeballs are."[21] And the eyeballs are moving online. In the United States, more than half of the entire adult population went online during the 2008 election to take part in or get information about candidates and campaigns. The Internet is now second only to television as a leading source for campaign news, having surpassed newspapers as a source of news in 2008.[22]

This means that future candidates must harness the ability to find supporters and empower them wherever they are, and that means a multifaceted strategy using Web and other new media. David All said the potential is there for future candidates to go beyond Obama's success, but it hinges on having the right new media vision and strategy. According to All, "Any candidate, at any level, can and should use modern media strategies to propel himself or herself to victory. A candidate must have the wherewithal to utilize what's out there and package themselves in an appropriate manner."[23]

Social Networks and Politics

One of the most successful areas for the Obama new media team was its strategy involving social networking. In addition to establishing a presence on both Facebook and MySpace, the campaign set up its own social networking site, called my.barackobama.com, which made it easy for supporters to link with other volunteers, give money to the campaign, and watch their personal fundraising thermometers rise as they encouraged friends and family to donate, and even allowed the campaign to use volunteers to take part in a virtually organized national phone bank. More than two million Americans registered at the site and used it during the campaign.[24]

The site included a custom interface that allowed visitors to obtain lists of voters from the Democratic National Party database. Volunteers were encouraged to call several voters and report information back to the campaign through the networking site. It's estimated that information was recorded through this site about the opinions of two hundred million Americans, and that Obama's Web operation, and those of other Democratic candidates, helped grow the DNC database to ten times its size in 2004.[25]

The success of the Obama campaign in this area has prompted many candidates considering a run in 2010 to look at pursuing a social networking strategy. But many are not sure where to begin. If a candidate has unlimited funds, he or she can build a site similar to my.barackobama.com. However, most candidates are not rolling in money and need a less expensive option. For candidates in small races, establishing a presence on Facebook and MySpace is enough. Jonathan Karush suggested those sites can provide candidates with a way to organize and motivate supporters. He acknowledged, "Aggregator sites like Facebook are capturing a massive amount of online time in one location, providing a more structured outlet for campaigns to push message, organizing, and fundraising."[26] The largest growing demographic on Facebook is people over the age of fifty, said David All, and "This site isn't going anywhere fast and will be a continued tool that must be utilized by any serious candidate for years to come."[27] But when running in higher-profile races involving larger numbers of potential voters, some consultants say that it might pay to invest in your own site. While it might be prohibitively expensive to build a social networking site from scratch, there are software programs that can be customized for political candidates.

WeTheCitizens is one of several companies offering software that allows a combination of networking and real-world activities. The software's aim is to get volunteers out knocking on doors for candidates. Early clients included Georgia governor Sonny Perdue and Rudy Guiliani's presidential primary campaign. A less expensive alternative might be Politics4All, which is a free service that allows candidates and advocacy groups to create profile pages and identify supporters. A more premium package for candidates—which isn't free—allows them to use an online donation tool, as well as receive demographic information based on U.S. Census data.[28] These are only two of the many software companies hoping to capitalize on Obama's new media success.

Early indications are that candidates in smaller races are scrambling to get on the social media bandwagon. Even mayoral and city council members in cities such as St. Petersburg, Florida, are making use of these platforms. Candidates in St. Petersburg are building a presence on Facebook, and invitations to join these political campaigns are finding their way onto members' pages. Candidates are also providing links to Twitter from campaign Web sites.[29] Twitter has unlimited potential, predicted David All and he said a candidate now has to be on Twitter to be taken seriously: "Twitter has created an entire new universe for conversation and discourse and the candidates that properly understand that very well may be the ones who end up winning."[30]

One thing that some people caution against is jumping into social networking without a well-defined strategy. Developing a new media presence is important, but one consultant cautions that candidates have to avoid buying into the hype surrounding these new technologies and focus on tools that will actually help them in their campaigns, not just capitalize on the buzz surrounding new media. According to one strategist, "You've got to think about what is really true."[31] In other words, a candidate should not try to use new media without having an understanding about how it might benefit his or her campaign.

There are countless politicians in current races with little guidance about how to use social networking. Most of them have profiles on Facebook or are on Twitter because they have heard that these are tools they should be using. But that doesn't mean they are using them very well. Instead of tweeting about serious topics, many candidates are posting updates about such mundane topics as their morning workouts, their TV show preferences, and their children's latest exploits, and that is probably not going to be effective. "Most of these people have not figured out how to use new digital tools for campaign purposes," remarked Darrell West, an expert on digital technology and social networking with the Brookings Institution. "They're viewing it as informal conversations as opposed to serious political communications, and they're wasting their time."[32]

But not all political consultants are sure that social networking always leads to a profitable investment of time and money for candidates. According to one Republican strategist, "There's no doubt that MySpace and Facebook can gather significant numbers of supporters, but I think the jury is out on whether or not those individuals can be mobilized from online to offline."[33] And, for candidates, that mobilization is crucial. While it is important for a candidate to identify and message his or her supporters, it is also crucial that those supporters be given opportunities to work for the candidate—whether it is knocking on doors to hand out campaign literature or asking others to donate to the campaign. The Obama campaign was able to engineer that mobilization, but it is not something that automatically happens just because a candidate has a social networking site.

It is important to have someone involved with the campaign who understands how to use new media. In fact, some people point out that technology does not stop moving, which makes it more important to find someone who is an expert in this area. Some experts point to an eventual convergence of the Web, texting, Twitter, and other social media on apps for smartphones such as the iPhone and BlackBerry. In fact, smartphones may become more like mini-laptop computers, which makes it even more important for political candidates to develop cell phone number lists. It is also possible that candidates could take advantage of the GPS function in cell phones that is predicted to be available in about half the phones in use by 2010.[34] Such technology could enable supporters to easily locate fellow volunteers to contact for the campaign, or even make door-to-door campaigning a thing of the past. "Most social networking tools, including Facebook, Twitter, and YouTube, either didn't exist or weren't a factor four years ago," noted Micah Sifry. "It's impossible to imagine what will be available by the next election cycle."[35] For a political candidate, the key is to stay on top of the technology, and that usually requires hiring people with specialized knowledge.

Sending a Message

Although both the Obama and the McCain campaigns made use of e-mail, most consultants see texting as the future of one-on-one campaign messaging. Micah Sifry, whose politics and technology blog attracted comments from both Republicans and Democrats during the election, says technology is changing politics. "Today's technologies are becoming as commonplace and mainstream as the telephone was to past generations," he noted. "It is fundamentally changing how candidates and the public interact."[36] One study reported that 77 percent of Internet experts said mobile phones will become "the primary Internet communications platform for a majority of people across the world."[37] Those surveyed said they expect the computing power of phones to continue to increase, as well as the implementation of universal standards for the devices.

This makes it even more important for candidates and parties to compile cell phone number lists. Barack Obama's team reportedly collected more than two million cell phone numbers by announcing his vice presidential candidate by text.[38] Texting has become quite frequent in American society, with sporting events, companies, and even television shows such as American Idol asking people to use their phones to text information or vote. Messages are limited to 160 characters, but that has not slowed the rate of texting. In October 2008, it is estimated that more than twenty-nine billion text messages were sent, which is more than the number of cell phone calls placed that month.[39]

The problem for candidates is that cell phone numbers are not usually published, and there is no central phone directory that can be used as a basis to build a candidate's phone list. So, the collection of phone numbers is often a problem for candidates. Plus, there's the fact that some people don't want to receive text messages from political candidates. Text message lists are opt-in only lists, so if a person is sent a text message, he or she must initiate the relationship by opting in. Candidates generally provide a way for supporters to sign up for text messages from the campaign Web site, but that is a relatively slow way to build a call list.

Other techniques suggested by political strategists include:

- Asking supporters to forward a text message to their friends. When this is built around a contest, it can generate a lot of new numbers.
- Encouraging people attending a political event to text their comments and thoughts during the proceedings.

- Making sure that a text number or shortcode (five or six letters that function as a phone number for text) is printed on all campaign literature and prominently displayed on the campaign Web site.

Although many candidates are concentrating on building text message lists, consultants and strategists warn against abandoning e-mail. One Republican strategist still labels e-mail as the "killer app." David All noted that "If you can't master e-mail, you can't master the world of modern media. Nothing is more important in the fight for the Internet than e-mail."[40] Because texting is limited to 160 characters, e-mail is often touted as the best way to urge supporters to take a particular action or expand on a candidate's ideas.

Because the demographics of those using e-mail now skews older, professionals advocate using both e-mail and texting. While there may be some overlap, this strategy can help campaigns make sure they are getting the message to younger voters who may focus on texting and rarely check e-mail. David All warned, "You have an entire generation of folks under age 25 no longer using e-mails, not even using Facebook; a majority are using text messaging."[41] Texting lists are going to be required for future candidates to keep in touch with and motivate younger voters.

Obama was also the first presidential candidate to purchase ad space inside a video game. They were placed inside nine video games and appeared as billboards and other signage. Because game consoles are connected to the Internet, the ads were available in different states at different times. The billboards in the games reminded players that early voting had begun in their states and directed them to the campaign Web site.[42] Advertising Age noted the placement as historic, but not surprising: "We as advertisers have used the gaming space to reach the 18- to 34-year-old demographic, so why shouldn't a presidential candidate use it as well? Of course, as Gamepolitics.com brings up, there's the issue of ad integration into T- or M-rated titles that may conflict with a candidate's family values."[43] For future candidates who want to make use of video game ads, the rating of the games is something that should be considered. While few candidates probably want to place ads in Grand Theft Auto, sports games such as the popular "Madden" football series might make an attractive buy for some candidates. The key is to find supporters wherever they are in cyberspace. Gaming ads present another avenue through which candidates might be able to connect with younger Americans.

DIY: Empowering Volunteers

Another area that is important for current and future candidates is the ability of the Internet and new media to provide opportunities for volunteers to organize their own "mini" campaigns for a candidate. While candidates such as Howard Dean and Ron Paul pursued a more "bottom-up" campaign organization, neither of them was able to simultaneously flatten the organization and maintain control of the campaign. Andrew Rasiej, founder of the Personal Democracy Forum, noted, "As far as major political circles were concerned, Howard Dean failed, and therefore the Internet didn't work."[44] Republican Ron Paul tried a different approach, building a Web site to use as a campaign hub, but allowing volunteers to organize campaign events and fundraising. The result was characterized by one observer as "Internet anarchy."[45] While Paul saw some success and was able to raise a significant amount of money via the Internet, the campaign never really gained traction.

Obama, on the other hand, managed to control the chaos that is a natural outgrowth of a more "bottom-up" campaign organization. Supporters were given the freedom to use my.barackobama.com to organize activities on their own, but resources were provided to help them achieve greater success. For instance, volunteers were "trained" in the basics of community organizing and received tips on how to host parties, raise money, and even canvass door-to-door using materials they could download from the social networking site. One Obama technology officer said the key to mobilizing the volunteers was the ability to move people from simply observing to actually working for the campaign. The campaign managed to tightly integrate online activity with tasks that supporters could do in their own neighborhoods, cities, and states.[46] The campaign also managed to succeed in maintaining control of its overall message while empowering supporters.

This ability to empower volunteers is the characteristic that really sets apart the 2008 election. It is not just that Web sites were more powerful, that text messaging was used for the first time, or that social networking pulled in millions of supporters. New media changed the power equation in campaigns, and in ways that transformed campaign organization. "I think we'll be analyzing this election for years to come as a seminal, transformative race," predicted Mark McKinnon, who was an adviser to President George W. Bush's campaigns in 2000 and 2004. He noted 2008 was "the year the paradigm got turned upside down and truly became bottom up instead of top down."[47] Terry Nelson, the political director of Bush's 2004 campaign, agreed: "We are in the midst of a fundamental transformation of how campaigns are run, and it's not over yet."[48]

Part of this transformation lies in the ability of volunteers to create their own campaign materials and distribute them via the Web. In the 2004 campaign, the "JibJab" animated videos went viral and landed the creators on late-night talk shows. But that content was created by professionals and simply distributed via the Web. In 2008, some of the most creative modes of support or vitriolic attacks were launched on YouTube by average Americans—not the campaigns. Hundreds of unofficial songs and fake campaign ads were posted on YouTube, including a song by will.i.am of the group Black-Eyed Peas. His song "Yes We Can" was not created by the campaign, but was used by the campaign at several events. The song had more than three million views on YouTube and the song's video won an Emmy. Obama supporters produced and uploaded their own ads, including responses to Hillary Clinton's "3 a.m." ad. One Obama supporter gained media attention when he uploaded a remake of Apple's "1984" ad featuring Hillary Clinton. Supporters of Senator John McCain posted their own YouTube versions of everything ranging from Obama's birth heritage to salutes to McCain's patriotism.

In fact, checking out campaign ads on YouTube became somewhat tricky, as some of the volunteer-generated ads looked authentic enough to confuse some people, which was sometimes the aim. Wayne Friedman of MediaPost, a TV Watch blog, noted: "Now, candidates will need to take time to sift through real, faux, and in-between political messages running on the biggest video network on the Internet—because the damage can come far and wide through professional-looking TV commercials. The problem with YouTube is, now everybody becomes a political spinmeister."[49]

But for candidates, this level of volunteer participation in a campaign is a new frontier. Instead of trying to control volunteers and their video creations, candidates should be happy that volunteers are excited about a candidate. "Allowing open user-generated content provides volunteers with a way to participate in the campaign in a real way and tools to truly evangelize for the candidate," noted Todd Ziegler of the Bivings Report, a company providing research and analysis of Web-based communication. He pointed out that if only a few thousand people participate in this way, but each gets five others to give money to the candidate or start a blog in support, it can yield significant benefits for a campaign: "It seems to me that truly allowing your supporters to carry your message for you will ultimately result in more supporters, more donations and ultimately better online results."[50]

The same thing can happen when supporters make their own printed materials, signs, and posters, as many did for Obama in 2008. Homemade Obama posters, some sporting a personal interpretation of the campaign logo or featuring the candidate's face, sprang up in cities across the United States. The campaign did not discourage such personalization of materials, but made official campaign brochures and materials available in both printed and downloadable forms.

Controlling the Message

Of course, one potential problem is that candidates can lose control of their messages when supporters of another candidate publish negative materials on sites such as YouTube. Most political consultants and strategists say that controlling a candidate's message is vital to winning an election, so it is an area that cannot be overlooked. YouTube empowers average Americans to affect the political process like never before, and this is forcing candidates to change the way they campaign.[51] For instance, candidates must be even more careful than before not to make public gaffes or speak words that could be misinterpreted. Aside from the never-ending news cycle which is always looking for controversial political news, a candidate never knows when someone is recording his or her comments. Senator John McCain found himself defending a public appearance in which he sang the Beach Boys' tune "Barbara Ann," but substituted the words "Bomb, Bomb, Bomb, Bomb, Bomb, Iran." The footage was apparently recorded on someone's camera phone and found its way onto YouTube, where thousands of people watched the senator happily sing the song to a campaign crowd in 2007.[52] This public relations gaffe was compounded when Democratic supporters took the video and reedited it—with at least one showing him as Dr. Strangelove—and posted their new creations on YouTube. MoveOn.org took the original McCain video and used part of it in a television commercial blasting the Arizona senator.

Not only must candidates now be ultra aware of what they say in public, but they must also invest in expert help regarding how their information is displayed on Web search engines. Research shows that people usually use three to five words when searching for information on Google or another search engine, mainly because it yields a much higher success rate.[53] Candidates should work to make sure that their information—the official campaign Web site and related official information—is the first link to pop up in a search engine. This is generally done through search optimization. Republican presidential candidate Mitt Romney was one of many candidates who used paid listings for his Web site to appear when certain search keyword strings were entered. This meant that when an individual typed in particular keyword strings such as "war in Iraq" or even a misspelling of his name, his official Web site was the among the first listings to pop up in Google. Both Romney and Senator John McCain invested heavily in Google AdWords, which is a keyword bidding program.[54]

Because this is a new area for political candidates, most of them are following the lead of companies and small businesses, many of which already use these techniques to boost traffic on their sites and direct individuals to their own messages. This technique holds great potential for candidates to not only direct potential voters to their Web sites, but also to pull them into volunteer-built sites where they can find information regarding issues or attacks on opponents. Search optimization can help with message control, and it should be used by future candidates.

Many of the old methods of message control are simply outdated. Gone are the days when Ronald Reagan's staff could control the flow of information to the press through a "message of the day," or when group construction of campaign news was all that the public would see about a national election. While political reporters for more traditional media often follow common "scripts" regarding news coverage of political campaigns,[55] those reporting or posting information through new media are not following any set rules, and they often have a political bias that is expressed in their comments. This is an area for future research by communication scholars, as it is a process that is evolving. While Obama was good at focusing on and controlling his message, details regarding how that was accomplished are still forthcoming. For current and future candidates, this area could simply be one in which they try to learn from mistakes made by other candidates and find a balance that works within their respective campaigns.

CONCLUSION

One thing that is abundantly clear is that current and future candidates will need to make an investment in online technology and people. Without the right individuals developing the campaign Web site and overseeing a new media strategy, much time and energy are wasted. In the span of just four years, new media have ballooned into some of the most important tools in a candidate's campaign. As pointed out earlier, some of these platforms were not even available in 2004, yet had matured quickly enough to make a major contribution in the 2008 campaign. The pace of technology has the capacity to outstrip a campaign's ability to harness its potential, which makes it imperative that candidates hire individuals and firms that can help make these evolving new tools productive parts of the campaign.

Another thing to remember is that new media cannot take the place of campaign basics such as personal voter contact, door-to-door campaigning, and the hosting of intimate campaign gatherings. These must still be done, but new media make it possible for volunteers to organize and take on many of these activities by themselves. This frees up the candidate, and it allows opinion leaders—noted by Lazarsfeld, Berelson, and Gaudet in 1948 as important for changes in the attitudes of the mass public[56]—to influence their friends, family members, and neighbors. The candidate will still need to personally solicit some funds, especially in smaller races in which the Web will play less of a role. Money still has to be moved from wealthy individuals to campaign coffers, and it often takes a phone call or personal chat with a candidate to complete that transfer.

A final point to remember is that a campaign might have unlimited funds, put together an incredibly talented online team, and provide team leaders with the tools to put together an effective campaign, yet still lose the election. That's because assembling the greatest talent cannot overcome a poor candidate. A candidate still needs to be perceived by the public as intelligent, strong, decisive, a good leader, charismatic, and empathetic. A good candidate should also be able to stir the emotions of voters. Obama's campaign manager in 2008 noted, "Without the candidate who excites people, you can have the greatest strategy and machinery, and it won't matter."[57] Technology alone cannot win a campaign, but good candidates will find it hard to win without it in the future. When the two things come together, the odds of success will be greatly increased.

In the end, it seems that political campaigns continue the trend of adapting to new technology and making technology work for them. In the case of new media, this adaptation can be a benefit for both political candidates and the voting public, as it provides a way for volunteers to more fully participate in electoral politics, and it provides candidates with a less expensive, yet more expansive, way to engage the public. It will be interesting to see how these new media platforms have evolved by the 2012 campaigns.

NOTES

1. Micah L. Sifry, "Covering the Web as a Force in Electoral Politics," *Nieman Reports*, 2008, www.nieman.harvard.edu/reportsitem.aspx?id=100026 (9 July 2009).

2. Aaron Smith, "The Internet's Role in Campaign 2008," Pew Internet and American Life Project, April 2009, pewresearch.org/pubs/1192/internet-politics-campaign-2008 (9 June 2009).

3. Smith, "Internet's Role."

4. David Talbot, "Personalized Campaigning," *Reviews*, March/April 2009, 80–82.

5. Jonathan Karush, e-mail message to author, 11 July 2009.

6. Samuel Greengard, "The First Internet President," *Communications of the ACM*, February 2009, 18.

7. David All, e-mail message to author, 15 July 2009.

8. Pippa Norris, *A Virtuous Circle* (Cambridge: Cambridge University Press), 2000.

9. Aaron Smith and Lee Rainie, "The Internet and the 2008 Election," Pew Internet and American Life Project, June 2008, www.pewinternet.org/Reports/2008/The-Internet-and-the-2008-Election.aspx (15 June 2008).

10. David Talbot, "How Obama *Really* Did It," *TechnologyReview.com*, September/October 2008, 78–83, www.technologyreview.com (10 July 2009).

11. Jose Antonio Vargas, "Obama Raised Half a Billion Online," *Washington Post*, 20 November 2008, voices.washingtonpost.com/44/2008/11/20/obama_raised_half_a_billion_on.html (3 July 2009).

12. Vargas, "Obama Raised."

13. Vargas, "Obama Raised."

14. Boyce Upholt, "New Media, New Cycle," *Politics*, 11 June 2009, www.politicsmagazine.com/blog_post/show/399 (3 July 2009).

15. Jonathan Karush, e-mail message to author, 11 July 2009.

16. Upholt, "New Media."

17. Upholt, "New Media."

18. Cyrus Krohn, "Slate Alum Cyrus Krohn, Now Online Guru for the RNC, is Injecting Consumer Savvy into E-campaigning," *Politics*, November 2008, 22–23.

19. Upholt, "New Media."

20. Jonathan Karush, e-mail to author, 11 July 2009.

21. Krohn, "Slate alum," 23.

22. Smith, "Internet's Role."

23. David All, e-mail to author, 15 July 2009.

24. Samuel Greengard, "The First Internet President," *Society*, February 2009, 16–18.

25. Talbot, "Personalized Campaigning," 81.

26. Jonathan Karush, e-mail to author, 11 July 2009.

27. David All, e-mail to author, 15 July 2009.

28. Joel Berg, "Trickle-Down Webonomics," November 2008, 59.

29. Cristina Silva, "St. Petersburg Political Campaigns Tap into Facebook, Twitter, Blogs," *St. Petersburg Times*, 11 February 2009, www.tampabay.com/news/politics/local/article974736.ece (14 July 2009).

30. David All, e-mail to author, 15 July 2009.

31. Upholt, "New Media."

32. Erin Einhorn, "How Tweet it is for These Candidates: City Politicians Discover Facebook, Twitter," *New York Daily News*, 13 July 2009, www.nydailynews.com/ny_local/2009/07/13/2009-07-13_how_tweet_it_is_for_these_candidates_city_politicians_discover_facebook_twitter.html (14 July 2009).

33. Krohn, "Slate alum," 23.

34. Andrew Charlesworth, "The Ascent of the Smartphone," IET Knowledge Network, 16 Feb. 2009, kn.theiet.org/magazine/issues/0903/smartphone-0903.cfm (20 July 2009).

35. Berg, "Trickle-Down," 18.

36. Greengard, "The First," 17.

37. Bill Greenwood, "Pew Surveys Tackle Internet's Future, Online Politics' Present," *Information Today* 26, no. 3 (March 2009).

38. Dane Strother, "Get Text Savvy—or You're Toast," *Politics*, November 2008, 62–63.

39. Strother, "Get Text," 62.

40. David All, e-mail to author, 15 July 2009.

41. Talbot, "How Obama," 82.

42. Devlin Barrett, "Ads for Obama Campaign: 'It's in the game,'" MSNBC, 14 October 2008, www.msnbc.msn.com/id/27184857/ (20 July 2009).

43. Craig Daitch, "Obama Says 'Yes We Can!' to In-game Advertising," *Advertising Age*, 13 October 2008, adage.com/digitalnext/article?article_id=131675 (20 July 2009).

44. Talbot, "How Obama," 81.

45. Talbot, "How Obama," 82.

46. Talbot, "How Obama," 81.

47. Adam Nagourney, "The '08 Campaign: Sea Change for Politics as We Know It," *New York Times*, 4 November 2008, 1(A).

48. Nagourney, "The '08 Campaign," 1.

49. Wayne Friedman, "Fake TV Commercials on YouTube: 1984 All Over Again," *MediaPost*, 19 March 2007, www.mediapost.com/publications/index .cfm?fa=Articles.showArticle&art_aid=57302 (16 July 2009).

50. Todd Ziegler, "Does User-Generated Content Work for Political Campaigns?" *The Bivings Report*, 6 April 2007, www.bivingsreport.com/2007/does-user-generated -content-work-for-political-campaigns/ (16 July 2009).

51. Paul Steinhauser, "The YouTube-ification of Politics: Candidates Losing Control," 18 July 2007, www.cnn.com/2007/POLITICS/07/18/youtube.effect/index .html (17 July 2009).

52. Declan McCullagh, "YouTube Deletes Video of McCain Singing 'Bomb Iran,'" *CNET News*, news.cnet.com/2100-1025_3-6178173.html (17 July 2009).

53. Arve Overland, "The 15 Steps to Getting Found Through Search Engines," *New Politics Institute*, 17 May 2006, www.newpolitics.net/node/86?full_report=1 (17 July 2009).

54. Sarah Lai Stirland, "Which Presidential Candidates Have Mastered Google?" *Wired*, 16 Augugst 2007, www.wired.com/politics/law/news/2007/08/election_ adwords (17 July 2009).

55. Girish J. Gulati, Marion R. Just, and Ann N. Crigler, "News Coverage of Political Campaigns," in *Political Communication Research*, ed. Lynda Lee Kaid (Mahwah, NJ: Lawrence Erlbaum, 2004), 237–56.

56. Richard E. Petty, Joseph R. Priester, and Pablo Brinol, "Mass Media Attitude Change: Implications of the Elaboration Likelihood Model of Persuasion," in *Media Effects: Advances in Theory and Research*, ed. Jennings Bryant and Dolf Zillman (Mahwah, NJ: Lawrence Erlbaum, 2002), 155–98.

57. Nagourney, "The '08 Campaign," 1.

Bibliography

Armstrong, Jerome, and Markso Moulitsas. *Crashing the Gate: Grassroots and the Rise of People-Powered Politics.* White River Junction, VT: Chelsea Green Publishing, 2006.

Baumann, Michael. "Campaign '08: The Power of the Post." *Information Today* 25, no. 9 (2008): 25.

Bedard, Paul. "YouTube Not Just for White House Hopefuls." *U.S. News & World Report* 143, no. 5 (August 2007): 15.

Beirne, Mike. "Marketers Find Facebook, MySpace Ripe for Politics." *Brandweek* 40, no. 34, (September 2008): 10.

Berg, Joel. "Trickle-Down Webonomics." *Politics (Campaigns & Elections)* 29, no. 11 (November 2008): 59.

Bimber, Bruce, and Richard Davis. *Campaigning Online: The Internet in U.S. Elections.* New York: Cambridge University Press, 2003.

Bitzer, Lloyd F. "Political Rhetoric." Pp. 225–48 in *Handbook of Political Communication,* edited by Dan Nimmo and Keith Sanders. Beverly Hills, CA: Sage, 1981.

"Blog mentions via Technorati," *TechPresident.com.* n.d. techpresident.com/scrape_plot/technorati/2008 (10 July 2009).

Boynton, G. R. "Our Conversations About Governing." Pp. 91–114 in *Political Communication Research,* edited by David Paletz. Norwood, NJ: Ablex, 1996.

Caraley, Demetrios. "Elections and Dilemmas of American Democratic Governance: Reflections." *Political Science Quarterly* 104, no. 1 (1989): 19–40.

Cornfield, Michael. "Game-Changers: New Technology and the 2008 Presidential Election." Pp. 205–30 in *The Year of Obama: How Barack Obama Won the White House,* edited by Larry J. Sabato. New York: Longman, 2010.

Davis, Gene. "Suffocation via Emails?" *Denver Daily News,* 2008. www.thedenverdailynews.com/article.php?aID=2211 (11 July 2009).

Denton, Robert E., Jr. *The Primetime Presidency of Ronald Reagan.* New York: Praeger, 1988.

Denton, Robert E., Jr., and Jim Kuypers. *Politics and Communication in America.* Long Grove, IL: Waveland Press, 2008.

Drezner, Daniel W., and Henry Farrell. "Blogs, Politics and Power." Special issue of *Public Choice* 134, no. 1–2 (January 2008).

Dulio, David A., Donald L. Groff, and James A. Thurber. "Untangled Web: Internet Use during the 1998 Election." *PS: Political Science and Politics* 32, no. 1 (1991): 53–58.

Feld, Peter. "What Obama Can Teach You About Millennial Marketing." *Advertising Age* 79, no. 31 (August 2008): 1–23.

Feldmann, Linda. "GOP YouTube Debates: Good Marks for New Views of Candidates." *Christian Science Monitor*, 30 November 2007, 1.

"Flickring Here, Twittering There." *Economist* 388, no. 8593 (16 August 2008): 30–31.

Friedenberg, Robert. *Communication Consultants in Political Campaigns.* Westport, CT: Praeger, 1997.

Graff, Garrett M. *The First Campaign: Globalization, the Web & the Race for the White House.* New York: Farrar, Straus and Giroux, 2007.

Gronbeck, Bruce E. "The Web, Campaign 07-08, and Engaged Citizens." Pp. 228–42 in *The 2008 Presidential Campaign: A Communication Perspective.* Lanham, MD: Rowman & Littlefield, 2009.

Gulati, Girish J. "No Laughing Matter: The Role of New Media in the 2008 Election." Pp. 187–203 in *The Year of Obama: How Barack Obama Won the White House*, edited by Larry J. Sabato. New York: Longman, 2010.

Harfoush, Rahaf. *Yes We Did! An Inside Look at How Social Media Built the Obama Brand.* Berkeley, CA: New Riders Press, 2009.

Hendricks, John Allen, and Shannon K. McCraw. "Coverage of Political Campaigns." Pp. 181–88 in *American Journalism: History, Principles Practices*, edited by W. David Sloan and Lisa Mullikin Parcell. Jefferson, NC: McFarland & Company, Inc., 2002.

Herrnson, Paul S., Atiya Kai Stokes-Brown, and Matthew Hindman. "Campaign Politics and the Digital Divide: Constituency Characteristic Considerations, and Candidate Internet Use in State Legislative Elections." *Political Research Quarterly* 60, no. 1 (2007): 31–42.

Hindman, Matthew. "The Real Lessons of Howard Dean: Reflections on the First Digital Campaign." *Perspectives on Politics* 3, no. 1 (2005): 121–28.

Huffington Post, ed. *The Huffington Post Complete Guide to Blogging.* New York: Simon and Schuster, 2008.

Itzkoff, Dave. "Obama Ads Appear in Video Game." *New York Times*, 15 October 2008, C2.

Jamieson, Kathleen Hall. *Eloquence in an Electronic Age.* New York: Oxford University Press, 1988.

Johnson, Dennis W., ed. *Campaigning for President 2008: Strategy and Tactics, New Voices and New Techniques.* New York: Routledge, 2009.

Johnson, Thomas J., Barbara K. Kaye, Shannon L. Bichard, and W. Joann Wong. "Every Blog Has Its Day: Politically-Interested Internet Users' Perceptions of Blog

Credibility." *Journal of Computer-Mediated Communication* 31, no. 1 (2007). jcmc.indiana.edu/vol13/issue1/johnson.html (10 July 2009).

Kaye, Kate. *Campaign 08: A Turning Point for Digital Media.* Scotts Valley, CA: CreateSpace, 2009.

Kestenbaum, David. "The Digital Divide Between McCain and Obama." *NPR*, 3 April 2008, www.npr.org (4 April 2009).

King, David C. "Catching Voters in the Web in the Elections of 1998." Pp. 99–123 in *Democracy.com: Governance in a Networked World*, edited by Elaine Ciulla Karmack and Joseph S. Nye, Jr. Hollis, NH: Hollis Publishing, 1999.

Kline, David, and Dan Bernstein, eds. *Blog! How the World of Blogs and Bloggers is Changing Our Culture.* New York: CDS Books, 2005.

Krohn, Cyrus. "Slate Alum Cyrus Krohn, Now Online Guru for the RNC, Is Injecting Consumer Savvy Into E-Campaigning." *Politics* (November 2008): 22–23.

Li, Charlene, and Josh Bernoff. *Groundswell: Winning in a World Transformed by Social Technologies.* Boston: Harvard Business School Press, 2008.

Nagourney, Adam. "The '08 Campaign: Sea Change for Politics as We Know It." *New York Times*, 4 November 2008, 1(A).

Nimmo, Dan, and David Swanson. "The Field of Political Communication: Beyond the Voter Persuasion Paradigm." Pp. 7–47 in *New Directions in Political Communication: A Resource Book*, edited by David Swanson and Dan Nimmo. Newbury Park, CA: Sage, 1990.

Panagopoulos, Costas. *Politicking Online:The Transformation of Election Campaign Communications.* Piscataway, NJ: Rutgers University Press, 2009.

Peter, Ian. "Ian Peter's History of the Internet," *Net History* 2003, www.nethistory.info (8 June 2009).

PEW Research Center for People and the Press. "More Than a Quarter of Voters Read Political Blogs: Liberal Dems Top Conservative Reps in Donations, Activism." 23 October 2008. people-press.org/reports/pdf/464.pdf (15 July 2009).

Price, Michelle. "Live Blogging Election 2008: How Social Media Changed This Election." *Social Media Savvy*, 4 November 2008. socialmediasavvy.com/2008/11/live-blogging-election-2008-how-social-media-changed-this-election/ (3 August 2009).

Puopolo, Sonia T. "The Web and U.S. Senate Campaigns 2000." *American Behavioral Scientist* 44, no. 12 (2001): 2030–47.

Rapaport, Richard. "Net vs. Norm." *Best of the Web*, 2000. www.forbes.com/asap/2000/0529/053_print.html (8 June 2009).

Siegel, Lee. *Against the Machine: How the Web Is Reshaping Culture and Commerce—and Why It Matters.* New York: Spiegel & Grau, 2009.

Sifry, Micah L. "Covering the Web as a Force in Electoral Politics." *Nieman Reports*, 2008. www.nieman.harvard.edu/reportsitem.aspx?id=100026 (9 July 2009).

Smith, Aaron. "The Internet's Role in Campaign 2008," *Pew Internet and American Life Project*, 2009. www.pewinternet.org/Reports/2009/6--The-Internets-Role-in-Campaign-2008.aspx (20 July 2009).

Smith, Aaron, and Lee Rainie. "The Internet and the 2008 Election." *Pew Internet and American Life Project*, June 2008. www.pewinternet.org/Reports/2008/The-Internet-and-the-2008-Election.aspx (15 June 2008).

Smith, Ben, and Jonathan Martin. "Untraceable E-mails Spread Obama Rumor." *Politico*, 2007. www.politico.com/news/stories/1007/6314.html (1 July 2009).

Spaeth, Merrie. "Presidential Politics and Public Relations in 2008: Marshall McLuhan 2.0." *Journalism Studies* 10, no. 3 (June 2009): 442.

Stromer-Galley, Jennifer. "On-line Interaction and Why Candidates Avoid It." *Journal of Communication* 50, no. 4 (2000): 111–32.

Strother, Dane. "Get Text-Savvy—Or You're Toast." *Politics (Campaigns & Elections)* 29, no. 11 (November 2008): 62–63.

Trippi, Joe. *The Revolution Will Not Be Televised.* New York: HarperCollins, 2008.

Upholt, Boyce. "New Media, New Cycle." *Politics*, 11 June 2009. www.politics magazine.com/blog_post/show/399 (3 July 2009).

Vargas, Jose Antonio. "Obama Raised Half a Billion Online." *Washington Post*, 2008. voices.washingtonpost.com/44/2008/11/20/obama_raised_half_a_billion_on.html (8 June 2009).

Whitney, Michael. "The McCain Campaign's 'Reckless' Email Strategy," *TechPresident*, 20 May 2008. techpresident.com/blog-entry/mccain-campaigns-reckless-email-strategy (18 June 2009).

Williams, Andrew, and John Tedesco, ed. *The Internet Election.* Lanham, MD: Rowman & Littlefield, 2006.

Winograd, Morley, and Michael Hais. *Millennial Makeover: My Space, YouTube and the Future of American Politics.* New Brunswick, NJ: Rutgers University Press, 2008.

Wolfe, Alan. "The New Pamphleteers." *New York Times Book Review*, 11 July 2004. www.nytimes.com/2004/07/11/books/the-new-pamphleteers.html?fta=y (31 August 2009).

Ziegler, Todd. "Does User-Generated Content Work for Political Campaigns?" *The Bivings Report*, 6 April 2007. www.bivingsreport.com/2007/does-user-generated-content-work-for-political-campaigns (16 July 2009).

Index

164 *Index*

About the Editors

John Allen Hendricks is director of the Division of Communication and Contemporary Culture and professor of communication at Stephen F. Austin State University. He is editor of the "Series in New Media Studies" book series for Lexington Books, and has written numerous chapters and journal articles on political communication. He is a member of the Board of Directors of the Broadcast Education Association (BEA) and past president of the Oklahoma Broadcast Education Association (OBEA), and serves on the editorial board of the *Journal of Radio and Audio Media*. He is past chair of both the political communication and mass communication divisions of the Southern States Communication Association (SSCA). He was chair of the Department of Communication and Theatre at Southeastern Oklahoma State University from 1999 to 2003. He earned a Ph.D. in mass communication with a specialization in advertising from the University of Southern Mississippi.

Robert E. Denton, Jr., holds the W. Thomas Rice Chair of Leadership Studies in the Pamplin College of Business and is a professor in the Department of Communication at Virginia Polytechnic Institute and State University (Virginia Tech). He served as the founding director of the Rice Center for Leader Development from 1996 to 2007. He currently serves as head of the Department of Communication, a position he previously held from 1988 until 1996. He has degrees in political science and communication from Wake Forest University and Purdue University. In addition to numerous articles, essays, and book chapters, he is author, coauthor, or editor of nineteen books. The most recent titles include *Politics and Communication in America: Campaigns, Media, and Governing in the 21st Century* (with Jim Kuypers, 2008) and *The 2008 Presidential Campaign: A Communication Perspective* (2009).

About the Contributors

Jody C. Baumgartner is assistant professor of political science at East Carolina University. He has several books to his credit, including *Modern Presidential Electioneering: An Organizational and Comparative Approach* (2000); *Checking Executive Power* (coedited with Naoko Kada, 2003); *The American Vice Presidency Reconsidered* (2006); *Conventional Wisdom and American Elections: Exploding Myths, Exploring Misconceptions* (with Peter Francia, 2007); and *Laughing Matters: Humor and American Politics in the Media Age* (coedited with Jonathan Morris, 2007). He has written or collaborated on two dozen articles and book chapters on political humor, the vice presidency, and other subjects. He received his Ph.D. in political science from Miami University in 1998, specializing in the study of campaigns and elections.

Jenn Burleson Mackay is assistant professor in the Department of Communication at Virginia Tech. Mackay's primary research interests are journalistic ethics and credibility. Her research also has delved into other ethical issues, such as how teens and children are used as sources for the news media and how the credibility of the news media can be affected by the design of news Web sites. Mackay coedited the book *Media Bias: Finding It, Fixing It*. Her research has been published in *Journalism and Mass Communication Quarterly*, *Journal of Mass Media Ethics*, *Mass Communication & Society*, and *Journalism Practice*. Mackay has worked in both television and newspaper newsrooms. She is a former reporter for *The Roanoke Times* in Virginia. Mackay earned her Ph.D. from the University of Alabama.

Jonathan S. Morris is associate professor of political science at East Carolina University. Morris conducts research in the fields of political communication, public opinion, and the U.S. Congress. He has authored *Laughing Matters: Humor and American Politics in the Media Age*, as well as over a dozen articles in refereed journals. Morris worked for U.S. Representative Sherrod Brown as an American Political Science Association Congressional Fellow. He received his Ph.D. in political science from Purdue University.

Eric E. Otenyo is associate professor of politics and international affairs at Northern Arizona University. His teaching and research interests are in the presidency, e-government, and comparative public administration generally. He is the coauthor of *Managerial Discretion in Government Decision Making: Beyond the Street Level* (with Jacqueline Vaughn, 2007) and *The First World Presidency: George H. W. Bush, 1989–1993* (with Nancy Lind, 2009). His published work also appears in numerous scholarly journals including the *International Journal of Public Administration*, *Public Organization Review*, *Public Resistance*, and the *International Journal of Services, Economics, and Management*. He received an MPA from Syracuse University and a Ph.D. in political science from Miami University, Oxford, Ohio.

Larry Powell is a professor in the Department of Communication Studies at the University of Alabama at Birmingham (UAB). He is the author or co-author of four books, including *Political Campaign Communication: Inside and Out* (coauthored with Joseph Cowart, 2003) and *Interviewing: Situations and Contexts* (with Jonathan Amsbary, 2006). Powell teaches courses in mass communication and communication management at UAB. He has published articles in numerous scholarly journals and is ranked as one of the top fifty communication researchers in the nation. In addition to his academic career, Powell has worked as a consultant for a number of statewide and local political campaigns in more than twenty states. Powell earned his bachelor's and master's degrees from Auburn University in 1970 and 1971 respectively. In 1975, he earned his Ph.D. from the University of Florida. He has been a member of the UAB faculty since 1998.

Melissa M. Smith is assistant professor of communication at Mississippi State University. Her research specializes in political communication with an emphasis on technology and campaigns. She also researches in the area of religion and politics. Her work has been published in *Communication Research Reports*, the *Journal of Media and Religion*, and *Politics* magazine. She has several years' experience as a newspaper reporter and television news producer that complement her teaching and scholarship. She earned her Ph.D. from the University of Alabama.

Nancy Snow is associate professor at Syracuse University where she teaches in the dual degree master's program in public diplomacy sponsored by the S.I. Newhouse School of Communications and the Maxwell School of Citizenship and Public Affairs. Snow is on leave as tenured associate professor of communications at California State University, Fullerton, and adjunct professor of communications in the Annenberg School at the University of Southern California. Snow is the author or coeditor of six books, including the *Routledge Handbook of Public Diplomacy* (with Philip Taylor), *Propaganda, Inc.*, and *Information War*. Snow's latest book is *Persuader-in-Chief: Global Opinion and Persuasion in the Age of Obama*, whose second edition includes contributions from participants in her spring 2009 Obama Think Tank course at Syracuse University. She is senior fellow in the USC Center on Public Diplomacy and lifetime member of the Public Diplomacy Council at Georgetown University and Fulbright Association. Snow received her Ph.D. in international relations (magna cum laude) from the School of International Service at the American University, Washington, DC. She regularly blogs about American popular culture and politics for the Huffington Post. Reach her at www.nancysnow.com.

Frederic I. Solop is professor and chair of the Department of Politics and International Affairs at Northern Arizona University. Before serving as chair, Solop was the director of the Social Research Laboratory at Northern Arizona University for nine years. His primary areas of research and publication include American politics, political participation, public opinion, elections, and social movements. Solop has been working in the area of Internet democracy since 2000 when he published his research on the first binding Internet election to be organized in the United States (the Arizona Democratic Party Primary). Since that time, Solop has continued studying the relationship between technology and politics, with a specific focus today on the role of social media in political participation and governance. Solop earned his Ph.D. from Rutgers University.

Brandon C. Waite is an emerging media fellow with the Center for Media Design at Ball State University, where he teaches graduate-level courses on the presidency and interest groups. Waite's research interests center on the nexus between technology and politics. He attended Appalachian State University in Boone, North Carolina, and received undergraduate degrees in English and political science in 2000 and an M.A. in political science in 2003. Waite earned his Ph.D. from the University of Tennessee in 2008.